The
History of Spiritualism

By
ARTHUR CONAN DOYLE, M.D., LL.D.

Président d'Honneur de la Fédération Spirite Internationale,
President of the London Spiritualist Alliance, and President
of the British College of Psychic Science

Volume I

With Eight Plates

CASSELL AND COMPANY, LTD
London, New York, Toronto and Melbourne

First published 1926

Printed in Great Britain

To

SIR OLIVER LODGE, F.R.S.

A great leader both in physical and in psychic science

In token of respect

This work is dedicated

PREFACE.

THIS work has grown from small disconnected chapters into a narrative which covers in a way the whole history of the Spiritualistic movement. This genesis needs some little explanation. I had written certain studies with no particular ulterior object save to gain myself, and to pass on to others, a clear view of what seemed to me to be important episodes in the modern spiritual development of the human race. These included the chapters on Swedenborg, on Irving, on A. J. Davis, on the Hydesville incident, on the history of the Fox sisters, on the Eddys and on the life of D. D. Home. These were all done before it was suggested to my mind that I had already gone some distance in doing a fuller history of the Spiritualistic movement than had hitherto seen the light—a history which would have the advantage of being written from the inside and with intimate personal knowledge of those factors which are characteristic of this modern development.

It is indeed curious that this movement, which many of us regard as the most important in the history of the world since the Christ episode, has never had a historian from those who were within it, and who had large personal experience of its development. Mr. Frank Podmore brought together a large number of the facts, and, by ignoring those which did not suit his purpose, endeavoured to suggest the worthlessness of most of the rest, especially the physical phenomena, which in his view were mainly the result of fraud. There is a history of Spiritualism by Mr. McCabe which turns everything to fraud, and which is itself a misnomer, since the public would buy a book with such a title under the impression that it was a serious record instead of a travesty. There is also a history by J. Arthur Hill which is written from a strictly psychic research point of view, and is far behind the real provable facts. Then we have " Modern American Spiritualism : A Twenty Years' Record," and " Nineteenth Century Miracles," by that great woman and splendid propagandist, Mrs. Emma Hardinge Britten, but these deal only with phases, though they are exceedingly valuable. Finally —and best of all—there is " Man's Survival After Death," by the Rev. Charles L. Tweedale ; but this is rather a very fine connected exposition of the truth of the cult than a deliberate consecutive history. There are general histories of mysticism, like those of Ennemoser and Howitt, but there is no clean-cut, comprehensive story of the successive developments of this world-wide movement. Just before going to press a book has appeared by Campbell-Holms which is a very useful compendium of psychic facts, as its title, . " The Facts of Psychic Science and Philosophy," implies, but here again it cannot claim to be a connected history.

It was clear that such a work needed a great deal of research—far more than I in my crowded life could devote to it. It is true that my time was in any case dedicated to it, but the literature is vast, and there were many aspects of the movement which claimed my attention. Under these circumstances I claimed and obtained the loyal assistance of Mr. W. Leslie Curnow, whose knowledge of the subject and whose industry have proved to be invaluable. He has dug assiduously into that vast quarry ; he has separated out the ore from the rubbish, and in every way he has been of the greatest assistance. I had originally expected no more than raw material, but he has occasionally given me the finished article, of which I have gladly availed myself, altering it only to the extent of getting my own personal point of view. I cannot admit too fully the loyal assistance which he has given me, and if I have not conjoined his name with my own upon the title-page it is for reasons which he understands and in which he acquiesces.

ARTHUR CONAN DOYLE.

The Psychic Bookshop,
Abbey House,
Victoria Street, S.W.

CONTENTS

xi

LIST OF ILLUSTRATIONS

THE HISTORY OF SPIRITUALISM

CHAPTER I

THE STORY OF SWEDENBORG

IT is impossible to give any date for the early appearances of external intelligent power of a higher or lower type impinging upon the affairs of men. Spiritualists are in the habit of taking March 31, 1848, as the beginning of all psychic things, because their own movement dates from that day. There has, however, been no time in the recorded history of the world when we do not find traces of preternatural interference and a tardy recognition of them from humanity. The only difference between these episodes and the modern movement is that the former might be described as a case of stray wanderers from some further sphere, while the latter bears the sign of a purposeful and organized invasion. But as an invasion might well be preceded by the appearance of pioneers who search out the land, so the spirit influx of recent years was heralded by a number of incidents which might well be traced to the Middle Ages or beyond them. Some term must be fixed for a commencement of the narrative, and perhaps no better one can be found than the story of the great Swedish seer,

Emanuel Swedenborg, who has some claim to be the father of our new knowledge of supernal matters.

When the first rays of the rising sun of spiritual knowledge fell upon the earth they illuminated the greatest and highest human mind before they shed their light on lesser men. That mountain peak of mentality was this great religious reformer and clairvoyant medium, as little understood by his own followers as ever the Christ has been.

In order fully to understand Swedenborg one would need to have a Swedenborg brain, and that is not met with once in a century. And yet by our power of comparison and our experience of facts of which Swedenborg knew nothing, we can realize some part of his life more clearly than he could himself. The object of this study is not to treat the man as a whole, but to endeavour to place him in the general scheme of psychic unfolding treated in this work, from which his own Church in its narrowness would withhold him.

Swedenborg was a contradiction in some ways to our psychic generalizations, for it has been the habit to say that great intellect stands in the way of personal psychic experience. The clean slate is certainly most apt for the writing of a message. Swedenborg's mind was no clean slate, but was criss-crossed with every kind of exact learning which mankind is capable of acquiring. Never was there such a concentration of information. He was primarily a great mining engineer and authority on metallurgy. He was a military engineer who helped to turn the fortunes of

one of the many campaigns of Charles XII of Sweden.
He was a great authority upon astronomy and physics,
the author of learned works upon the tides and the
determination of latitude. He was a zoologist and an
anatomist. He was a financier and political economist
who anticipated the conclusions of Adam Smith.
Finally, he was a profound Biblical student who had
sucked in theology with his mother's milk, and lived
in the stern Evangelical atmosphere of a Lutheran
pastor during the most impressionable years of his
life. His psychic development, which occurred when
he was fifty-five, in no way interfered with his mental
activity, and several of his scientific pamphlets were
published after that date.

With such a mind it is natural enough that he
should be struck by the evidence for extra-mundane
powers which comes in the way of every thoughtful
man, but what is not natural is that he should himself
be the medium for such powers. There is a sense in
which his mentality was actually detrimental and
vitiated his results, and there was another in which it
was to the highest degree useful. To illustrate this
one has to consider the two categories into which his
work may be divided.

The first is the theological. This seems to most
people outside the chosen flock a useless and perilous
side of his work. On the one hand he accepts the
Bible as being in a very particular sense the work of
God. Upon the other he contends that its true meaning is entirely different from its obvious meaning, and
that it is he, and only he, who, by the help of angels,

3

is able to give the true meaning. Such a claim is intolerable. The infallibility of the Pope would be a trifle compared with the infallibility of Swedenborg if such a position were admitted. The Pope is at least only infallible when giving his verdict on points of doctrine ex cathedra with his cardinals around him. Swedenborg's infallibility would be universal and unrestricted. Nor do his explanations in the least commend themselves to one's reason. When, in order to get at the true sense of a God-given message, one has to suppose that a horse signifies intellectual truth, an ass signifies scientific truth, a flame signifies improvement, and so on and on through countless symbols, we seem to be in a realm of make-believe which can only be compared with the ciphers which some ingenious critics have detected in the plays of Shakespeare. Not thus does God send His truth into the world. If such a view were accepted the Swedenborgian creed could only be the mother of a thousand heresies, and we should find ourselves back again amid the hair-splittings and the syllogisms of the mediæval schoolmen. All great and true things are simple and intelligible. Swedenborg's theology is neither simple nor intelligible, and that is its condemnation.

When, however, we get behind his tiresome exegesis of the Scriptures, where everything means something different from what it obviously means, and when we get at some of the general results of his teaching, they are not inharmonious with liberal modern thought or with the teaching which has been received from the Other Side since spiritual communication became open. Thus the general proposition that this world is a laboratory of souls, a forcing-ground where the material refines out the spiritual, is not to be disputed. He rejects the Trinity in its ordinary sense, but rebuilds it in some extraordinary sense which would be equally objectionable to a Unitarian. He admits that every system has its divine purpose and that virtue is not confined to Christianity. He agrees with the Spiritualist teaching in seeking the true meaning of Christ's life in its power as an example, and he rejects atonement and original sin. He sees the root of all evil in selfishness, yet he admits that a healthy egoism, as Hegel called it, is essential. In sexual matters his theories are liberal to the verge of laxity. A Church he considered an absolute necessity, as if no individual could arrange his own dealings with his Creator. Altogether, it is such a jumble of ideas, poured forth at such length in so many great Latin volumes, and expressed in so obscure a style, that every independent interpreter of it would be liable to found a new religion of his own. Not in that direction does the worth of Swedenborg lie.

That worth is really to be found in his psychic powers and in his psychic information which would have been just as valuable had no word of theology ever come from his pen. It is these powers and that information to which we will now turn.

Even as a lad young Swedenborg had visionary moments, but the extremely practical and energetic manhood which followed submerged that more delicate side of his nature. It came occasionally to the surface, however, all through his life, and several instances have been put on record which show that he possessed those powers which are usually called "travelling clairvoyance," where the soul appears to leave the body, to acquire information at a distance, and to return with news of what is occurring elsewhere. It is a not uncommon attribute of mediums, and can be matched by a thousand examples among Spiritualistic sensitives, but it is rare in people of intellect, and rare also when accompanied by an apparently normal state of the body while the phenomenon is proceeding. Thus, in the oft-quoted example of Gothenburg, where the seer observed and reported on a fire in Stockholm, 300 miles away, with perfect accuracy, he was at a dinner-party with sixteen guests, who made valuable witnesses. The story was investigated by no less a person than the philosopher Kant, who was a contemporary.

These occasional incidents were, however, merely the signs of latent powers which came to full fruition quite suddenly in London in April of the year 1744. It may be remarked that though the seer was of a good Swedish family and was elevated to the Swedish nobility, it was none the less in London that his chief books were published, that his illumination was begun and finally that he died and was buried. From the day of his first vision he continued until his death, twenty-seven years later, to be in constant touch with the other world. "The same night the world of spirits, hell and heaven, were convincingly opened to

6

me, where I found many persons of my acquaintance of all conditions. Thereafter the Lord daily opened the eyes of my spirit to see in perfect wakefulness what was going on in the other world, and to converse, broadawake, with angels and spirits."

In his first vision Swedenborg speaks of " a kind of vapour steaming from the pores of my body. It was a most visible watery vapour and fell downwards to the ground upon the carpet." This is a close description of that ectoplasm which we have found to be the basis of all physical phenomena. The substance has also been called " ideoplasm," because it takes on in an instant any shape with which it is impressed by the spirit. In this case it changed, according to his account, into vermin, which was said to be a sign from his Guardians that they disapproved of his diet, and was accompanied by a clairaudient warning that he must be more careful in that respect.

What can the world make of such a narrative? They may say that the man was mad, but his life in the years which followed showed no sign of mental weakness. Or they might say that he lied. But he was a man who was famed for his punctilious veracity. His friend Cuno, a banker of Amsterdam, said of him, " When he gazed upon me with his smiling blue eyes it was as if truth itself was speaking from them." Was he then self-deluded and honestly mistaken? We have to face the fact that in the main the spiritual observations which he made have been confirmed and extended since his time by innumerable psychic observers. The true verdict is that he was the first and in many ways the greatest of the whole line of mediums, that he was subject to the errors as well as to the privileges which mediumship brings, that only by the study of mediumship can his powers be really understood, and that in endeavouring to separate him from Spiritualism his New Church has shown a complete misapprehension of his gifts, and of their true place in the general scheme of Nature. As a great pioneer of the Spiritual movement his position is both intelligible and glorious. As an isolated figure with incomprehensible powers, there is no place for him in any broad comprehensive scheme of religious thought.

It is interesting to note that he considered his powers to be intimately connected with a system of respiration. Air and ether being all around us, it is as if some men could breathe more ether and less air and so attain a more etheric state. This, no doubt, is a crude and clumsy way of putting it, but some such idea runs through the work of many schools of psychic thought. Laurence Oliphant, who had no obvious connexion with Swedenborg, wrote his book " Sympneumata " in order to explain it. The Indian system of Yoga depends upon the same idea. But anyone who has seen an ordinary medium go into trance is aware of the peculiar hissing intakes with which the process begins and the deep expirations with which it ends. A fruitful field of study lies there for the Science of the future. Here, as in other psychic matters, caution is needed. The author has known several cases where tragic results have followed upon an ignorant use of deep-breathing psychic exercises. Spiritual, like electrical power, has its allotted use, but needs some knowledge and caution in handling.

Swedenborg sums up the matter by saying that when he communed with spirits he would for an hour at a time hardly draw a breath, " taking in only enough air to serve as a supply to his thoughts." Apart from this peculiarity of respiration, Swedenborg was normal during his visions, though he naturally preferred to be secluded at such times. He seems to have been privileged to examine the other world through several of its spheres, and though his theological habit of mind may have tinctured his descriptions, on the other hand the vast range of his material knowledge gave him unusual powers of observation and comparison. Let us see what were the main facts which he brought back from his numerous journeys, and how far they coincide with those which have been obtained since his day by psychic methods.

He found, then, that the other world, to which we all go after death, consisted of a number of different spheres representing various shades of luminosity and happiness, each of us going to that for which our spiritual condition has fitted us. We are judged in automatic fashion, like going to like by some spiritual law, and the result being determined by the total result of our life, so that absolution or a death-bed repentance can be of little avail. He found in these spheres that the scenery and conditions of this world were closely reproduced, and so also was the general framework of society. He found houses in which families lived, temples in which they worshipped, halls in which they assembled for social purposes, palaces in which rulers might dwell.

Death was made easy by the presence of celestial beings who helped the new-comer into his fresh existence. Such new-comers had an immediate period of complete rest. They regained consciousness in a few days of our time.

There were both angels and devils, but they were not of another order to ourselves. They were all human beings who had lived on earth and who were either undeveloped souls, as devils, or highly developed souls, as angels.

We did not change in any way at death. Man lost nothing by death, but was still a man in all respects, though more perfect than when in the body. He took with him not only his powers but also his acquired modes of thought, his beliefs and his prejudices.

All children were received equally, whether baptized or not. They grew up in the other world. Young women mothered them until the real mother came across.

There was no eternal punishment. Those who were in the hells could work their way out if they had the impulse. Those in the heavens were also in no permanent place, but were working their way to something higher.

There was marriage in the form of spiritual union in the next world. It takes a man and a woman to make a complete human unit. Swedenborg, it may be remarked, was never married in life.

There was no detail too small for his observation in the spirit spheres. He speaks of the architecture, the artisans' work, the flowers and fruits, the scribes, the embroidery, the art, the music, the literature, the science, the schools, the museums, the colleges, the libraries and the sports. It may all shock conventional minds, though why harps, crowns and thrones should be tolerated and other less material things denied, it is hard to see.

Those who left this world old, decrepit, diseased, or deformed, renewed their youth, and gradually assumed their full vigour. Married couples continued together if their feelings towards each other were close and sympathetic. If not, the marriage was dissolved. "Two real lovers are not separated by the death of one, since the spirit of the deceased dwells with the spirit of the survivor, and this even to the death of the latter, when they again meet and are reunited, and love each other more tenderly than before."

Such are some gleanings out of the immense store of information which God sent to the world through Swedenborg. Again and again they have been repeated by the mouths and the pens of our own Spiritualistic illuminates. The world has so far disregarded it, and clung to outworn and senseless conceptions. Gradually the new knowledge is making its way, however, and when it has been entirely accepted the true greatness of the mission of Swedenborg will be recognized, while his Biblical exegesis will be forgotten.

The New Church, which was formed in order to

sustain the teaching of the Swedish master, has allowed itself to become a backwater instead of keeping its rightful place as the original source of psychic knowledge. When the Spiritualistic movement broke out in 1848, and when men like Andrew Jackson Davis supported it with philosophic writings and psychic powers which can hardly be distinguished from those of Swedenborg, the New Church would have been well advised to hail this development as being on the lines indicated by their leader. Instead of doing so, they have preferred, for some reason which is difficult to understand, to exaggerate every point of difference and ignore every point of resemblance, until the two bodies have drifted into a position of hostility. In point of fact, every Spiritualist should honour Swedenborg, and his bust should be in every Spiritualist temple, as being the first and greatest of modern mediums. On the other hand, the New Church should sink any small differences and join heartily in the new movement, contributing their churches and organization to the common cause.

It is difficult on examining Swedenborg's life to discover what are the causes which make his present-day followers look askance at other psychic bodies. What he did then is what they do now. Speaking of Polhem's death the seer says : " He died on Monday and spoke with me on Thursday. I was invited to the funeral. He saw the hearse and saw them let down the coffin into the grave. He conversed with me as it was going on, asking me why they had buried him when he was alive. When the priest pronounced that

EMANUEL SWEDENBORG (*Ætat. 80*)

From an engraving by Battersby in "*The European Magazine,*" 1787

he would rise again at the Day of Judgment he asked
why this was, when he had risen already. He wondered that such a belief could obtain, considering that
he was even now alive."

This is entirely in accord with the experience of
a present-day medium. If Swedenborg was within
his rights, then the medium is so also.

Again : " Brahe was beheaded at 10 in the morning and spoke to me at 10 that night. He was with
me almost without interruption for several days."

Such instances show that Swedenborg had no more
scruples about converse with the dead than the Christ
had when He spoke on the mountain with Moses and
Elias.

Swedenborg has laid down his own view very
clearly, but in considering it one has to remember
the time in which he lived and his want of experience
of the trend and object of the new revelation. This
view was that God, for good and wise purposes, had
separated the world of spirits from ours and that communication was not granted except for cogent reasons
—among which mere curiosity should not be counted.
Every earnest student of the psychic would agree with
it, and every earnest Spiritualist is averse from turning
the most solemn thing upon earth into a sort of pas-
time. As to having a cogent reason, our main reason
is that in such an age of materialism as Swedenborg
can never have imagined, we are endeavouring to prove
the existence and supremacy of spirit in so objective
a way that it will meet and beat the materialists on
their own ground. It would be hard to imagine any

reason more cogent than this, and therefore we have every right to claim that if Swedenborg were now living he would have been a leader in our modern psychic movement.

Some of his followers, notably Dr. Garth Wilkinson, have put forward another objection thus : " The danger of man in speaking with spirits is that we are all in association with our likes, and being full of evil these similar spirits, could we face them, would but confirm us in our own state of views."

To this we can only reply that though it is specious it is proved by experience to be false. Man is not naturally bad. The average human being is good. The mere act of spiritual communication in its solemnity brings out the religious side. Therefore as a rule it is not the evil but the good influence which is encountered, as the beautiful and moral records of séances will show. The author can testify that in nearly forty years of psychic work, during which he has attended innumerable séances in many lands, he has never on any single occasion heard an obscene word or any message which could offend the ears of the most delicate female. Other veteran Spiritualists bring the same testimony. Therefore, while it is undoubtedly true that evil spirits are attracted to an evil circle, in actual practice it is a very rare thing for anyone to be incommoded thereby. When such spirits come the proper procedure is not to repulse them, but rather to reason gently with them and so endeavour to make them realize their own condition and what they should do for self-improvement. This has occurred many times within the author's personal experience and with the happiest results.

Some little personal account of Swedenborg may fitly end this brief review of his doctrines, which is primarily intended to indicate his position in the general scheme. He must have been a most frugal, practical, hard-working and energetic young man, and a most lovable old one. Life seems to have mellowed him into a very gentle and venerable creature. He was placid, serene, and ever ready for conversation which did not take a psychic turn unless his companions so desired. The material of such conversations was always remarkable, but he was afflicted with a stammer which hindered his enunciation. In person he was tall and spare, with a spiritual face, blue eyes, a wig to his shoulders, dark clothing, knee-breeches, buckles, and a cane.

Swedenborg claimed that a heavy cloud was formed round the earth by the psychic grossness of humanity, and that from time to time there was a judgment and a clearing up, even as the thunderstorm clears the material atmosphere. He saw that the world, even in his day, was drifting into a dangerous position owing to the unreason of the Churches on the one side and the reaction towards absolute want of religion which was caused by it. Modern psychic authorities, notably Vale Owen, have spoken of this ever-accumulating cloud, and there is a very general feeling that the necessary cleansing process will not be long postponed.

A notice of Swedenborg from the Spiritualistic

standpoint may be best concluded by an extract from his own diary. He says : " All confirmations in matters pertaining to theology are, as it were, *glued fast into the brains*, and can with difficulty be removed, and while they remain, genuine truths can find no place." He was a very great seer, a great pioneer of psychic knowledge, and his weakness lay in those very words which he has written.

The general reader who desires to go further will find Swedenborg's most characteristic teachings in his " Heaven and Hell," " The New Jerusalem," and " Arcana Cœlestia." His life has been admirably done by Garth Wilkinson, Trobridge, and Brayley Hodgetts, the present president of the English Swedenborg Society. In spite of all his theological symbolism, his name must live eternally as the first of all modern men who has given a description of the process of death, and of the world beyond, which is not founded upon the vague ecstatic and impossible visions of the old Churches, but which actually corresponds with the descriptions which we ourselves obtain from those who endeavour to convey back to us some clear idea of their new existence.

CHAPTER II.

EDWARD IRVING: THE SHAKERS

THE story of Edward Irving and his experience of spiritual manifestations in the years from 1830 to 1833 are of great interest to the psychic student, and help to bridge the gap between Swedenborg on one side and Andrew Jackson Davis on the other. The facts are as follows :

Edward Irving was of that hard-working poorer-class Scottish stock which has produced so many great men. Of the same stock and at the same time and district came Thomas Carlyle. Irving was born in Annan in the year 1792. After a hard, studious youth, he developed into a very singular man. In person he was a giant and a Hercules in strength, his splendid physique being only marred by a bad outward cast of one eye—a defect which, like Byron's lame foot, seemed in some sort to present an analogy to the extremes in his character. His mind, which was virile, broad and courageous, was warped by early training in the narrow school of the Scottish Church, where the hard, crude views of the old Covenanters—an impossible Protestantism which represented a reaction against an impossible Catholicism —still poisoned the human soul. His mental position was strangely contradictory, for while he had inherited this cramped theology he had failed to inherit much which is the very birthright of the poorer Scot. He was opposed to all that was liberal, and even such obvious measures of justice as the Reform Bill of 1832 found in him a determined opponent.

This strange, eccentric, and formidable man had his proper environment in the 17th century, when his prototypes were holding moorland meetings in Galloway and avoiding, or possibly even attacking with the arms of the flesh, the dragoons of Claverhouse. But, live when he might, he was bound to write his name in some fashion on the annals of his time. We read of his strenuous youth in Scotland, of his rivalry with his friend Carlyle in the affections of the clever and vivacious Jane Welsh, of his enormous walks and feats of strength, of his short career as a rather violent school-teacher at Kirkcaldy, of his marriage to the daughter of a minister in that town, and finally of his becoming curate or assistant to the great Dr. Chalmers, who was, at that time, the most famous clergyman in Scotland, and whose administration of his parish in Glasgow is one of the outstanding chapters in the history of the Scottish Church. In this capacity he gained that man-to-man acquaintance with the poorer classes which is the best and most practical of all preparations for the work of life. Without it, indeed, no man is complete.

There was at that time a small Scottish church in Hatton Garden, off Holborn, in London, which had lost its pastor and was in a poor position, both spiritually and financially. The vacancy was offered to Dr. Chalmers's assistant, and after some heart-searchings was accepted by him. Here his sonorous eloquence and his thoroughgoing delivery of the Gospel message began to attract attention, and suddenly the strange Scottish giant became the fashion. The humble street was blocked by carriages on a Sunday morning, and some of the most distinguished men and women in London scrambled for a share of the very scanty accommodation. There is evidence that this extreme popularity did not last, and possibly the preacher's habit of expounding a text for an hour and a half was too much for the English weakling, however acceptable north of the Tweed. Finally a move was made to a larger church in Regent Square which could hold two thousand people, and there were sufficient stalwarts to fill this in decent fashion, though the preacher had ceased to excite the interest of his earlier days. Apart from his oratory, Irving seems to have been a conscientious and hard-working pastor, striving assiduously for the temporal needs of the more humble of his flock, and ever ready at all hours of the day or night to follow the call of duty.

Soon, however, there came a rift between him and the authorities of his Church. The matter in dispute made a very fine basis for a theological quarrel of the type which has done more harm in the world than the smallpox. The question was whether the Christ had in Him the possibility of sin, or whether the Divine portion of His being was a complete and absolute bar to physical temptations. The assessors contended that the association of such ideas as sin and Christ was a blasphemy. The obdurate clergyman, however, replied with some show of reason that unless the Christ had the capacity for sin, and successfully resisted it, His earthly lot was not the same as ours, and His virtues deserved less admiration. The matter was argued out in London with immense seriousness and at intolerable length, with the result that the presbytery declared its unanimous disapproval of the pastor's views. As, however, his congregation in turn expressed their unqualified approval, he was able to disregard the censure of his official brethren.

But a greater stumbling-block lay ahead, and Irving's encounter with it has made his name live as all names live which associate themselves with real spiritual issues. It should first be understood that Irving was deeply interested in Biblical prophecy, especially the vague and terrible images of St. John, and the strangely methodical forecasts of Daniel. He brooded much over the years and the days which were fixed as the allotted time before the days of wrath should precede the Second Coming of the Lord. There were others at that time—1830 and onwards—who were deeply immersed in the same sombre speculations. Among these was a wealthy banker named Drummond, who had a large country house at Albury, near Guildford. At this house these Biblical students used to assemble from time to time, discussing and comparing their views with such thoroughness that it was not unusual for their sittings to extend over a week, each day being fully taken up from breakfast to supper. This band was called the "Albury Prophets." Excited by the political portents which led up to the Reform Bill, they all considered that the foundations of the deep had been loosened. It is hard to imagine what their reaction would have been had they lived to witness the Great War. As it was, they were convinced that the end of all things was at hand, and they looked out eagerly for signs and portents, twisting the vague and sinister words of the prophets into all manner of fantastic interpretations.

Finally, above the monotonous horizon of human happenings there did actually appear a strange manifestation. There had been a legend that the spiritual gifts of earlier days would reassert themselves before the end, and here apparently was the forgotten gift of tongues coming back into the experience of mankind. It had begun in 1830 on the western side of Scotland, where the names of the sensitives, Campbell and MacDonald, spoke of that Celtic blood which has always been more alive to spiritual influences than the heavier Teutonic strain. The Albury Prophets were much exercised in their minds, and an emissary was sent from Mr. Irving's church to investigate and report. He found that the matter was very real. The people were of good repute, one of them, indeed, a woman whose character could best be described as saintly. The strange tongues in which they both talked broke out at intervals, and the manifestation was accompanied by healing miracles and other signs of power. Clearly it was no fraud or pretence, but a real influx of some strange force which carried one back to apostolic times. The faithful waited eagerly for further developments.

These were not long in coming, and they broke out in Irving's own church. It was in July, 1831, that it was rumoured that certain members of the congregation had been seized in this strange way in their own homes, and discreet exhibitions were held in the vestry and other secluded places. The pastor and his advisers were much puzzled as to whether a more public demonstration should be tolerated. The matter settled itself, however, after the fashion of affairs of the spirit, and in October of the same year the prosaic Church of Scotland service was suddenly interrupted by the strange outcry of the possessed. It came so suddenly and with such vehemence, both at the morning and afternoon service, that a panic set in in the church, and had it not been for their giant pastor thundering out, " Oh, Lord, still the tumult of the people ! " a tragedy might have followed. There was also a good deal of hissing and uproar from those who were conservative in their tastes. Altogether the sensation was a considerable one, and the newspapers of the day were filled with it, though their comments were far from respectful or favourable.

The sounds came from both women and men, and consisted in the first instance of unintelligible noises which were either mere gibberish, or some entirely unknown language. " Sudden, doleful, and unintelligible sounds," says one witness. " There was a force and fulness of sound," said another description, " of which the delicate female organs would seem incapable." " It burst forth with an astounding and terrible crash," says a third. Many, however, were greatly impressed by these sounds, and among them was Irving himself. " There is a power in the voice to thrill the heart and overawe the spirit after a manner which I have never felt. There is a march and majesty and sustained grandeur of which I have never heard the like. It is likest to one of the simplest and most ancient chants in the cathedral service in so much that I have been led to think that these chants, which can be traced as high as Ambrose, are recollections of the inspired utterances of the primitive Church."

Soon, moreover, intelligible English words were added to the strange outbursts. These usually consisted of ejaculations and prayers, with no obvious sign of any supernormal character save that they broke out at unseasonable hours and independently of the will of the speaker. In some cases, however, these powers developed until the gifted one was able, while under the influence, to give long harangues, to lay down the law in most dogmatic fashion over points of doctrine, and to issue reproofs which occasionally were turned even in the direction of the long-suffering pastor.

There may have been—in fact, there probably was—a true psychic origin to these phenomena, but they had developed in a soil of narrow bigoted theology, which was bound to bring them to ruin. Even Swedenborg's religious system was too narrow to receive the full undistorted gifts of the spirit, so one can imagine what they became when contracted within the cramped limits of a Scottish church, where every truth must be shorn or twisted until it corresponds with some fantastic text. The new good wine will not go into the old narrow bottles. Had there been a fuller revelation, then doubtless other messages would have been received in other fashions which would have presented the matter in its just proportions, and checked one spiritual gift by others. But there was no development save towards chaos. Some of the teaching received could not be reconciled with orthodoxy, and was therefore obviously of the devil. Some of the sensitives condemned others as heretics. Voice was raised against voice. Worst of all, some of the chief speakers became convinced themselves that their own speeches were diabolical. Their chief reason seems to have been that they did not accord with their own spiritual convictions, which would seem to some of us rather an indication that they were angelic. They entered also upon the slippery path of prophecy, and were abashed when their own prophecies did not materialize.

Some of the statements which came through these sensitives, and which shocked their religious sensibilities, might seem to deserve serious consideration by a more enlightened generation. Thus one of these Bible-worshippers is recorded as saying, concerning the Bible Society, "That it was the curse going through the land, quenching the Spirit of God, by the letter of the Word of God." Right or wrong, such an utterance would seem to be independent of him who uttered it, and it is in close accord with many of the spiritual teachings which we receive to-day. So long as the letter is regarded as sacred, just so long can anything, even pure materialism, be proved from that volume. —

One of the chief mouthpieces of the spirit was a certain Robert Baxter—not to be confused with the Baxter who some thirty years later was associated with certain remarkable prophecies. This Robert Baxter seems to have been a solid, earnest, prosaic citizen who viewed the Scriptures much as a lawyer views a legal document, with an exact valuation of every phrase—especially of such phrases as fitted into his own hereditary scheme of religion. He was an honest man with a restless conscience, which continually worried him over the smaller details, while leaving him quite unperturbed as to the broad platform upon which his beliefs were constructed. This man was powerfully affected by the influx of spirit— to use his own phrase, " his mouth was opened in power." According to him, January 14, 1832, was the beginning of those mystical 1,260 days which were to precede the Second Coming and the end of the world. Such a prediction must have been particularly sympathetic to Irving with his millennial dreams. But long before the days were fulfilled Irving was in his grave, and Baxter had forsworn those voices which had, in this instance at least, deceived him.

Baxter has written a pamphlet with the portentous title, " Narrative of Facts, Characterising the Supernatural Manifestations, in Members of Mr.

Irving's Congregation, and other Individuals, in England and Scotland, and formerly in the Writer Himself." Spiritual truth could no more come through such a mind than white light could come through a prism, and yet in this account he has to admit the occurrence of many things which seem clearly preternatural, mixed up with much that is questionable, and some things which are demonstrably false. The object of the pamphlet is mainly to forswear his evil and invisible guides, so that he may return to the safe if flattish bosom of the Scottish Church. It is noticeable, however, that a second member of Irving's congregation wrote an answering pamphlet with an even longer title, which showed that Baxter was right so long as he was prompted by the spirit, and wrong in his Satanic inferences. This pamphlet is interesting as containing letters from various people who possessed the gift of tongues, showing that they were earnest-minded folk who were incapable of any conscious deception.

What is an impartial psychic student who is familiar with more modern phases to say to this development ? Personally it seems to the author to have been a true psychic influx, blanketed and smothered by a petty sectarian theology of the letter-perfect description for which the Pharisees were reproved. If he may venture his individual opinion, it is that the perfect recipient of spiritual teaching is the earnest man who has worked his way through all the orthodox creeds, and whose mind, eager and receptive, is a blank surface ready to register a new impression exactly as received. He becomes the true child and pupil of other-world teaching, and all other types of Spiritualist appear to be compromises. This does not alter the fact that personal nobility of character may make the honest compromiser a far higher type than the pure Spiritualist, but it applies only to the actual philosophy. The field of Spiritualism is infinitely broad, and on it every variety of Christian, as well as the Moslem, the Hindu or the Parsee, can dwell in brotherhood. But a mere acceptance of spirit return and communion is not enough. Many savages have that. We need a moral code as well, and whether we regard Christ as a benevolent teacher or as a divine ambassador, His actual ethical teaching in one form or another, even if not coupled with His name, is an essential thing for the upliftment of mankind. But always it must be checked by reason, and acted upon in the spirit and not according to the letter.

This, however, is digression. In the voices of 1831 there are the signs of real psychic power. It is a recognized spiritual law that all psychic manifestations become distorted when seen through the medium of narrow sectarian religion. It is also a law that pompous, inflated persons attract mischievous entities and are the butts of the spirit world, being made game of by the use of large names and by prophecies which make the prophet ridiculous. Such were the guides who descended upon the flock of Mr. Irving, and produced various effects, good or bad, according to the instrument used.

The unity of the Church, which had been shaken by the previous censure of the presbytery, dissolved under this new trial. There was a large secession, and the building was claimed by the trustees. Irving and the stalwarts who were loyal to him wandered forth in search of new premises, and found them in the hall used by Robert Owen, the Socialist, philanthropist, and free-thinker, who was destined twenty years later to be one of the pioneer converts to Spiritualism. Here, in Gray's Inn Road, Irving rallied the faithful. It cannot be denied that the Church, as he organized it, with its angel, its elders, its deacons, its tongues, and its prophecies, was the best reconstruction of a primitive Christian Church that has ever been made. If Peter or Paul reincarnated in London they would be bewildered, and possibly horrified, by St. Paul's or by Westminster Cathedral, but they would certainly have been in a perfectly familiar atmosphere in the gathering over which Irving presided. A wise man recognizes that God may be approached from innumerable angles. The minds of men and the spirit of the times vary in their reaction to the great central cause, and one can only insist upon a broad charity both in oneself and in others. It was in this that Irving seems to have been wanting. It was always by the standard of that which was a sect among sects that he would measure the universe. There were times when he was vaguely conscious of this, and it may be that those wrestlings with Apollyon, of which he complains, even as Bunyan and the Puritans of old used to complain, had a strange explanation. Apollyon was really the Spirit of Truth, and the inward struggle was not between Faith and Sin, but was really between the darkness of inherited dogma, and the light of inherent and instinctive reason, God-given, and rising for ever in revolt against the absurdities of man.

But Irving lived very intensely and the successive crises through which he had passed had broken him down. These contests with argumentative theologians and with recalcitrant members of his flock may seem trivial things to us when viewed far off down the vista of years, but to him, with his eager, earnest, storm-torn soul, they were vital and terrible. To the un-fettered mind this sect or that seems a matter of indifference, but to Irving, both from heredity and from education, the Scottish Church was the ark of God, and yet he, its zealous, faithful son, driven by his own conscience, had rushed forth and had found the great gates which contained Salvation slammed and barred behind him. He was a branch cut from the tree, and he withered. It is a true simile, and it is more than a simile, for it became an actual physical fact. This giant in early middle age wilted and shrank. His great frame stooped. His cheeks became hollow and wan. His eyes shone with the bale-ful fever which was consuming him. And so, working to the very end and with the words, "If I die, I die with the Lord," upon his lips, his soul passed forth into that clearer and more golden light where the tired brain finds rest and the anxious spirit enters into a peace and assurance which life has never given.

Apart from this isolated incident of Irving's Church, there was one other psychic manifestation of those days which led more directly to the Hydesville revelation. This was the outbreak of spiritual phenomena among the Shaker communities in the United States, which has received less attention than it deserves.

These good people seem to have had affiliations on the one side with the Quakers, and, on the other, with the refugees from the Cevennes, who came to England to escape the persecution of Louis XIV. Even in England their harmless lives did not screen them from the persecution of the bigots, and they were forced to emigrate to America about the time of the War of Independence. There they founded settlements in various parts, living simple cleanly lives upon communistic principles, with sobriety and chastity as their watchword. It is not surprising that as the psychic cloud of other-world power slowly settled upon the earth it should have found its first response from such altruistic communities. In 1837 there were sixty such bodies in existence, and all of them responded in various degrees to the new power. They kept their experiences very strictly to themselves at the time, for as their elders subsequently explained, they would certainly have been all consigned to Bedlam had they told what had actually occurred. Two books, however, " Holy Wisdom " and " The Sacred Roll," which arose from their experiences, appeared afterwards.

The phenomena seem to have begun with the usual warning noises, and to have been followed by the obsession from time to time of nearly all the community. Everyone, man and woman, proved to be open to spirit possession. The invaders only came, however, after asking permission, and at such intervals as did not interfere with the work of the community. The chief visitants were Red Indian spirits, who came collectively as a tribe. "One or two elders might be in the room below, and there would be a knock at the door and the Indians would ask whether they might come in. Permission being given, a whole tribe of Indian spirits would troop into the house, and in a few minutes you would hear 'Whoop!' here and 'Whoop!' there all over the house." The whoops emanated, of course, from the vocal organs of the Shakers themselves, but while under the Indian control they would talk Indian among themselves, dance Indian dances, and in all ways show that they were really possessed by the Redskin spirits.

One may well ask why should these North American aborigines play so large a part not only in the inception, but in the continuance of this movement? There are few physical mediums in this country, as well as in America, who have not a Red Indian guide, whose photograph has not infrequently been obtained by psychic means, still retaining his scalp-locks and his robes. It is one of the many mysteries which we have still to solve. We can only say for certain, from our own experience, that such spirits are powerful in producing physical phenomena, but that they never present the higher teaching which comes to us either from European or from Oriental spirits. The physical phenomena are still, however, of very great importance, as calling the attention of sceptics to the matter, and therefore the part assigned to the Indians is a very vital one. Men of the rude open-air type seem in spirit life to be especially associated with the crude manifestations of spirit activity, and it has been repeatedly asserted, though it is hard to say how it could be proved, that their chief organizer was an adventurer who in life was known as Henry Morgan, and died as Governor of Jamaica, a post to which he had been appointed in the time of Charles II. Such unproved assertions are, it must be admitted, of no value in our present state of knowledge, but they should be put on record as further information may in time shed some new light upon them. John King, which is the spirit name of the alleged Henry Morgan, is a very real being, and there are few Spiritualists of experience who have not seen his heavily-bearded face and heard his masterful voice. As to the Indians who are his colleagues or his subordinates, one can but hazard the conjecture that they are children of Nature who are nearer perhaps to the primitive secrets than other more complex races. It may be that their special work is of the nature of an expiation and atonement—an explanation which the author has heard from their lips.

These remarks may well seem a digression from the actual experience of the Shakers, but the difficulties raised in the mind of the inquirer arise largely from the number of new facts, without any order or explanation, which he is forced to encounter. His mind has no possible pigeon-hole into which they can be fitted. Therefore, the author will endeavour in these pages to provide so far as possible from his own experience, or from that of those upon whom he can rely, such sidelights as may make the matter more intelligible, and give at least a hint of those laws which lie behind, and are as binding upon spirits as upon ourselves. Above all, the inquirer must cast away for ever the idea that the discarnate are necessarily wise or powerful entities. They have their individuality and their limitations, even as we have, and these limitations become the more marked when they have to manifest themselves through so foreign a substance as matter.

The Shakers had among them a man of outstanding intelligence named F. W. Evans, who gave a very clear and entertaining account of all this matter, which may be sought by the curious in the *New York Daily Graphic* of November 24, 1874, and has been largely copied into Colonel Olcott's work, " People From the Other World."

Mr. Evans and his associates after the first disturbance, physical and mental, caused by this spirit irruption, settled down to study what it really meant. They came to the conclusion that the matter could be divided into three phases. The first phase was the actual proving to the observer that the thing was real. The second phase was one of instruction, as even the humblest spirit can bring information as to his own experience of after-death conditions. The third phase was called the missionary phase and was the practical application. The Shakers came to the unexpected conclusion that the Indians were there not to teach but to be taught. They proselytized them, therefore, exactly as they would have done in life. A similar experience has occurred since then in very many Spiritualistic circles, where humble and lowly spirits have come to be taught that which they should have learned in this world had true teachers been available. One may well ask why the higher spirits over there do not supply this want? The answer given to the author upon one notable occasion was, " These people are very much nearer to you than to us. You can reach them where we fail."

It is clear from this that the good Shakers were never in touch with the higher guides—possibly they did not need guidance—and that their visitors were on a low plane. For seven years these visitations continued. When the spirits left they informed their hosts that they were going, but that presently they would return, and that when they did so they would pervade the world and enter the palace as well as the cottage. It was just four years later that the Rochester knockings broke out. When they did so, Elder Evans and another Shaker visited Rochester and saw the Fox sisters. Their arrival was greeted with great enthusiasm from the unseen forces, who proclaimed that this was indeed the work which had been foretold.

One remark of Elder Evans is worth transcribing. When asked, " Don't you think your experience is much the same as that of monks and nuns in the Middle Ages? " he did not answer. " Ours were angelic but these others were diabolical," as would have been said had the situation been reversed, but he replied with fine candour and breadth of mind, " Certainly. That is the proper explanation of them through all the ages. The visions·of Saint Theresa were Spiritualistic visions just such as we have frequently had vouchsafed to the members of our society." When further asked whether magic and necromancy did not belong to the same category, he answered, " Yes. That is when Spiritualism is used for selfish ends." It is clear that there were men living nearly a century ago who were capable of instructing our wise men of to-day.

That very remarkable woman, Mrs. Hardinge Britten, has recorded in her " Modern American Spiritualism " how she came in close contact with the Shaker community, and was shown by them the records, taken at the time, of their spiritual visitation. In them it was stated that the new era was to be inaugurated by an extraordinary discovery of material as well as of spiritual wealth. This is a most remarkable prophecy, as it is a matter of history that the goldfields of California were discovered within a very short time of the psychic outburst. A Swedenborg with his doctrine of correspondences might perhaps contend that the one was complementary to the other.

This episode of the Shaker manifestations is a very distinct link between the Swedenborg pioneer work and the period of Davis and the Fox sisters. We shall now consider the career of the former, which is intimately associated with the rise and progress of the modern psychic movement.

CHAPTER III

ANDREW JACKSON DAVIS was one of the most remarkable men of whom we have any exact record. Born in 1826 on the banks of the Hudson, his mother was an uneducated woman, with a visionary turn which was allied to vulgar superstition, while his father was a drunken worker in leather. He has written the details of his own childhood in a curious book, " The Magic Staff," which brings home to us the primitive and yet forceful life of the American provinces in the first half of last century. The people were rude and uneducated, but their spiritual side was very much alive, and they seem to have been reaching out continually for some new thing. It was in these country districts of New York in the space of a few years that both Mormonism and modern Spiritualism were evolved.

There never could have been a lad with fewer natural advantages than Davis. He was feeble in body and starved in mind. Outside an occasional school primer he could only recall one book that he had ever read up to his sixteenth year. Yet in that poor entity there lurked such spiritual forces that before he was twenty he had written one of the most profound and original books of philosophy ever pro-

36

duced. Could there be a clearer proof that nothing came from himself, and that he was but a conduit pipe through which flowed the knowledge of that vast reservoir which finds such inexplicable outlets ? The valour of a Joan of Arc, the sanctity of a Theresa, the wisdom of a Jackson Davis, the supernormal powers of a Daniel Home, all come from the same source.

In his later boyhood, Davis's latent psychic powers began to develop. Like Joan, he heard voices in the fields—gentle voices which gave him good advice and comfort. Clairvoyance followed this clairaudience. At the time of his mother's death, he had a striking vision of a lovely home in a land of brightness which he conjectured to be the place to which his mother had gone. His full capacity was tapped, however, by the chance that a travelling showman who exhibited the wonders of mesmerism came to the village and experimented upon Davis, as well as on many other young rustics who desired to experience the sensation. It was soon found that Davis had very remarkable clairvoyant powers.

These were developed not by the peripatetic mesmerist, but by a local tailor named Levingston, who seems to have been a pioneer thinker. He was so intrigued by the wonderful gifts of his subject, that he abandoned his prosperous business and devoted his whole time to working with Davis and to using his clairvoyant powers for the diagnosis of disease. Davis had developed the power, common among psychics, of seeing without the eyes, including things which could not be seen in any case by human vision. At first, the gift was used as a sort of amusement in reading the letters or the watches of the assembled rustics when his eyes were bandaged. In such cases all parts of the body can assume the function of sight, and the reason probably is that the etheric or spiritual body, which possesses the same organs as the physical, is wholly or partially disengaged, and that it registers the impression. Since it might assume any posture, or might turn completely round, one would naturally get vision from any angle, and an explanation is furnished of such cases as the author met in the north of England, where Tom Tyrrell, the famous medium, used to walk round a room, admiring the pictures, with the back of his head turned towards the walls on which they were hung. Whether in such cases the etheric eyes see the picture, or whether they see the etheric duplicate of the picture, is one of the many problems which we leave to our descendants.

Levingston used Davis at first for medical diagnosis. He described how the human body became transparent to his spirit eyes, which seemed to act from the centre of his forehead. Each organ stood out clearly and with a special radiance of its own which was dimmed in case of disease. To the orthodox medical mind, with which the author has much sympathy, such powers are suspect as opening a door for quackery, and yet he is bound to admit that all that was said by Davis has been corroborated within his own experience by Mr. Bloomfield, of Melbourne, who described to him the amazement which he felt when this power came suddenly upon him in the street, and revealed the anatomy of two persons who were walking in front of him. So well attested are such powers that it has been not unusual for medical men to engage clairvoyants as helpers in diagnosis. Hippocrates says, " The affection's suffered by the body the soul sees with shut eyes." Apparently, then, the ancients knew something of such methods. Davis's ministrations were not confined to those who were in his presence, but his soul or etheric body could be liberated by the magnetic manipulation of his employer, and could be sent forth like a carrier pigeon with the certainty that it would come home again bearing any desired information. Apart from the humanitarian mission on which it was usually engaged it would sometimes roam at will, and he has described in wonderful passages how he would see a translucent earth beneath him, with the great veins of mineral beds shining through like masses of molten metal, each with its own fiery radiance.

It is notable that at this earlier phase of Davis's psychic experience he had no memory when he returned from trance of what his impressions had been. They were registered, however, upon his subconscious mind, and at a later date he recalled them all clearly. For the time he was a source of instruction to others but remained ignorant himself.

Until then his development had been on lines which are not uncommon, and which could be matched within the experience of every psychic student. But then there occurred an episode which was entirely novel and which is described in close detail in the

autobiography. Put briefly, the facts were these.
On the evening of March 6, 1844, Davis was suddenly
possessed by some power which led him to fly from
the little town of Poughkeepsie, where he lived, and
to hurry off, in a condition of semi-trance, upon a
rapid journey. When he regained his clear per-
ceptions he found himself among wild mountains, and
there he claims to have met two venerable men with
whom he held intimate and elevating communion, the
one upon medicine and the other upon morals. All
night he was out, and when he inquired his whereabouts next morning he was told that he was in the
Catskill Mountains and forty miles from his home.
The whole narrative reads like a subjective experience,
a dream or a vision, and one would not hesitate to
place it as such were it not for the details of his reception and the meal he ate upon his return. It
is a possible alternative that the flight into the mountains was a reality and the interviews a dream. He
claims that he afterwards identified his two mentors
as Galen and Swedenborg, which is interesting as being
the first contact with the dead which he had ever
recognized. The whole episode seems visionary, and
had no direct bearing upon the lad's remarkable future.

He felt higher powers stirring within him, and it
was remarked to him that when he was asked profound questions in the mesmeric trance he always
replied, " I will answer that in my book." In his
nineteenth year he felt that the hour for writing the
book had come. The mesmeric influence of Levingston did not, for some reason, seem suited for this, and

a Dr. Lyon was chosen as the new mesmerist. Lyon threw up his practice and went with his singular protégé to New York, where they presently called upon the Rev. William Fishbough to come and act as amanuensis. The intuitional selection seems to have been justified, for he also at once gave up his work and obeyed the summons. Then, the apparatus being ready, Lyon threw the lad day after day into the magnetic trance, and his utterances were taken down by the faithful secretary. There was no money and no publicity in the matter, and even the most sceptical critic cannot but admit that the occupation and objects of these three men were a wonderful contrast to the money-making material world which surrounded them. They were reaching out to the beyond, and what can man do that is nobler?

It is to be understood that a pipe can carry no more than its own diameter permits. The diameter of Davis was very different from that of Swedenborg. Each got knowledge while in an illuminated state. But Swedenborg was the most learned man in Europe, while Davis was as ignorant a young man as could be found in the State of New York. Swedenborg's revelation was perhaps the greater, though more likely to be tinged by his own brain. The revelation of Davis was incomparably the greater miracle.

Dr. George Bush, Professor of Hebrew in the University of New York, who was one of those pre-

I can solemnly affirm that I have heard Davis correctly quote the Hebrew language in his lectures, and display a knowledge of geology which would have been astonishing in a person of his age, even if he had devoted years to the study. He has discussed, with the most signal ability, the profoundest questions of historical and biblical archæ- ology, of mythology, of the origin and affinity of language, and the progress of civilization among the different nations of the globe, which would do honour to any scholar of the age, even if in reaching them he had the advantage of access to all the libraries in Christendom. Indeed, if he had acquired all the information he gives forth in these lectures, not in the two years since he left the shoemaker's bench, but in his whole life, with the most assiduous study, no prodigy of intellect of which the world has ever heard would be for a moment compared with him, yet not a single volume or page has he ever read.

Davis has a remarkable pen-picture of himself at that moment. He asks us to take stock of his equip- ment. " The circumference of his head is unusually small," says he. " If size is the measure of power, then this youth's mental capacity is unusually limited. His lungs are weak and unexpanded. He had not dwelt amid refining influences—manners ungentle and awkward. He has not read a book save one. He knows nothing of grammar or the rules of lan- guage, nor associated with literary or scientific per- sons." Such was the lad of nineteen from whom there now poured a perfect cataract of words and ideas which are open to the criticism not of simplicity, but of being too complex and too shrouded in learned terms, although always with a consistent thread of reason and method beneath them.

It is very well to talk of the subconscious mind, but this has usually been taken as the appearance of ideas which have been received and then submerged. When, for example, the developed Davis could recall what had happened in his trances during his undeveloped days, that was a clear instance of the emerging of the buried impressions. But it seems an abuse of words to talk of the unconscious mind when we are dealing with something which could never by normal means have reached any stratum of the mind, whether conscious or not.

Such was the beginning of Davis's great psychic revelation which extended eventually over many books and is all covered by the name of the " Harmonial Philosophy." Of its nature and its place in psychic teaching we shall treat later.

In this phase of his life Davis claims still to have been under the direct influence of the person whom he afterwards identified as Swedenborg—a name quite unfamiliar to him at the time. From time to time he received a clairaudient summons to " go up into the mountain." This mountain was a hill on the farther bank of the Hudson opposite Poughkeepsie. There on the mountain he claims that he met and spoke with a venerable figure. There seems to have been none of the details of a materialization, and the incident has no analogy in our psychic experience, save indeed—and one speaks with all reverence—when the Christ also went up into a mountain and communed with the forms of Moses and Elias. There the analogy seems complete.

Davis does not appear to have been at all a religious man in the ordinary conventional sense, although he was drenched with true spiritual power. His views, so far as one can follow them, were very critical as regards Biblical revelation, and, to put it at the lowest, he was no believer in literal interpretation. But he was honest, earnest, unvenal, anxious to get the truth and conscious of his responsibility in spreading it.

For two years the unconscious Davis continued to dictate his book upon the secrets of Nature, while the conscious Davis did a little self-education in New York with occasional restorative visits to Poughkeepsie. He had begun to attract the attention of some serious people, Edgar Allan Poe being one of his visitors. His psychic development went on, and before he reached his twenty-first year he had attained a state when he needed no second person to throw him into trance but could do it for himself. His subconscious memory too was at last opened, and he was able to go over the whole long vista of his experiences. It was at this time that he sat by a dying woman and observed every detail of the soul's departure, a wonderful description of which is given in the first volume of the " Great Harmonia." Although this description has been issued as a separate pamphlet it is not as well known as it should be, and a short epitome of it may interest the reader.

He begins by the consoling reflection that his own soul-flights, which were death in everything save duration, had shown him that the experience was

" interesting and delightful," and that those symptoms
which appear to be signs of pain are really the unconscious reflexes of the body, and have no significance.
He then tells how, having first thrown himself into
what he calls the " Superior condition," he thus
observed the stages from the spiritual side. " The
material eye can only see what is material, and the
spiritual what is spiritual," but as everything would
seem to have a spiritual counterpart the result is the
same. Thus when a spirit comes to us it is not us
that it perceives but our etheric bodies, which are,
however, duplicates of our real ones.

It was this etheric body which Davis saw emerging
from its poor outworn envelope of protoplasm, which
finally lay empty upon the bed like the shrivelled
chrysalis when the moth is free. The process began
by an extreme concentration in the brain, which
became more and more luminous as the extremities
became darker. It is probable that man never thinks
so clearly, or is so intensely conscious, as he becomes
after all means of indicating his thoughts have left him.
Then the new body begins to emerge, the head disen-
gaging itself first. Soon it has completely freed itself,
standing at right-angles to the corpse, with its feet near
the head, and with some luminous vital band between
which corresponds to the umbilical cord. When the
cord snaps a small portion is drawn back into the dead
body, and it is this which preserves it from instant
putrefaction. As to the etheric body, it takes some
little time to adapt itself to its new surroundings, and
in this instance it then passed out through the open

doors. " I saw her pass through the adjoining room,
out of the door and step from the house into the
atmosphere. . . . Immediately upon her emergement
from the house she was joined by two friendly spirits
from the spiritual country, and after tenderly recog-
nizing and communing with each other the three, in
the most graceful manner, began ascending obliquely
through the ethereal envelopment of our globe.
They walked so naturally and fraternally together
that I could scarcely realize the fact that they trod the
air—they seemed to be walking on the side of a
glorious but familiar mountain. I continued to gaze
upon them until the distance shut them from my
view."

Such is the vision of Death as seen by A. J. Davis
—a very different one from that dark horror which has
so long obsessed the human imagination. If this be
the truth, then we can sympathize with Dr. Hodgson
in his exclamation, " I can hardly bear to wait."
But is it true ? We can only say that there is a great
deal of corroborative evidence.

Many who have been in the cataleptic condition, or who have been so ill that they have sunk into
deep coma, have brought back impressions very consistent with Davis's explanation, though others have
returned with their minds completely blank. The
author, when at Cincinnati in 1923, was brought into
contact with a Mrs. Monk, who had been set down
as dead by her doctors, and for an hour or so had
experienced a post-mortem existence before some
freak of fate restored her to life. She wrote a short

account of her experience, in which she had a vivid remembrance of walking out of the room, just as Davis described, and also of the silver thread which continued to unite her living soul ·to her comatose body. A remarkable case was reported in *Light*, also (March 25, 1922), in which the five daughters of a dying woman, all of them clairvoyant, watched and reported the process of their mother's death. There again the description of the process was very analogous to that given, and yet there is sufficient difference in this and other accounts to suggest that the sequence of events is not always regulated by the same laws. Another variation of extreme interest is to be found in a drawing done by a child medium which depicts the soul leaving the body and is described in Mrs. De Morgan's "From Matter to Spirit" (p. 121). This book, with its weighty preface by the celebrated mathematician Professor De Morgan, is one of the pioneer works of the spiritual movement in Great Britain. When one reflects that it was published in 1863 one's heart grows heavy at the success of those forces of obstruction, reflected so strongly in the Press, which have succeeded for so many years in standing between God's message and the human race.

The prophetic power of Davis can only be got over by the sceptic if he ignores the record. Before 1856 he prophesied in detail the coming of the motor-car and of the typewriter. In his book, "The Penetralia," appears the following:

" *Question :* Will utilitarianism make any discoveries in other locomotive directions ? "

" Yes; look out about these days for carriages and travelling saloons on country roads—without horses, without steam, without any visible motive power— moving with greater speed and far more safety than at present. Carriages will be moved by a strange and beautiful and simple admixture of aqueous and atmospheric gases—so easily condensed, so simply ignited, and so imparted by a machine somewhat resembling our engines, as to be entirely concealed and manageable between the forward wheels. These vehicles will prevent many embarrassments now experienced by persons living in thinly populated territories. The first requisite for these land-locomotives will be good roads, upon which with your engine, without your horses, you may travel with great rapidity. These carriages seem to me of uncomplicated construction."

" He was next asked:

" Do you perceive any plan by which to expedite the art of writing ? "

" Yes; I am almost moved to invent an automatic psychographer—that is, an artificial soul-writer. It may be constructed something like a piano, one brace or scale of keys to represent the elementary sounds; another and lower tier to represent a combination, and still another for a rapid re-combination; so that a person, instead of playing a piece of music, may touch off a sermon or a poem."

So, too, this seer, in reply to a query regarding what was then termed " atmospheric navigation," felt " deeply impressed " that " the necessary mechanism—to transcend the adverse currents of air, so that

ANDREW JACKSON DAVIS

we may sail as easily and safely and pleasantly as birds
—is dependent on a new motive power. This power
will come. It will not only move the locomotive on
the rail, and the carriage on the country road, but the
aerial cars also, which will move through the sky from
country to country."

He predicted the coming of Spiritualism in his
" Principles of Nature," published in 1847, where he
says:

It is a truth that spirits commune with one another
while one is in the body and the other in the higher spheres
—and this, too, when the person in the body is unconscious
of the influx, and hence cannot be convinced of the fact ;
and this truth will ere long present itself in the form of a
living demonstration. And the world will hail with delight
the ushering-in of that era when the interiors of men will
be opened, and the spiritual communion will be established such as is now being enjoyed by the inhabitants of
Mars, Jupiter and Saturn.

In this matter Davis's teaching was definite, but
it must be admitted that in a good deal of his work he
is indefinite and that it is hard reading, for it is dis-
figured by the use of long words, and occasionally he
even invents a vocabulary of his own. It was, however, on a very high moral and intellectual level, and
might be best described as an up-to-date Christianity
with Christ's ethics applied to modern problems and
entirely freed from all trace of dogma. " Docu-
mentary Religion," as Davis called it, was not in his
opinion religion at all. That name could only be
applied to the personal product of reason and spiritu-

ality. Such was the general line of teaching, mixed up with many revelations of Nature, which was laid down in the successive books of the " Harmonial Philosophy " which succeeded " Nature's Divine Revelations," and occupied the next few years of his life. Much of the teaching appeared in a strange paper called "The Univercœlum," and much was spread by lectures in which he laid before the public the results of his revelations.

In his spiritual vision Davis saw an arrangement of the universe which corresponds closely with that which Swedenborg had already noted, and with that afterwards taught by the spirits and accepted by the Spiritualists. He saw a life which resembled that of earth, a life that may be called semi-material, with pleasures and pursuits that would appeal to our natures which had been by no means changed by death. He saw study for the studious, congenial tasks for the energetic, art for the artistic, beauty for the lover of Nature, rest for the weary ones. He saw graduated phases of spiritual life, through which one slowly rose to the sublime and the celestial. He carried his magnificent vision onward beyond the present universe, and saw it dissolve once more into the fire-mist from which it had consolidated, and then consolidate once more to form the stage on which a higher evolution could take place, the highest class here starting as the lowest class there. This process he saw renew itself innumerable times, covering trillions of years, and ever working towards refinement and purification. These spheres he pictured as concentric rings round the world, but as he admits that neither time nor space define themselves clearly in his visions, we need not take their geography in too literal a sense. The object of life was to qualify for advancement in this tremendous scheme, and the best method of human advancement was to get away from sin— not only the sins which are usually recognized, but also those sins of bigotry, narrowness and hardness, which are very especially blemishes not of the ephemeral flesh but of the permanent spirit. For this purpose the return to simple life, simple beliefs, and primitive brotherhood was essential. Money, alcohol, lust, violence and priestcraft—in its narrow sense—were the chief impediments to racial progress.

It must be admitted that Davis, so far as one can follow his life, lived up to his own professions. He was very humble-minded, and yet he was of the stuff that saints are made of. His autobiography extends only to 1857, so that he was little over thirty when he published it, but it gives a very complete and sometimes an involuntary insight into the man. He was very poor, but he was just and charitable. He was very earnest, and yet he was patient in argument and gentle under contradiction. The worst motives were imputed to him, and he records them with a tolerant smile. He gives a full account of his first two marriages, which were as unusual as everything else about him, but which reflect nothing but credit upon him. From the date at which " The Magic Staff " finishes he seems to have carried on the same life of alternate writing and lecturing, winning more and more the ear of the world, until he died in the year 1910 at the age of eighty-four. The last years of his life he spent as keeper of some small book-store in Boston. The fact that his " Harmonial Philosophy " has now passed through some forty editions in the United States is a proof that the seed which he scattered so assiduously has not all fallen upon barren ground.

What is of importance to us is the part played by Davis at the commencement of the spiritual revelation. He began to prepare the ground before that revelation occurred. He was clearly destined to be closely associated with it, for he was aware of the material demonstration at Hydesville upon the very day when it occurred. From his notes there is quoted the sentence, under the vital date of March 31, 1848: " About daylight this morning a warm breathing passed over my face and I heard a voice, tender and strong, saying, ' Brother, the good work has begun—behold, a living demonstration is born.' I was left wondering what could be meant by such a message." It was the beginning of the mighty movement in which he was to act as prophet. His own powers were themselves supernormal upon the mental side, just as the physical signs were upon the material side. Each supplemented the other. He was, up to the limit of his capacity, the soul of the movement, the one brain which had a clear vision of the message which was heralded in so novel and strange a way. No man can take the whole message, for it is infinite, and rises ever higher as we come into contact with higher beings, but Davis interpreted it so well for his

day and generation that little can be added even now
to his conception.

He had advanced one step beyond Swedenborg,
though he had not Swedenborg's mental equipment
with which to marshal his results. Swedenborg had
seen a heaven and hell, even as Davis saw it and has
described it with fuller detail. Swedenborg did not,
however, get a clear vision of the position of the dead
and the true nature of the spirit world with the possibility of return as it was revealed to the American
seer. This knowledge came slowly to Davis. His
strange interviews with what he described as " materialized spirits " were exceptional things, and he drew
no common conclusions from them. It was later when
he was brought into contact with actual spiritual
phenomena that he was able to see the full meaning of
them. This contact was not established at Rochester,
but rather at Stratford in Connecticut, where Davis
was a witness of the Poltergeist phenomena which
broke out in the household of a clergyman, Dr.
Phelps, in the early months of 1850. A study of
these led him to write a pamphlet, " The Philosophy
of Spiritual Intercourse," expanded afterwards to a
book which contains much which the world has not
yet mastered. Some of it, in its wise restraint, may
also be commended to some Spiritualists. " Spiritualism is useful as a living demonstration of a future
existence," he says. " Spirits have aided me many
times, but they do not control either my person or my
reason. They can and do perform kindly offices for
those on earth. But benefits can only be secured on

the condition that we allow them to become our teachers and not our masters—that we accept them as companions, not as gods to be worshipped." Wise words—and a modern restatement of the vital remark of Saint Paul that the prophet must not be subject to his own gifts.

In order to explain adequately the life of Davis one has to ascend to supernormal conditions. But even then there are alternative explanations. When one considers the following undeniable facts :

1. That he claims to have seen and heard the materialized form of Swedenborg before he knew anything of his teachings.
2. That *something* possessed this ignorant youth, which gave him great knowledge.
3. That this knowledge took the same broad sweeping universal lines which were characteristic of Swedenborg.
4. But that they went one step farther, having added just that knowledge of spirit power which Swedenborg may have attained after his death.

Considering these four points, then, is it not a feasible hypothesis that the power which controlled Davis was actually Swedenborg ? It would be well if the estimable but very narrow and limited New Church took such possibilities into account. But whether Davis stood alone, or whether he was the reflection of one greater than himself, the fact remains that he was a miracle man, the inspired, learned, uneducated apostle of the new dispensation. So permanent has been his influence that the well-known artist and critic Mr. E. Wake Cook, in his remarkable book " Retrogression in Art," harks back to Davis's teaching as the one modern influence which could recast the world. Davis left his mark deep upon Spiritualism. " Summerland," for example, as a name for the modern Paradise, and the whole system of Lyceum schools with their ingenious organization, are of his devising. As Mr. Baseden Butt has remarked, " Even to-day the full and final extent of his influence is extremely difficult, if not impossible, to assess." *

* *Occult Review*, Feb., 1925.

CHAPTER IV

THE HYDESVILLE EPISODE

WE have now traced various disconnected and irregular uprushes of psychic force in the cases which have been set forth, and we come at last to the particular episode which was really on a lower level than those which had gone before, but which occurred within the ken of a practical people who found means to explore it thoroughly and to introduce reason and system into what had been a mere object of aimless wonder. It is true that the circumstances were lowly, the actors humble, the place remote, and the communication sordid, being based on no higher motive than revenge. When, however, in the everyday affairs of this world one wishes to test whether a telegraphic wire is in operation, one notices whether a message comes through, and the high or low nature of that message is quite a secondary consideration. It is said that the first message which actually came through the Transatlantic cable was a commonplace inquiry from the testing engineer. None the less, kings and presidents have used it since. So it is that the humble spirit of the murdered pedlar of Hydesville may have opened a gap into which the angels have thronged. There is good and bad and all that is intermediate on the Other Side as on this side of the veil. The company you attract depends upon yourself and your own motives.

Hydesville is a typical little hamlet of New York State, with a primitive population which was, no doubt, half-educated, but was probably, like the rest of those small American centres of life, more detached from prejudice and more receptive of new ideas than any other set of people at that time. This particular village, situated about twenty miles from the rising town of Rochester, consisted of a cluster of wooden houses of a very humble type. It was in one of these, a residence which would certainly not pass the requirements of a British district council surveyor, that there began this development which is already, in the opinion of many, by far the most important thing that America has given to the commonweal of the world. It was inhabited by a decent farmer family of the name of Fox—a name which, by a curious coincidence, has already been registered in religious history as that of the apostle of the Quakers. Besides the father and mother, who were Methodists in religion, there were two children resident in the house at the time when the manifestations reached such a point of intensity that they attracted general attention. These children were the daughters—Margaret, aged fourteen, and Kate, aged eleven. There were several other children out in the world, of whom only one, Leah, who was teaching music in Rochester, need come into this narrative.

The little house had already established a somewhat uncanny reputation. The evidence to this effect was collected and published very shortly after the event, and seems to be as reliable as such evidence can be. In view of the extreme importance of everything which bears upon the matter, some extracts from these depositions must be inserted, but to avoid dislocation of the narrative the evidence upon this point has been relegated to the Appendix. We will therefore pass at once to the time of the tenancy of the Fox family, who took over the house on December 11, 1847. It was not until the next year that the sounds heard by the previous tenants began once more. These sounds consisted of rapping noises. A rap would seem to be the not unnatural sound to be produced by outside visitors when they wished to notify their presence at the door of human life and desired that door to be opened for them. Just such raps (all unknown to these unread farmers) had occurred in England in 1661 at the house of Mr. Mompesson, at Tedworth.* Raps, too, are recorded by Melancthon as having occurred at Oppenheim, in Germany, in 1520, and raps were heard at the Epworth Vicarage in 1716. Here they were once more, and at last they were destined to have the closed door open.

The noises do not seem to have incommoded the Fox family until the middle of March, 1848. From that date onwards they continually increased in intensity. Sometimes they were a mere knocking; at other times they sounded like the movement of furniture. The children were so alarmed that they refused

---

* "Saducismus Triumphatus," by Rev. Joseph Glanvil.

to sleep apart and were taken into the bedroom of their parents. So vibrant were the sounds that the beds thrilled and shook. Every possible search was made, the husband waiting on one side of the door and the wife on the other, but the rappings still continued. It was soon noticed that daylight was inimical to the phenomena, and this naturally strengthened the idea of trickery, but every possible solution was tested and failed. Finally, upon the night of March 31 there was a very loud and continued outbreak of inexplicable sounds. It was on this night that one of the great points of psychic evolution was reached, for it was then that young Kate Fox challenged the unseen power to repeat the snaps of her fingers. That rude room, with its earnest, expectant, half-clad occupants with eager upturned faces, its circle of candlelight, and its heavy shadows lurking in the corners, might well be made the subject of a great historical painting. Search all the palaces and chancelleries of 1848, and where will you find a chamber which has made its place in history as secure as this little bedroom of a shack?

The child's challenge, though given with flippant words, was instantly answered. Every snap was echoed by a knock. However humble the operator at either end, the spiritual telegraph was at last working, and it was left to the patience and moral earnestness of the human race to determine how high might be the uses to which it was put in the future. Unexplained forces were many in the world, but here was a force claiming to have independent intelligence at the back of it. That was the supreme sign of a new departure.

Mrs. Fox was amazed at this development, and at the further discovery that the force could apparently see as well as hear, for when Kate snapped her fingers without sound the rap still responded. The mother asked a series of questions, the answers to which, given in numerals, showed a greater knowledge of her own affairs than she herself possessed, for the raps insisted that she had had seven children, whereas she protested that she had borne only six, until one who had died early came back to her mind. A neighbour, Mrs. Redfield, was called in, and her amusement was changed to wonder, and finally to awe, as she also listened to correct answers to intimate questions.

The neighbours came flocking in as some rumours of these wonders got about, and the two children were carried off by one of them, while Mrs. Fox went to spend the night at Mrs. Redfield's. In their absence the phenomena went on exactly the same as before, which disposes once for all of those theories of cracking toes and dislocating knees which have been so frequently put forward by people unaware of the true facts.)

Having formed a sort of informal committee of investigation, the crowd, in shrewd Yankee fashion, spent a large part of the night of March 31 in playing question and answer with the unseen intelligence. According to its own account he was a spirit; he had been injured in that house; he rapped out the name of a former occupant who had injured him; he was thirty-one years old at the time of death (which was five years before); he had been murdered for money; he had been buried in the cellar ten feet deep. On descending to the cellar, dull, heavy thumps, coming apparently from under the earth, broke out when the investigator stood at the centre. There was no sound at other times. That, then, was the place of burial ! It was a neighbour named Duesler who, first of all modern men, called over the alphabet and got answers by raps on the letters. In this way the name of the dead man was obtained—Charles B. Rosma. The idea of connected messages was not developed until four months later, when Isaac Post, a Quaker, of Rochester, was the pioneer. These, in very brief outline, were the events of March 31, which were continued and confirmed upon the succeeding night, when not fewer than a couple of hundred people had assembled round the house. Upon April 2 it was observed that the raps came in the day as well as at night.

Such is a synopsis of the events of the night of March 31, 1848, but as it was the small root out of which sprang so great a tree, and as this whole volume may be said to be a monument to its memory, it would seem fitting that the story should be given in the very words of the two original adult witnesses. Their evidence was taken within four days of the occurrence, and forms part of that admirable piece of psychic research upon the part of the local committee which will be described and commented upon later. Mrs. Fox deposed :

On the night of the first disturbance we all got up, lighted a candle and searched the entire house, the noises continuing during the time, and being heard near the same place. Although not very loud, it produced a jar of the bedsteads and chairs that could be felt when we were in bed. It was a tremulous motion, more than a sudden jar. We could feel the jar when standing on the floor. It continued on this night until we slept. I did not sleep until about twelve o'clock. On March 30th we were disturbed all night. The noises were heard in all parts of the house. My husband stationed himself outside of the door while I stood inside, and the knocks came on the door between us. We heard footsteps in the pantry, and walking downstairs ; we could not rest, and I then concluded that the house must be haunted by some unhappy restless spirit. I had often heard of such things, but had never witnessed anything of the kind that I could not account for before.

On Friday night, March 31st, 1848, we concluded to go to bed early and not permit ourselves to be disturbed by the noises, but try and get a night's rest. My husband was here on all these occasions, heard the noises, and helped search. It was very early when we went to bed on this night—hardly dark. I had been so broken of my rest I was almost sick. My husband had not gone to bed when we first heard the noise on this evening. I had just lain down. It commenced as usual. I knew it from all other noises I had ever heard before. The children, who slept in the other bed in the room, heard the rapping, and tried to make similar sounds by snapping their fingers.

My youngest child, Cathie, said : " Mr. Splitfoot, do as I do," clapping her hands. The sound instantly followed her with the same number of raps. When she stopped, the sound ceased for a short time. Then Margaretta said, in sport, " Now, do just as I do. Count one, two, three, four," striking one hand against the other at the same time; and the raps came as before. She was afraid to repeat them. Then Cathie said in her childish simplicity, " Oh, mother, I know what it is. To-morrow is April-fool day, and it's somebody trying to fool us."

I then thought I could put a test that no one in the place could answer. I asked the noise to rap my different children's ages, successively. Instantly, each one of my children's ages was given correctly, pausing between them sufficiently long to individualize them until the seventh, at which a longer pause was made, and then three more emphatic raps were given, corresponding to the age of the little one that died, which was my youngest child.

I then asked : " Is this a human being that answers my questions so correctly ? " There was no rap. I asked: " Is it a spirit ? If it is, make two raps." Two sounds were given as soon as the request was made. I then said : " If it was an injured spirit, make two raps," which were instantly made, causing the house to tremble. I asked : " Were you injured in this house ? " The answer was given as before. " Is the person living that injured you ? " Answered by raps in the same manner. I ascertained by the same method that it was a man, aged thirty-one years, that he had been murdered in this house, and his remains were buried in the cellar ; that his family consisted of a wife and five children, two sons and three daughters, all living at the time of his death, but that his wife had since died. I asked : " Will you continue to rap if I call my neighbours that they may hear it too ? " The raps were loud in the affirmative.

My husband went and called in Mrs. Redfield, our nearest neighbour. She is a very candid woman. The girls were sitting up in bed clinging to each other, and trembling with terror. I think I was as calm as I am now. Mrs. Redfield came immediately (this was about half-past seven), thinking she would have a laugh at the children. But when she saw them pale with fright, and nearly speechless, she was amazed, and believed there was something more serious than she had supposed. I asked a few questions for her, and was answered as before. He told her age exactly. She then called her husband, and the same questions were asked and answered.

Then Mr. Redfield called in Mr. Duesler and wife, and several others. Mr. Duesler then called in Mr. and Mrs. Hyde, also Mr. and Mrs. Jewell. Mr. Duesler asked many questions, and received answers. I then named all the neighbours I could think of, and asked if any of them had injured him, and received no answer. Mr. Duesler then asked questions and received answers . He asked : " Were you murdered ? " Raps affirmative. " Can your murderer be brought to justice ? " No sound. " Can he be punished by the law ? " No answer. He then said : " If your murderer cannot be punished by the law, manifest it by raps," and the raps were made clearly and distinctly. In the same way, Mr. Duesler ascertained that he was murdered in the east bedroom about five years ago and that the murder was committed by a Mr. —— on a Tuesday night at twelve o'clock ; that he was murdered by having his throat cut with a butcher knife ; that the body was taken down to the cellar ; that it was not buried until the next night ; that it was taken through the buttery, down the stairway, and that it was buried ten feet below the surface of the ground. It was also ascertained that he was murdered for his money, by raps affirmative.

" How much was it—one hundred ? " No rap. " Was it two hundred ? " etc., and when he mentioned five hundred the raps replied in the affirmative.

Many called in who were fishing in the creek, and all heard the same questions and answers. Many remained in the house all night. I and my children left the house.

My husband remained in the house with Mr. Redfield all night. On the next Saturday the house was filled to overflowing. There were no sounds heard during day, but they commenced again in the evening. It was said that there were over three hundred persons present at the time. On Sunday morning the noises were heard throughout the day by all who came to the house.

On Saturday night, April 1st, they commenced digging in the cellar ; they dug until they came to water, and then gave it up. The noise was not heard on Sunday evening nor during the night. Stephen B. Smith and wife (my daughter Marie), and my son David S. Fox and wife, slept in the room this night.

I have heard nothing since that time until yesterday. In the forenoon of yesterday there were several questions answered in the usual way by rapping. I have heard the noise several times to-day.

I am not a believer in haunted houses or supernatural appearances. I am very sorry that there has been so much excitement about it. It has been a great deal of trouble to us. It was our misfortune to live here at this time ; but I am willing and anxious that the truth should be known, and that a true statement should be made. I cannot account for these noises ; all that I know is that they have been heard repeatedly, as I have stated. I have heard this rapping again this (Tuesday) morning, April 4. My children also heard it.

I certify that the foregoing statement has been read to me, and that the same is true ; and that I should be willing to take my oath that it is so, if necessary."

(Signed) Margaret Fox.

April 11, 1848.

Statement by John D. Fox

I have heard the above statement of my wife, Margaret Fox, read, and hereby certify that the same is true in all its particulars. I heard the same rappings which she has spoken of, in answer to the questions, as stated by her. There have been a great many questions besides those asked, and answered in the same way. Some have been asked a great many times, and they have always received the same answers. There has never been any contradiction whatever.

I do not know of any way to account for those noises, as being caused by any natural means. We have searched every nook and corner in and about the house, at different times, to ascertain, if possible, whether anything or anybody was secreted there that could make the noise, and have not been able to find anything which would or could explain the mystery. It has caused a great deal of trouble and anxiety.

Hundreds have visited the house, so that it is impossible for us to attend to our daily occupations ; and I hope that, whether caused by natural or supernatural means, it will be ascertained soon. The digging in the cellar will be resumed as soon as the water settles, and then it can be ascertained whether there are any indications of a body ever having been buried there ; and if there are, I shall have no doubt but that it is of supernatural origin.

(*Signed*) JOHN D. FOX.

April 11, 1848.

The neighbours had formed themselves into a committee of investigation, which for sanity and efficiency might be a lesson to many subsequent researchers. They did not begin by imposing their own conditions, but they started without prejudice to record the facts exactly as they found them. Not only did they collect and record the impressions of everyone concerned, but they actually had the evidence in printed form within a month of the occurrence. The author has in vain attempted to get an original copy of the pamphlet, " A Report of the Mysterious Noises heard in the House of Mr. John D. Fox," published at Canandaigua, New York, but he has been presented with a facsimile of the original, and it is his considered opinion that the fact of human survival and power of communication was definitely proved to any mind capable of weighing evidence from the day of the appearance of that document.

The statement made by Mr. Duesler, chief of the committee, gives important testimony to the occurrence of the noises and jars in the absence of the Fox girls from the house, and disposes once and for ever of all suspicion of their complicity in these events. Mrs. Fox, as we have seen, referring to the night of Friday, March 31, said: " I and my children left the house." Part of Mr. Duesler's statement reads:

I live within a few rods of the house in which these sounds have been heard. The first I heard anything about them was a week ago last Friday evening (March 31st). Mrs. Redfield came over to my house to get my wife to go over to Mrs. Fox's. Mrs. R. appeared to be very much agitated. My wife wanted me to go over with them, and I accordingly went. . . . This was about nine o'clock in the evening. There were some twelve or fourteen persons present when I left them. Some were so frightened that they did not want to go into the room. I went into the room and sat down on the bed. Mr. Fox asked a question and I heard the rapping, which they had spoken of, distinctly. I felt the bedstead jar when the sounds were produced.

The Hon. Robert Dale Owen,* a member of the United States Congress, and formerly American Minister to Naples, supplies a few additional particulars in his narrative, written after conversations with Mrs. Fox and her daughters, Margaret and Catharine. Describing the night of March 31, 1848, he says ("Footfalls, etc.," p. 287):

The parents had had the children's beds removed into their bedroom, and strictly enjoined them not to talk of noises even if they heard them. But scarcely had the mother seen them safely in bed and was retiring to rest herself when the children cried out, "Here they are again!" The mother chid them, and lay down. Thereupon the noises became louder and more startling. The children sat up in bed. Mrs. Fox called in her husband. The night being windy, it suggested itself to him that it might be the rattling of the sashes. He tried several, shaking them to see if they were loose. Kate, the youngest girl, happened to remark that as often as her father shook a window-sash the noises seemed to reply. Being a lively child, and in a measure accustomed to what was going on, she turned to where the noise was, snapped her fingers, and called out, "Here, old Splitfoot, do as I do." *The knocking instantly responded.* That was the very commencement. Who can tell where the end will be? . . . Mr. Mompesson, in bed with his little daughter (about Kate's age) whom the sound seemed chiefly to follow, "observed that it would exactly answer, in drumming, anything that was beaten or called for." But his curiosity led him no further. Not so Kate Fox. She tried, by silently bringing together her thumb and forefinger, whether she could still obtain a response. Yes! It could see, then, as well as hear!

* Author of "Footfalls on the Boundary of Another World" (1860), and "The Debatable Land" (1871).

She called her mother. " Only look, mother ! " she said, bringing together her finger and thumb as before. And as often as she repeated the noiseless motion, just so often responded the raps.

In the summer of 1848 Mr. David Fox, with the assistance of Mr. Henry Bush, Mr. Lyman Granger, of Rochester, and others, resumed digging in the cellar. At a depth of five feet they found a plank, and further digging disclosed charcoal and quicklime, and finally human hair and bones, which were pronounced by expert medical testimony to belong to a human skeleton. It was not until fifty-six years later that a further discovery was made which proved beyond all doubt that someone had really been buried in the cellar of the Fox house.

This statement appeared in the *Boston Journal* (a non-Spiritualistic paper) of November 23, 1904, and runs as follows:

Rochester, N.Y., Nov. 22nd, 1904 : The skeleton of the man supposed to have caused the rappings first heard by the Fox sisters in 1848 has been found in the walls of the house occupied by the sisters, and clears them from the only shadow of doubt held concerning their sincerity in the discovery of spirit communication.

The Fox sisters declared they learned to communicate with the spirit of a man, and that he told them he had been murdered and buried in the cellar. Repeated excavations failed to locate the body and thus give proof positive of their story.

The discovery was made by school-children playing in the cellar of the building in Hydesville known as the " Spook House," where the Fox sisters heard the wonderful rappings. William H. Hyde, a reputable citizen of Clyde, who owns the house, made an investigation and found an almost entire human skeleton between the earth and crumbling cellar walls, undoubtedly that of the wandering pedlar who, it was claimed, was murdered in the east room of the house, and whose body was hidden in the cellar.

Mr. Hyde has notified relatives of the Fox sisters, and the notice of the discovery will be sent to the National Order of Spiritualists, many of whom remember having made pilgrimage to the " Spook House," as it is commonly called. The finding of the bones practically corroborates the sworn statement made by Margaret Fox, April 11, 1848.

There was discovered a pedlar's tin box as well as the bones, and this box is now preserved at Lilydale, the central country head-quarters of the American Spiritualists, to which also the old Hydesville house has been transported.

These discoveries settle the question for ever and prove conclusively that there *was* a crime committed in the house, and that this crime was indicated by psychic means. When one examines the result of the two diggings one can reconstruct the circumstances. It is clear that in the first instance the body was buried with quicklime in the centre of the cellar. Later the criminal was alarmed by the fact that this place was too open to suspicion and he had dug up the body, or the main part of it, and reburied it under the wall where it would be more out of the way. The work had been done so hurriedly, however, or in such imperfect light, that some clear traces were left, as has been seen, of the original grave.

Was there independent evidence of such a crime ? In order to find it we have to turn to the deposition of Lucretia Pulver, who served as help during the tenancy of Mr. and Mrs. Bell, who occupied the house four years before. She describes how a pedlar came to the house and how he stayed the night there with his wares. Her employers told her that she might go home that night.

I wanted to buy some things off the pedlar but had no money with me, and he said he would call at our house next morning and sell them to me. I never saw him after this. About three days after this they sent for me to come back. I accordingly came back. . . .

I should think this pedlar of whom I have spoken was about thirty years of age. I heard him conversing with Mrs. Bell about his family. Mrs. Bell told me that he was an old acquaintance of theirs—that she had seen him several times before. One evening, about a week after this, Mrs. Bell sent me down to the cellar to shut the outer door. In going across the cellar I fell down near the centre of it. It appeared to be uneven and loose in that part. After I got upstairs, Mrs. Bell asked me what I screamed for and I told her. She laughed at me being frightened, and said it was only where the rats had been at work in the ground. A few days after this, Mr. Bell carried a lot of dirt into the cellar just at night and was at work there some time. Mrs. Bell told me that he was filling up the rat-holes.

A short time after this Mrs. Bell gave me a thimble which she said she had bought of this pedlar. About three months after this I visited her and she said the pedlar had been there again and she showed me another thimble which she said she had bought from him. She showed me some other things which she said she had bought from him.

It is worth noting that a Mrs. Lape in 1847 had claimed to have actually *seen* an apparition in the house, and that this vision was of a middle-sized man who wore grey pants, a black frock-coat and black cap. Lucretia Pulver deposed that the pedlar in life wore a black frock-coat and light-coloured pants.

On the other hand, it is only fair to add that the Mr. Bell who occupied the house at that time was not a man of notorious character, and one would willingly concede that an accusation founded entirely upon psychic evidence would be an unfair and intolerable thing. It is very different, however, when the proofs of a crime have actually been discovered, and the evidence then centres merely upon which tenant was in possession at that particular time. The deposition of Lucretia Pulver assumes vital importance in its bearing upon this matter.

There are one or two points about the case which would bear discussion. One is that a man with so remarkable a name as Charles B. Rosma should never have been traced, considering all the publicity which the case acquired. This would certainly at the time have appeared a formidable objection, but with our fuller knowledge we appreciate how very difficult it is to get names correctly across. A name apparently is a purely conventional thing, and as such very different from an idea. Every practising Spiritualist has received messages which were correct coupled with names which were mistaken. It is possible that the real name was Ross, or possibly Rosmer, and that this error prevented identification. Again, it is curious that he should not have known that his body had been moved from the centre of the cellar to the wall, where it was eventually found. We can only record the fact without attempting to explain it.

Again, granting that the young girls were the mediums and that the power was drawn from them, how came the phenomena when they had actually been removed from the house? To this one can only answer that though the future was to show that the power did actually emanate from these girls, none the less it seemed to have permeated the house and to have been at the disposal of the manifesting power for a time at least when the girls were not present.

The Fox family were seriously troubled by the disturbances—Mrs. Fox's hair turned white in a week —and as it became apparent that these were associated with the two young daughters, these were sent from home. But in the house of her brother, David Fox, where Margaret went, and in that of her sister Leah, whose married name was Mrs. Fish, at Rochester, where Catharine was staying, the same sounds were heard. Every effort was made to conceal these manifestations from the public, but they soon became known. Mrs. Fish, who was a teacher of music, was unable to continue her profession, and hundreds of people flocked to her house to witness the new marvels. It should be stated that either this power was contagious, or else it was descending upon many individuals independently from some common source. Thus Mrs. Leah Fish, the elder sister, received it, though in a less degree than Kate or Margaret. But it was no longer confined to the Fox family. It was like some psychic cloud descending from on high and showing itself on those persons who were susceptible. Similar sounds were heard in the home of Rev. A. H. Jervis, a Methodist minister, living in Rochester. Strong physical phenomena also began in the family of Deacon Hale, of Greece, a town close to Rochester. A little later Mrs. Sarah A. Tamlin and Mrs. Benedict, of Auburn, developed remarkable mediumship. Mr. Capron, the first historian of the movement, describes Mrs. Tamlin as one of the most reliable mediums he had ever met, and says that though the sounds occurring in her presence were not so loud as those with the Fox family, the messages were equally trustworthy.

It speedily became evident, then, that these unseen forces were no longer attached to any building, but that they had transferred themselves to the girls. In vain the family prayed with their Methodist friends that relief would come. In vain also were exorcisms performed by the clergy of various creeds. Beyond joining with loud raps in the Amens, the unseen presences took no notice of these religious exercises.

The danger of blindly following alleged spirit guidance was clearly shown some months later in the neighbouring town of Rochester, where a man disappeared under suspicious circumstances. An enthusiastic Spiritualist had messages by raps which announced a murder. The canal was dragged and the wife of the missing man was actually ordered to enter the canal, which nearly cost her her life. Some months later the absentee returned, having fled to Canada to avoid a writ for debt. This, as may well be imagined, was a blow to the young cult. The public did not then understand what even now is so little understood, that death causes no change in the human spirit, that mischievous and humorous entities abound, and that the inquirer must use his own instincts and his own common sense at every turn. "Try the spirits that ye may know them." In the same year, in the same district, the truth of this new philosophy upon the one side, and its limitations and dangers on the other, were most clearly set forth. These dangers are with us still. The silly man, the arrogant inflated man, the cocksure man, is always a safe butt. Every observer has had some trick played upon him. The author has himself had his faith sorely shaken by deception until some compensating proof has come along to assure him that it was only a lesson which he had received, and that it was no more fiendish or even remarkable that disembodied intelligences should be hoaxers than that the same intelligence inside a human body should find amusement in the same foolish way.

The whole course of the movement had now widened and taken a more important turn. It was no longer a murdered man calling for justice. The pedlar seemed to have been used as a pioneer, and now that he had found the opening and the method, a myriad of Intelligences were swarming at his back. Isaac Post had instituted the method of spelling by raps, and messages were pouring through. According to these the whole system had been devised by the contrivance of a band of thinkers and inventors upon the spirit plane, foremost among whom was Benjamin Franklin, whose eager mind and electrical knowledge in earth life might well qualify him for such a venture. Whether this claim was true or not, it is a fact that Rosma dropped out of the picture at this stage, and that the intelligent knockings purported to be from the deceased friends of those inquirers who were prepared to take a serious interest in the matter and to gather in reverent mood to receive the messages. That they still lived and still loved was the constant message from the beyond, accompanied by many material tests, which confirmed the wavering faith of the new adherents of the movement. When asked for their methods of working and the laws which governed them, the answers were from the beginning exactly what they are now : that it was a matter concerned with human and spirit magnetism; that some who were richly endowed with this physical property were mediums; that this endowment was not necessarily allied to morality or intelligence ; and that the condition of harmony was especially necessary to secure good results. In seventy odd years we have learned very little more; and after all these years the primary law of harmony is invariably broken at the so-called test séances, the members of which imagine that they have disproved the philosophy when they obtain negative or disordered results, whereas they have actually confirmed it.

In one of the early communications the Fox sisters

were assured that " these manifestations would not be confined to them, but would go all over the world." This prophecy was soon in a fair way to be fulfilled, for these new powers and further developments of them, which included the discerning and hearing of spirits and the movement of objects without contact, appeared in many circles which were independent of the Fox family. In an incredibly short space of time the movement, with many eccentricities and phases of fanaticism, had swept over the Northern and Eastern States of the Union, always retaining that solid core of actual tangible fact, which might be occasionally simulated by impostors, but always reasserted itself to the serious investigator who could shake himself free from preconceived prejudice. Disregarding for the moment these wider developments, let us continue the story of the original circles at Rochester.

The spirit messages had urged upon the small band of pioneers a public demonstration of their powers in an open meeting at Rochester—a proposition which was naturally appalling to two shy country girls and to their friends. So incensed were the discarnate Guides by the opposition of their earthly agents that they threatened to suspend the whole movement for a generation, and did actually desert them completely for some weeks. At the end of that time communication was restored and the believers, chastened by this interval of thought, put themselves unreservedly into the hands of the outside forces, promising that they would dare all in the cause. It was no light matter. A few of the clergy, notably the

Methodist minister, the Rev. A. H. Jervis, rallied to their aid, but the majority thundered from their pulpits against them, and the mob eagerly joined in the cowardly sport of heretic-baiting. On November 14, 1849, the Spiritualists held their first meeting at the Corinthian Hall, the largest available in Rochester. The audience, to its credit, listened with attention to the exposition of facts from Mr. Capron, of Auburn, the principal speaker. A committee of five representative citizens was then selected to examine into the matter and to report upon the following evening, when the meeting would reassemble. So certain was it that this report would be unfavourable that the *Rochester Democrat* is stated to have had its leading article prepared, with the head-line: " Entire Exposure of the Rapping Humbug." The result, however, caused the editor to hold his hand. The committee reported that the raps were undoubted facts, though the information was not entirely correct, that is, the answers to questions were "not altogether right nor altogether wrong." They added that these raps came on walls and doors some distance from the girls, causing a sensible vibration. " They entirely failed to find any means by which it could be done."

This report was received with disapproval by the audience, and a second committee from among the dissentients was formed. This investigation was conducted in the office of a lawyer. Kate, for some reason, was away, and only Mrs. Fish and Margaret were present. None the less, the sounds continued as before, though a Dr. Langworthy was introduced to test the possibility of ventriloquism. The final report was that " the sounds were heard, and their thorough investigation had conclusively shown them to be produced neither by machinery nor ventriloquism, though what the agent is they were unable to determine."

Again the audience turned down the report of their own committee, and again a deputation was chosen from among the most extreme opponents, one of whom vowed that if he could not find out the trick he would throw himself over the falls of the Genesee River. Their examination was thorough to the length of brutality, and a committee of ladies was associated with it. The latter stripped the frightened girls, who wept bitterly under their afflictions. Their dresses were then tied tightly round their ankles and they were placed upon glass and other insulators. The committee was forced to report, " when they were standing on pillows with a handkerchief tied round the bottom of their dresses, tight to the ankles, we all heard the rapping on the wall and floor distinctly." The committee further testified that their questions, some of them mental, had been answered correctly.

So long as the public looked upon the movement as a sort of joke it was prepared to be tolerantly amused, but when these successive reports put the matter in a more serious light, a wave of blackguardism swept over the town, which reached such a pitch that Mr. Willetts, a gallant Quaker, was compelled at the fourth public meeting to declare that " the mob of ruffians who designed to lynch the girls should do

so, if they attempted it, over his dead body." There
was a disgraceful riot, the young women were
smuggled out by a back door, and reason and justice
were for the moment clouded over by force and folly.
Then, as now, the minds of the average men of the
world were so crammed with the things that do not
matter that they had no space for the things that do
matter. But Fate is never in a hurry, and the movement went on. Many accepted the findings of the
successive committees as being final, and indeed, it is
difficult to see how the alleged facts could have been
more severely tested. At the same time, this strong,
new, fermenting wine began to burst some of the old
bottles into which it was poured to the excusable
disgust of the public.

The many discreet, serious and religious circles
were for a season almost obscured by swollen-headed
ranters who imagined themselves to be in touch with
every high entity from the Apostles downwards, some
even claiming the direct afflatus of the Holy Ghost
and emitting messages which were only saved from
being blasphemous by their crudity and absurdity.
One community of these fanatics, who called themselves the Apostolic Circle of Mountain Cove, particularly distinguished themselves by their extreme claims
and furnished good material for the enemies of the
new dispensation. The great body of Spiritualists
turned away in disapproval from such exaggerations,
but were unable to prevent them. Many well-
attested supernormal phenomena came to support the
failing spirits of those who were distressed by the

excesses of the fanatics. On one occasion, which is particularly convincing and well-reported, two bodies of investigators in separate rooms, at Rochester, on February 20, 1850, received the same message simultaneously from some central force which called itself Benjamin Franklin. This double message was: "There will be great changes in the nineteenth century. Things that now look dark and mysterious to you will be laid plain before your sight. Mysteries are going to be revealed. The world will be enlightened." It must be admitted that, up to now, the prophecy has been only partially fulfilled, and it may at the same time be conceded that, with some startling exceptions, the forecasts of the spirit people have not been remarkable for accuracy, especially where the element of time is concerned.

The question has often been asked: "What was the purpose of so strange a movement at this particular time, granting that it is all that it claims to be?" Governor Tallmadge, a United States senator of repute, was one of the early converts to the new cult, and he has left it upon record that he asked this question upon two separate occasions in two different years from different mediums. The answer in each case was almost identical. The first said: "It is to draw mankind together in harmony, and to convince sceptics of the immortality of the soul." The second said: "To unite mankind and to convince sceptical minds of the immortality of the soul." Surely this is no ignoble ambition and does not justify those narrow and bitter attacks from ministers and the less progressive of their flocks from which Spiritualists have up to the present day had to suffer. The first half of the definition is particularly important, for it is possible that one of the ultimate results of this movement will be to unite religion upon a common basis so strong, and, indeed, so self-sufficient, that the quibbles which separate the Churches of to-day will be seen in their true proportions and will be swept away or disregarded. One could even hope that such a movement might spread beyond the bounds of Christianity and throw down some of the barriers which stand between great sections of the human race.

Attempts to expose the phenomena were made from time to time. In February, 1851, Dr. Austin Flint, Dr. Charles A. Lee, and Dr. C. B. Coventry of the University of Buffalo, published a statement *showing to their own satisfaction that the sounds occurring in the presence of the Fox sisters were caused by the snapping of knee-joints. It called forth a characteristic reply in the Press from Mrs. Fish and Margaret Fox, addressed to the three doctors:

> As we do not feel willing to rest under the imputation of being impostors, we are very willing to undergo a proper and decent examination, provided we can select three male and three female friends who shall be present on the occasion. We can assure the public that there is no one more anxious than ourselves to discover the origin of these mysterious manifestations. If they can be explained on "anatomical" or "physiological" principles, it is due to the world that the investigation be made, and that the

* Capron : " Modern Spiritualism, &c.," pp. 310-313.

" humbug " be exposed. As there seems to be much interest manifested by the public on that subject, we would suggest that as early an investigation as is convenient would be acceptable to the undersigned.

Ann L. Fish.
Margaretta Fox.

The investigation was held, but the results were negative. In an appended note to the doctors' report in the *New York Tribune*, the editor (Horace Greeley) observes:

> The doctors, as has already appeared in our columns, commenced with the assumption that the origin of the " rapping " sounds *must* be physical, and their primary cause the volition of the ladies aforesaid—in short, that these ladies were " The Rochester impostors." They appear, therefore, in the above statement, as the prosecutors of an impeachment, and ought to have selected other persons as judges and reporters of the trial. . . . It is quite probable that we shall have another version of the matter.

Much testimony in support of the Fox sisters was quickly forthcoming, and the only effect of the professors' " exposure " was to redouble the public interest in the manifestations.

There was also the alleged confession of Mrs. Norman Culver, who deposed, on April 17, 1851, that Catharine Fox had revealed to her the whole secret of how the raps were produced. It was an entire fabrication, and Mr. Capron published a crushing answer, showing that on the date when Catharine Fox was supposed to have made the confession to Mrs. Culver, she was residing at his house seventy miles distant.

Mrs. Fox and her three daughters began public sittings in New York in the spring of 1850, at Barnum's Hotel, and they attracted many curious visitors. The Press was almost unanimous in denunciation of them. A brilliant exception to this was found in Horace Greeley, already quoted, who wrote an appreciative article in his paper under his own initials. A portion of this will be found in the Appendix.

After a return to Rochester, the Fox family made a tour of the Western States, and then paid a second visit to New York, when the same intense public interest was displayed. They had obeyed the spirits' mandate to proclaim these truths to the world, and the new era that had been announced was now ushered in. When one reads the detailed accounts of some of these American sittings, and considers the brain power of the sitters, it is amazing to think that people, blinded by prejudice, should be so credulous as to imagine that it was all the result of deception. At that time was shown moral courage which has been conspicuously lacking since the reactionary forces in science and in religion combined to stifle the new knowledge and to make it dangerous for its professors. Thus in a single sitting in New York in 1850 we find that there were gathered round the table the Rev. Dr. Griswold, Fenimore Cooper the novelist, Bancroft the historian, Rev. Dr. Hawks, Dr. J. W. Francis, Dr. Marcy, Willis the Quaker poet, Bryant the poet, Bigelow of the *Evening Post*, and General Lyman. All of these were satisfied as to the facts, and the account winds up: " The manners and bearing of the ladies " (i.e. the three Fox sisters) " are such as to create a prepossession in their favour." The world since then has dug up much coal and iron; it has erected great structures and it has invented terrible engines of war, but can we say that it has advanced in spiritual knowledge or reverence for the unseen? Under the guidance of materialism the wrong path has been followed, and it becomes increasingly clear that the people must return or perish.

CHAPTER V

THE CAREER OF THE FOX SISTERS

FOR the sake of continuity the subsequent history of the Fox sisters will now be given after the events at Hydesville. It is a remarkable, and to Spiritualists a painful, story, but it bears its own lesson and should be faithfully recorded. When men have an honest and whole-hearted aspiration for truth there is no development which can ever leave them abashed or find no place in their scheme.

For some years the two younger sisters, Kate and Margaret, gave séances at New York and other places, successfully meeting every test which was applied to them. Horace Greeley, afterwards a candidate for the United States presidency, was, as already shown, deeply interested in them and convinced of their entire honesty. He is said to have furnished the funds by which the younger girl completed her very imperfect education.

During these years of public mediumship, when the girls were all the rage among those who had no conception of the religious significance of this new revelation, and who concerned themselves with it purely in the hope of worldly advantage, the sisters exposed themselves to the enervating influences of promiscuous séances in a way which no earnest

Spiritualist could justify. The dangers of such practices were not then so clearly realized as now, nor had it occurred to people that it is unlikely that high spirits would descend to earth in order to advise as to the state of railway stocks or the issue of love affairs. The ignorance was universal, and there was no wise mentor at the elbow of these poor pioneers to point the higher and the safer path. Worst of all, their jaded energies were renewed by the offer of wine at a time when one at least of them was hardly more than a child. It is said that there was some family predisposition towards alcoholism, but even without such a taint their whole procedure and mode of life were rash to the last degree. Against their moral character there has never been a breath of suspicion, but they had taken a road which leads to degeneration of mind and character, though it was many years before the more serious effects were manifest.

Some idea of the pressure upon the Fox girls at this time may be gathered from Mrs. Hardinge Britten's * description from her own observation. She talks of " pausing on the first floor to hear poor patient Kate Fox, in the midst of a captious, grumbling crowd of investigators, repeating hour after hour the letters of the alphabet, while the no less poor, patient spirits rapped out names, ages and dates to suit all comers." Can one wonder that the girls, with vitality sapped, the beautiful, watchful influence of the mother removed, and harassed by enemies, succumbed to a

* "Autobiography," p. 40.

gradually increasing temptation in the direction of stimulants ?

A remarkably clear light is thrown upon Margaret at this period in that curious booklet, "The Love Letters of Dr. Elisha Kane." It was in 1852 that Dr. Kane, afterwards the famous Arctic explorer, met Margaret Fox, who was a beautiful and attractive girl. To her Kane wrote those love letters which record one of the most curious courtships in literature. Elisha Kane, as his first name might imply, was a man of Puritan extraction, and Puritans, with their belief that the Bible represents the absolutely final word in spiritual inspiration and that they understand what that last word means, are instinctively antagonistic to a new cult which professes to show that new sources and new interpretations are still available.

He was also a doctor of medicine, and the medical profession is at the same time the most noble and the most cynically incredulous in the world. From the first Kane made up his mind that the young girl was involved in fraud, and formed the theory that her elder sister Leah was, for purposes of gain, exploiting the fraud. The fact that Leah shortly afterwards married a wealthy man named Underhill, a Wall Street insurance magnate, does not appear to have modified Kane's views as to her greed for illicit earnings. The doctor formed a close friendship with Margaret, put her under his own aunt for purposes of education whilst he was away in the Arctic, and finally married her under the curious Gretna Green kind of marriage law which seems to have prevailed at the time. Shortly afterwards he died (in 1857), and the widow, now calling herself Mrs. Fox-Kane, forswore all phenomena for a time, and was received into the Roman Catholic Church.

In these letters Kane continually reproaches Margaret with living in deceit and hypocrisy. We have very few of her letters, so that we do not know how far she defended herself. The compiler of the book, though a non-Spiritualist, says: " Poor girl, with her simplicity, ingenuousness and timidity, she could not, had she been so inclined, have practised the slightest deception with any chance of success." This testimony is valuable, as the writer was clearly intimately acquainted with everyone concerned. Kane himself, writing to the younger sister Kate, says: " Take my advice and never talk of the spirits either to friends or strangers. You know that with all my intimacy with Maggie after a whole month's trial I could make nothing of them. Therefore they are a great mystery."

Considering their close relations, and that Margaret clearly gave Kane every demonstration of her powers, it is inconceivable that a trained medical man would have to admit after a month that he could make nothing of it, if it were indeed a mere cracking of a joint. One can find no evidence for fraud in these letters, but one does find ample proof that these two young girls, Margaret and Kate, had not the least idea of the religious implications involved in these powers, or of the grave responsibilities of mediumship, and that they misused their gift in the direction of giving worldly advice, receiving promiscuous sitters, and answering comic or frivolous questions. If in such circumstances both their powers and their character were to deteriorate, it would not surprise any experienced Spiritualist. They deserved no better, though their age and ignorance furnished an excuse.

To realize their position one has to remember that they were little more than children, poorly educated, and quite ignorant of the philosophy of the subject. When a man like Dr. Kane assured Margaret that it was very wrong, he was only saying what was dinned into her ears from every quarter, including half the pulpits of New York. Probably she had an uneasy feeling that it *was* wrong, without in the least knowing why, and this may account for the fact that she does not seem to remonstrate with him for his suspicions. Indeed, we may admit that *au fond* Kane was right, and that the proceedings were in some ways unjustifiable. At that time they were very unvenal themselves, and had they used their gift, as D. D. Home used his, with no relation to worldly things, and for the purpose only of proving immortality and consoling the afflicted, then, indeed, they would have been above criticism. He was wrong in doubting their gift, but right in looking askance at some examples of their use of it.

In some ways Kane's position is hopelessly illogical. He was on most intimate and affectionate terms with the mother and the two girls, although if words have any meaning he thought them to be swindlers living

on the credulity of the public. "Kiss Katie for me,"
he says, and he continually sends love to the mother.

Already, young as they were, he had a glimpse of
the alcoholic danger to which they were exposed by
late hours and promiscuous company. "Tell Katie
to drink no champagne, and do you follow the same
advice," said he. It was sound counsel, and it would
have been well for themselves and for the movement
if they had both followed it; but again we must
remember their inexperienced youth and the constant
temptations.

Kane was a curious blend of the hero and the prig.
Spirit-rapping, unfortified by any of the religious or
scientific sanctions which came later, was a low-down
thing, a superstition of the illiterate, and was he, a
man of repute, to marry a spirit-rapper ? He vacil-
lated over it in an extraordinary way, beginning a
letter with claims to be her brother, and ending by
reminding her of the warmth of his kisses. "Now
that you have given me your heart, I will be a brother
to you," he says. He had a vein of real superstition
running through him which was far below the credulity which he ascribed to others. He frequently
alludes to the fact that by raising his right hand he
had powers of divination and that he had learned it
"from a conjurer in the Indies." Occasionally he is
a snob as well as a prig. "At the very dinner-table
of the President I thought of you"; and again: "You
could never lift yourself up to my thoughts and my
objects. I could never bring myself down to yours."
As a matter of fact, the few extracts given from her

letters show an intelligent and sympathetic mind. On at least one occasion we find Kane suggesting deceit to her, and she combating the idea.

There are four fixed points which can be established by the letters:

1. That Kane thought in a vague way that there was trickery ;
2. That in the years of their close intimacy she never admitted it;
3. That he could not even suggest in what the trickery lay;
4. That she did use her powers in a way which serious Spiritualists would deplore.

She really knew no more of the nature of these forces than those around her did. The editor says: " She had always averred that she never fully believed the rappings to be the work of spirits, but imagined some occult laws of nature were concerned." This was her attitude later in life, for on her professional card she printed that people must judge the nature of the powers for themselves.

It is natural that those who speak of the danger of mediumship, and especially of physical mediumship, should point to the Fox sisters as an example. But their case must not be exaggerated. In the year 1871, after more than twenty years of this exhausting work, we find them still receiving the enthusiastic support and admiration of many leading men and women of the day. It was only after forty years of public service that adverse conditions were manifested in their lives, and therefore, without in any way glossing over what is evil, we can fairly claim that their record hardly justifies those who allude to mediumship as a soul-destroying profession.

It was in this year—1871—that Kate Fox's visit to England was brought about through the generosity of Mr. Charles F. Livermore, a prominent banker of New York, in gratitude for the consolation he had received from her wonderful powers, and to advance the cause of Spiritualism. He provided for all her needs, and thus removed any necessity for her to give professional sittings. He also arranged for her to be accompanied by a congenial woman companion.

In a letter * to Mr. Benjamin Coleman, a well-known worker in the Spiritualist movement, Mr. Livermore says:

Miss Fox, taken all in all, is no doubt the most wonderful living medium. Her character is irreproachable and pure. I have received so much through her powers of mediumship during the past ten years which is solacing, instructive and astounding, that I feel greatly indebted to her, and desire to have her taken good care of while absent from her home and friends.

His further remarks have some bearing possibly on the later sad events of her life:

That you may the more thoroughly understand her idiosyncrasies, permit me to explain that she is a sensitive of the highest order and of childlike simplicity ; she feels keenly the atmospheres of everyone with whom she is brought in contact, and to that degree that at times she becomes exceedingly nervous and apparently capricious.

* *The Spiritual Magazine*, 1871, pp. 525-6.

For this reason I have advised her not to sit in dark séances, that she may avoid the irritation arising from the suspicion of sceptics, mere curiosity-mongers, and lovers of the marvellous.

The perfection of the manifestations to be obtained through her depends upon her surroundings, and in proportion as she is in rapport or sympathy with you does she seem receptive of spiritual power. The communications through her are very remarkable, and have come to me frequently from my wife (Estelle), in perfect idiomatic French, and sometimes in Spanish and Italian, whilst she herself is not acquainted with any of these languages. You will understand all this, but these explanations may be necessary for others. As I have said, *she will not give séances as a professional medium*, but I hope she will do all the good she can in furtherance of the great truth, in a quiet way, while she remains in England.

Mr. Coleman, who had a sitting with her in New York, says that he received one of the most striking evidences of spirit identity that had ever occurred to him in his experience of seventeen years. Mr. Cromwell F. Varley, the electrician who laid the Atlantic cable, in his evidence before the London Dialectical Society in 1869, spoke of interesting electrical experiments he made with this medium.

The visit of Kate Fox to England was evidently regarded as a mission, for we find Mr. Coleman advising her to choose only those sitters who are not afraid to have their names published in confirmation of the facts they have witnessed. This course seems to have been adopted to some extent, for there is preserved a fair amount of testimony to her powers from, among others, Professor William Crookes, Mr.

S. C. Hall, Mr. W. H. Harrison (editor of *The Spiritu-alist*), Miss Rosamund Dale Owen (who afterwards married Laurence Oliphant), and the Rev. John Page Hopps.

The new-comer began to hold sittings soon after her arrival. At one of the first of these, on November 24, 1871, a representative of *The Times* was present, and he published a detailed account of the séance, which was held jointly with D. D. Home, a close friend of the medium. This appeared in an article entitled " Spiritualism and Science," occupying three and a half columns of leading type. *The Times* Commissioner speaks of Miss Fox taking him to the door of the room and inviting him to stand by her and to hold her hands, which he did, " when loud thumps seemed to come from the panels, as if done with the fist. These were repeated at our request any number of times." He mentioned that he tried every test that he could think of, that Miss Fox and Mr. Home gave every opportunity for examination, and that their feet and hands were held.

In the course of a leading article on the above report and the correspondence that came from it, *The Times* (January 6, 1873) declared that there was no case for scientific inquiry:

Many sensible readers, we fear, will think we owe them an apology for opening our columns to a controversy on such a subject as Spiritualism and thus treating as an open or debatable question what should rather be dismissed at once as either an imposture or a delusion. But even an imposture may call for unmasking, and popular delusions however absurd, are often too important to be neglected by the wiser portion of mankind. . . . Is there, in reality, anything, as lawyers would say, to go to a jury with ? Well, on the one hand, we have abundance of alleged experience which can hardly be called evidence, and a few depositions of a more notable and impressive character. On the other hand, we have many accounts of convicted impostors, and many authentic reports of precisely such disappointments or discoveries as we should be led to expect.

On December 14, 1872, Miss Fox married Mr. H. D. Jencken, a London barrister-at-law, author of " A Compendium of Modern Roman Law," etc., and honorary general secretary of the Association for the Reform and Codification of the Law of Nations. He was one of the earliest Spiritualists in England.

The Spiritualist, in its account of the ceremony, says that the spirit people took part in the proceedings, for at the wedding breakfast loud raps were heard coming from various parts of the room, and the large table on which stood the wedding-cake was repeatedly raised from the floor.

A contemporary witness states that Mrs. Kate Fox-Jencken (as she came to be known) and her husband were to be met in the early 'seventies in good social circles in London. Her services were eagerly sought after by investigators.

John Page Hopps describes her at this time as " a small, thin, very intelligent, but rather simpering little woman, with nice, gentle manners and a quiet enjoyment of her experiments which entirely saved her from the slightest touch of self-importance or affectation of mystery."

Her mediumship consisted chiefly of raps (often of great power), spirit lights, direct writing, and the appearance of materialized hands. Full form materializations, which had been an occasional feature of her sittings in America, were rare with her in England. On a number of occasions objects in the séance-room were moved by spirit agency, and in some cases brought from another room.

It was about this time that Professor William Crookes conducted his inquiries into the medium's powers, and issued that whole-hearted report which is dealt with later when Crookes's early connexion with Spiritualism comes to be discussed. These careful observations show that the rappings constituted only a small part of Kate Fox's psychic powers, and that if they could be adequately explained by normal means they would still leave us amid mysteries. Thus Crookes recounts how, when the only people present besides himself and Miss Fox were his wife and a lady relative :

" I was holding the medium's two hands in one of mine, while her feet were resting on my feet. Paper was on the table before us, and my disengaged hand was holding a pencil.

" A luminous hand came down from the upper part of the room, and after hovering near me for a few seconds, took the pencil from my hand, rapidly wrote on a sheet of paper, threw the pencil down, and then rose over our heads, gradually fading into darkness."

Many other observers describe similar phenomena with this medium on various occasions.

A very extraordinary phase of Mrs. Fox-Jencken's mediumship was the production of luminous substances. In the presence of Mrs. Makdougall Gregory, Mr. W. H. Harrison, the editor of a London newspaper, and others, a hand appeared carrying some phosphorescent material, about four inches square, with which the floor was struck and a sitter's face touched.* The light proved to be cold. Miss Rosamund Dale Owen, in her account of this phenomenon,† describes the objects as " illumined crystals," and says that she has seen no materialization which gave so realistic a feeling of spirit nearness as did these graceful lights. The author can also corroborate the fact that these lights are usually cold, as on one occasion, with another medium, such a light settled for some seconds upon his face. Miss Owen also speaks of books and small ornaments being carried about, and a heavy musical box, weighing about twenty-five pounds, being brought from a side-table. A peculiarity of this instrument was that it had been out of order for months and could not be used until the unseen forces repaired it and wound it themselves.

Mrs. Jencken's mediumship was interwoven in the texture of her daily life. Professor Butlerof says that when he paid a morning social call on her and her

* *The Spiritualist,* Vol. VIII, p. 299.
† *Light,* 1884, p. 170.

husband in company with M. Aksakof he heard raps upon the floor. Spending an evening at the Jenckens' house, he reports that raps were numerous during tea. Miss Rosamund Dale Owen also refers* to the incident of the medium standing in the street at a shop window with two ladies, when raps joined in the conversation, the pavement vibrating under their feet. The raps are described as having been loud enough to attract the attention of passers by. Mr. Jencken relates many cases of spontaneous phenomena in their home life.

ˑA volume could be filled with details of the séances of this medium, but with the exception of one further record we must be content with agreeing with the dictum of Professor Butlerof, of the University of St. Petersburg, who, after investigating her powers in London, wrote in *The Spiritualist* (February 4, 1876):

From all that I was able to observe in the presence of Mrs. Jencken, I am forced to come to the conclusion that the phenomena peculiar to that medium are of a strongly objective and convincing nature, and they would, I think, be sufficient for the most pronounced but *honest* sceptic to cause him to reject ventriloquism, muscular action, and every such artificial explanation of the phenomena.

Mr. H. D. Jencken died in 1881, and his widow was left with two sons. These children showed wonderful mediumship at a very early age, particulars of which will be found in contemporary records.†
Mr. S. C. Hall, a well-known literary man and a

* *Light*, 1884, p. 39.
† *The Spiritualist*, Vol. IV, p. 138, and Vol. VII, p. 66.

prominent Spiritualist, describes* a sitting at his house in Kensington on his birthday, May 9, 1882, at which his deceased wife manifested her presence:

Many interesting and touching messages were conveyed to me by the usual writing of Mrs. Jencken. We were directed to put out the light. Then commenced a series of manifestations such as I have not often seen equalled, and very seldom surpassed. . . . I removed a small handbell from the table and held it in my own hand. I felt a hand take it from me, when it was rung in all parts of the room during at least five minutes. I then placed an accordion under the table, whence it was removed, and at a distance of three or four feet from the table round which we were seated, tunes were played. The accordion was played and the bell was rung in several parts of the room, while two candles were lit on the table. It was not, therefore, what is termed a dark sitting, although occasionally the lights were put out. During all the time Mr. Stack held one of the hands of Mrs. Jencken and I held the other —each frequently saying, " I have Mrs. Jencken's hand in mine."

About fifty flowers of heartsease were placed on a sheet of paper before me. I had received some heartsease flowers from a friend in the morning, but the vase that contained them was not in the sitting-room. I sent for it and found it intact. The bouquet had not been in the least disturbed. In what is called " Direct Writing " I found these words written in pencil in a very small hand, on a sheet of paper that lay before me, " I have brought you my token of love." At a sitting some days previously (when alone with Mrs. Jencken) I had received this message, " On your birthday I will bring you a token of love."

Mr. Hall adds that he had marked the sheet of

* *Light*, 1882, pp. 239-40.

paper with his initials, and, as an extra precaution, had torn off one of the corners in such a manner as to ensure recognition.

It is evident that Mr. Hall was greatly impressed by what he had seen. He writes: " I have witnessed and recorded many wonderful manifestations; I doubt if I have seen any more convincing than this; certainly none more refined; none that gave more conclusive evidence that pure and good and holy spirits alone were communicating." He states that he has consented to become Mrs. Jencken's " banker," presumably for funds for the education of her two boys. In view of what afterwards happened to this gifted medium, there is a sad interest in his concluding words:

I feel confidence approaching certainty that, in all respects, she will so act as to increase and not lessen her power as a medium while retaining the friendship and trust of the many who cannot but feel for her a regard in some degree resembling (as arising from the same source) that which the New Church accords to Emanuel Swedenborg, and the Methodists render to John Wesley. Assuredly Spiritualists owe to this lady a huge debt for the glad tidings she was largely the instrument, selected by Providence, to convey to them.

We have given this account in some detail because it shows that the gifts of the medium were at this time of a high and powerful order. A few years earlier, at a séance at her house on December 14, 1873, on the occasion of the first anniversary of her wedding, a spirit message was rapped out: " When shadows fall upon you, think of the brighter side." It was a prophetic message, for the end of her life was all shadows.

Margaret (Mrs. Fox-Kane) had joined her sister Kate in England in 1876, and they remained together for some years until the very painful incident occurred which has now to be discussed. It would appear that a very bitter quarrel broke out between the elder sister Leah (now Mrs. Underhill) and the two younger ones. It is probable that Leah may have heard that there was now a tendency to alcoholism, and may have interfered with more energy than tact. Some Spiritualists interfered also, and incurred the fury of the two sisters by some suggestion that Kate's children should be separated from her.

Looking round for some weapon—any weapon—with which they could injure those whom they so bitterly hated, it seems to have occurred to them—or, according to their subsequent statement, to have been suggested to them, with promises of pecuniary reward —that if they injured the whole cult by an admission of fraud they would wound Leah and her associates in their most sensitive part. On the top of alcoholic excitement and the frenzy of hatred there was added religious fanaticism, for Margaret had been lectured by some of the leading spirits of the Church of Rome and persuaded, as Home had been also for a short time, that her own powers were evil. She mentions Cardinal Manning as having influenced her mind in this way, but her statements are not to be taken too seriously. At any rate, all these causes combined and reduced her to a state which was perilously near madness. Before leaving London she had written to the *New York Herald* denouncing the cult, but stating in one sentence that the rappings were " the only part of the phenomena that is worthy of notice." On reaching New York, where, according to her own subsequent statement, she was to receive a sum of money for the newspaper sensation which she promised to produce, she broke out into absolute raving against her elder sister.

It is a curious psychological study, and equally curious is the mental attitude of the people who could imagine that the assertions of an unbalanced woman, acting not only from motives of hatred but also from —as she herself stated—the hope of pecuniary reward, could upset the critical investigation of a generation of observers.

None the less, we have to face the fact that she did actually produce rappings, or enable raps to be produced, at a subsequent meeting in the New York Academy of Music. This might be discounted upon the grounds that in so large a hall any prearranged sound might be attributed to the medium. More important is the evidence of the reporter of the *Herald*, who had a previous private performance. He describes it thus :

I heard first a rapping under the floor near my feet, then under the chair in which I was seated, and again under a table on which I was leaning. She led me to the door and I heard the same sound on the other side of it. Then when she sat down on the piano stool the instrument reverberated more loudly and the tap-tap resounded throughout its hollow structure.

This account makes it clear that she had the noises under control, though the reporter must have been more unsophisticated than most pressmen of my acquaintance, if he could believe that sounds varying both in quality and in position all came from some click within the medium's foot. He clearly did not know how the sounds came, and it is the author's opinion that Margaret did not know either. That she really had something which she could exhibit is proved, not only by the experience of the reporter but by that of Mr. Wedgwood, a London Spiritualist, to whom she gave a demonstration before she started for America. It is vain, therefore, to contend that there was no basis at all in Margaret's exposure. What that basis was we must endeavour to define.

The Margaret Fox-Kane sensation was in August and September, 1888—a welcome boon for the enterprising paper which had exploited it. In October Kate came over to join forces with her sister. It should be explained that the real quarrel, so far as is known, was between Kate and Leah, for Leah had endeavoured to get Kate's children taken from her on the grounds that the mother's influence was not for good. Therefore, though Kate did not rave, and though she volunteered no exposures in public or private, she was quite at one with her sister in the general plot to " down " Leah at all costs.

She was the one who caused my arrest last spring (she said) and the bringing of the preposterous charge that I was cruel to my children. I don't know why it is she has always been jealous of Maggie and me ; I suppose because we could do things in Spiritualism that she couldn't.

She was present at the Hall of Music meeting on October 21, when Margaret made her repudiation and produced the raps. She was silent on that occasion, but that silence may be taken as a support of the statements to which she listened.

If this were indeed so, and if she spoke as reported to the interviewer, her repentance must have come very rapidly. Upon November 17, less than a month after the famous meeting, she wrote to a lady in London, Mrs. Cottell, who was the tenant of Carlyle's old house, this remarkable letter from New York (*Light*, 1888, p. 619):

I would have written to you before this but my surprise was so great on my arrival to hear of Maggie's exposure of Spiritualism that I had no heart to write to anyone.

The manager of the affair engaged the Academy of Music, the very largest place of entertainment in New York City ; it was filled to overflowing.

. They made fifteen hundred dollars clear. I have often wished I had remained with you, and if I had the means I would now return to get out of all this.

I think now I could make money in proving that the knockings are not made with the toes. So many people come to me to ask me about this exposure of Maggie's that I have to deny myself to them.

They are hard at work to expose the whole thing if they can ; but they certainly cannot.

Maggie is giving public exposures in all the large places in America, but I have only seen her once since I arrived.

This letter of Kate's points to pecuniary temptation as playing a large part in the transaction. Maggie, however, seems to have soon found that there was little money in it, and could see no profit in telling lies for which she was not paid, and which had only proved that the Spiritualistic movement was so firmly established that it was quite unruffled by her treachery. For this or other reasons—let us hope with some final twinges of conscience as to the part she had played— she now admitted that she had been telling falsehoods from the lowest motives. The interview was reported in the New York Press, November 20, 1889, about a year after the onslaught.

" Would to God," she said, in a voice that trembled with intense excitement, " that I could undo the injustice I did the cause of Spiritualism when, under the strong psychological influence of persons inimical to it, I gave expression to utterances that had no foundation in fact. This retraction and denial has not come about so much from my own sense of what is right as from the silent impulse of the spirits using my organism at the expense of the hostility of the treacherous horde who held out promises of wealth and happiness in return for an attack on Spiritualism, and whose hopeful assurances were so deceitful. . . .

" Long before I spoke to any person on this matter, I was unceasingly reminded by my spirit control what I should do, and at last I have come to the conclusion that it would be useless for me further to thwart their promptings. . . . "

" Has there been no mention of a monetary consideration for this statement ? "

" Not the smallest; none whatever."

" Then financial gain is not the end which you are
looking to ? "

" Indirectly, yes. You know that even a mortal
instrument in the hands of the spirit must have the
maintenance of life. This I propose to derive from
my lectures. Not one cent has passed to me from any
person because I adopted this course."

" What cause led up to your exposure of the spirit
rappings ? "

" At that time I was in great need of money, and
persons—who for the present I prefer not to name—
took advantage of the situation; hence the trouble.
The excitement, too, helped to upset my mental
equilibrium."

" What was the object of the persons who induced
you to make the confession that you and all other
mediums traded on the credulity of people ? "

" They had several objects in view. Their first
and paramount idea was to crush Spiritualism, to
make money for themselves, and to get up a great
excitement, as that was an element in which they
flourish."

" Was there any truth in the charges you made
against Spiritualism ? "

" Those charges were false in every particular. I
have no hesitation in saying that. . . . "

" No, my belief in Spiritualism has undergone no
change. When I made those dreadful statements I

was not responsible for my words. Its genuineness is an incontrovertible fact. Not all the Herrmans that ever breathed can duplicate the wonders that are produced through some mediums. By deftness of fingers and smartness of wits they may produce writing on papers and slates, but even this cannot bear close investigation. Materialization is beyond their mental calibre to reproduce, and I challenge anyone to make the ' rap ' under the same conditions which I will. There is not a human being on earth can produce the ' raps ' in the same way as they are through me."

" Do you propose to hold séances ? "

" No, I will devote myself entirely to platform work, as that will find me a better opportunity to refute the foul slanders uttered by me against Spiritualism."

" What does your sister Kate say of your present course ? "

" She is in complete sympathy with me. She did not approve my course in the past. . . . "

" Will you have a manager for your lecture tour ? "

" No, sir. I have a horror of them. They, too, treated me most outrageously. Frank Stechen acted shamefully with me. He made considerable money through his management for me, and left me in Boston without a cent. All I got from him was five hundred and fifty dollars, which was given to me at the beginning of the contract."

To give greater authenticity to the interview, at her suggestion the following open letter was written to which she placed her signature:

128, West Forty-third Street,
New York City,
November 16, 1889.

To THE PUBLIC.

The foregoing interview having been read over to me I find nothing contained therein that is not a correct record of my words and truthful expression of my sentiments. I have not given a detailed account of the ways and means which were devised to bring me under subjection, and so extract from me a declaration that the spiritual phenomena as exemplified through my organism were a fraud. But I shall fully atone for this incompleteness when I get upon the platform.

The exactness of this interview was testified to by the names of a number of witnesses, including J. L. O'Sullivan, who was U.S. Minister to Portugal for twenty-five years. He said, " If ever I heard a woman speak truth, it was then."

So it may have been, but the failure of her lecture-agent to keep her in funds seems to have been the determining factor.

The statement would settle the question if we could take the speaker's words at face value, but unfortunately the author is compelled to agree with Mr. Isaac Funk, an indefatigable and impartial researcher, that Margaret at this period of her life could not be relied upon.

What is a good deal more to the purpose is that Mr. Funk sat with Margaret, that he heard the raps " all round the room " without detecting their origin, and that they spelt out to him a name and address which were correct and entirely beyond the knowledge of the medium. The information given was wrong, but, on the other hand, abnormal power was shown by reading the contents of a letter in Mr. Funk's pocket. Such mixed results are as puzzling as the other larger problem discussed in this chapter.

There is one factor which has been scarcely touched upon in this examination. It is the character and career of Mrs. Fish, afterwards Mrs. Underhill, who as Leah, the elder sister, plays so prominent a part in the matter. We know her chiefly by her book, " The Missing Link in Modern Spiritualism " (Knox & Co., New York, 1885). This book was written by a friend, but the facts and documents were provided by Mrs. Underhill, who checked the whole narrative. It is simply and even crudely put together, and the Spiritualist is bound to conclude that the entities with whom the Fox circle were at first in contact were not always of the highest order. Perhaps on another plane, as on this, it is the plebeians and the lowly who carry out spiritual pioneer work in their own rough way and open the path for other and more refined agencies. With this sole criticism, one may say that the book gives a sure impression of candour and good sense, and as a personal narrative of one who was so nearly concerned in these momentous happenings, it is destined to outlive most of our current literature and to be read with close attention and even with reverence by generations unborn. Those humble folk who watched over the new birth—Capron, of Auburn, who first lectured upon it in public ; Jervis, the gallant Methodist minister, who cried, "I know it is true, and

I will face the frowning world ! " ; George Willetts, the Quaker; Isaac Post, who called the first spiritual meeting; the gallant band who testified upon the Rochester platform while the rowdies were heating the tar—all of them are destined to live in history. Of Leah it can truly be said that she recognized the religious meaning of the movement far more clearly than her sisters were able to do, and that she set her face against that use of it for purely worldly objects which is a degradation of the celestial. The following passage is of great interest as showing how the Fox family first regarded this visitation, and must impress the reader with the sincerity of the writer:

The general feeling of our family . . . was strongly adverse to all this strange and uncanny thing. We regarded it as a great misfortune which had fallen upon us; how, whence or why we knew not. . . . We resisted it, struggled against it, and constantly and earnestly prayed for deliverance from it, even while a strange fascination attached to these marvellous manifestations thus forced upon us, against our will, by invisible agencies and agents whom we could neither resist, control nor understand. If our will, earnest desires and prayers could have prevailed or availed, the whole thing would have ended then and there, and the world outside of our little neighbourhood would never have heard more of the Rochester Rappings, or of the unfortunate Fox family.

These words give the impression of sincerity, and altogether Leah stands forth in her book, and in the evidence of the many witnesses quoted, as one who was worthy to play a part in a great movement.

Both Kate Fox-Jencken and Margaret Fox-Kane

died in the early 'nineties, and their end was one of sadness and gloom. The problem which they present is put fairly before the reader, avoiding the extremes of the too sensitive Spiritualist who will not face the facts, and the special-pleading sceptics who lay stress upon those parts of the narrative which suit their purpose and omit or minimize everything else. Let us see, at the cost of a break in our narrative, if any sort of explanation can be found which covers the double fact that what these sisters could do was plainly abnormal, and yet that it was, to some extent at least, under their control. It is not a simple problem, but an exceedingly deep one which exhausts, and more than exhausts, the psychic knowledge which is at this date available, and was altogether beyond the reach of the generation in which the Fox sisters were alive.

The simple explanation which was given by the Spiritualists of the time is not to be set aside readily—and least readily by those who know most. It was that a medium who ill-uses her gifts and suffers debasement of moral character through bad habits, becomes accessible to evil influences which may use her for false information or for the defilement of a pure cause. That may be true enough as a *causa causans*. But we must look closer to see the actual how and why.

The author is of opinion that the true explanation will be found by coupling all these happenings with the recent investigations of Dr. Crawford upon the means by which physical phenomena are produced.

MARGARETTA FOX-KANE   KATE FOX-JENCKEN   LEAH UNDERHILL

He showed very clearly, as is detailed in a subsequent chapter, that raps (we are dealing at present only with that phase) are caused by a protrusion from the medium's person of a long rod of a substance having certain properties which distinguish it from all other forms of matter. This substance has been closely examined by the great French physiologist, Dr. Charles Richet, who has named it " ectoplasm." These rods are invisible to the eye, partly visible to the sensitive plate, and yet conduct energy in such a fashion as to make sounds and strike blows at a distance.

Now, if Margaret produced the raps in the same fashion as Crawford's medium, we have only to make one or two assumptions which are probable in themselves, and which the science of the future may definitely prove in order to make the case quite clear. The one assumption is that a centre of psychic force is formed in some part of the body from which the ectoplasm rod is protruded. Supposing that centre to be in Margaret's foot, it would throw a very clear light upon the evidence collected in the Seybert inquiry. In examining Margaret and endeavouring to get raps from her, one of the committee, with the permission of the medium, placed his hand upon her foot. Raps at once followed. The investigator cried: " This is the most wonderful thing of all, Mrs. Kane. I distinctly feel them in your foot. There is not a particle of motion in your foot, but there is an unusual pulsation."

This experiment by no means bears out the idea of joint dislocation or snapping toes. It is, however, exactly what one could imagine in the case of a centre from which psychic power was projected. This power is in material shape and is drawn from the body of the medium, so that there must be some nexus. This nexus may vary. In the case quoted it was in Margaret's foot. It was observed by the Buffalo doctors that there was a subtle movement of a medium at the moment of a rap. The observation was correct, though the inference was wrong. The author has himself distinctly seen in the case of an amateur medium a slight general pulsation when a rap was given—a recoil, as it were, after the discharge of force.

Granting that Margaret's power worked in this way, we have now only to discuss whether ectoplasmic rods can under any circumstances be protruded at will. So far as the author knows, there are no observations which bear directly upon the point. Crawford's medium seems always to have manifested when in trance, so that the question did not arise. In other physical phenomena there is some reason to think that in their simpler form they are closely connected with the medium, but that as they progress they pass out of her control and are swayed by forces outside herself. Thus the ectoplasm pictures photographed by Madame Bisson and Dr. Schrenck Notzing (as shown in his recent book) may in their first forms be ascribed to the medium's thoughts or memories taking visible shape in ectoplasm, but as she becomes lost in trance they take the form of figures which in extreme cases are endowed with independent life. If there be a general analogy between the two classes of phenomena, then it is entirely possible that Margaret had some control over the expulsion of ectoplasm which caused the sound, but that when the sound gave forth messages which were beyond her possible knowledge, as in the case instanced by Funk, the power was no longer used by her but by some independent intelligence.

It is to be remembered that no one is more ignorant of how effects are produced than the medium, who is the centre of them. One of the greatest physical mediums in the world told the author once that he had never witnessed a physical phenomenon, as he was himself always in trance when they occurred; the opinion of any one of the sitters would be more valuable than his own. Thus in the case of these Fox sisters, who were mere children when the phenomena began, they knew little of the philosophy of the subject, and Margaret frequently said that she did not understand her own results. If she found that she had herself some power of producing the raps, however obscure the way by which she did it, she would be in a frame of mind when she might well find it impossible to contradict Dr. Kane when he accused her of being concerned in it. Her confession, too, and that of her sister, would to that extent be true, but each would be aware, as they afterwards admitted, that there was a great deal more which could not be explained and which did not emanate from themselves.

There remains, however, one very important point to be discussed—the most important of all to those who accept the religious significance of this movement. It is a most natural argument for those who are un-versed in the subject to say, " Are these your fruits ? Can a philosophy or religion be good which has such an effect upon those who have had a prominent place in its establishment ? " No one can cavil at such an objection, and it calls for a clear answer, which has often been made and yet is in need of repetition.

Let it then be clearly stated that there is no more connexion between physical mediumship and morality than there is between a refined ear for music and morality. Both are purely physical gifts. The musician might interpret the most lovely thoughts and excite the highest emotions in others, influencing their thoughts and raising their minds. Yet in himself he might be a drug-taker, a dipsomaniac, or a pervert. On the other hand, he might combine his musical powers with an angelic personal character. There is simply no connexion at all between the two things, save that they both have their centre in the same human body.

So it is in physical mediumship. We all, or nearly all, exude a certain substance from our bodies which has very peculiar properties. With most of us, as is shown by Crawford's weighing chairs, the amount is negligible. With one in 100,000 it is considerable. That person is a physical medium. He or she gives forth a raw material which can, we hold, be used by independent external forces. The individual's char-acter has nothing to do with the matter. Such is the result of two generations of observation.

If it were exactly as stated, then, the physical medium's character would be in no way affected by his gift. Unfortunately, that is to understate the case. Under our present unintelligent conditions, the physical medium is subjected to certain moral risks which it takes a strong and well-guarded nature to withstand. The failures of these most useful and devoted people may be likened to those physical injuries, the loss of fingers and hands, incurred by those who have worked with the X-rays before their full properties were comprehended. Means have been taken to overcome these physical dangers after a certain number have become martyrs for science, and the moral dangers will also be met when a tardy reparation will be made to the pioneers who have injured themselves in forcing the gates of knowledge. These dangers lie in the weakening of the will, in the extreme debility after phenomenal sittings, and the temptation to gain temporary relief from alcohol, in the temptation to fraud when the power wanes, and in the mixed and possibly noxious spirit influences which surround a promiscuous circle, drawn together from motives of curiosity rather than of religion. The remedy is to segregate mediums, to give them salaries instead of paying them by results, to regulate the number of their sittings and the character of the sitters, and thus to remove them from influences which overwhelmed the Fox sisters as they have done other of the strongest mediums in the past. On the other hand, there are physical mediums who retain such high motives and work upon such religious lines that they are the salt of the earth. It is the same power which is used by the Buddha and by the Woman of Endor. The objects and methods of its use are what determine the character.

The author has said that there is little connexion between physical mediumship and morality. One could imagine the ectoplasmic flow being as brisk from a sinner as from a saint, impinging upon material objects in the same way and producing results which would equally have the good effect of convincing the materialist of forces outside his ken. This does not apply, however, to internal mediumship, taking the form not of phenomena but of teaching and messages, given either by spirit voice, human voice, automatic writing, or any other device. Here the vessel is chosen that it may match what it contains. One could not imagine a small nature giving temporary habitation to a great spirit. One must be a Vale Owen before one gets Vale Owen messages. If a high medium degenerated in character, I should expect to find the messages cease or else share in the degeneration. Hence, too, the messages of a divine spirit such as is periodically sent to cleanse the world, of a mediæval saint, of Joan of Arc, of Swedenborg, of Andrew Jackson Davis, or of the humblest automatic writer in London, provided that the impulse is a true one, are really the same thing in various degrees. Each is a genuine breath from beyond, and yet each intermediary tinges with his or her personality the message which comes through. So, as in a glass darkly, we see this wondrous mystery, so vital and yet so undefined. It is its very greatness which prevents it from being defined. We have done a little, but we hand back many a problem to those who march behind us. They may look upon our own most advanced speculation as elementary, and yet may see vistas of thought before them which will stretch to the uttermost bounds of their mental vision.

CHAPTER VI

FIRST DEVELOPMENTS IN AMERICA

HAVING dealt with the history of the Fox family and the problems which that history raises, we shall now return to America and note the first effects of this invasion from another sphere of being.

These effects were not entirely excellent. There were follies on the part of individuals and extravagances on that of communities.

One of these, based on communications received through the mediumship of Mrs. Benedict, was the Apostolic Circle. It was started by a small group of men, strong believers in a second advent, who sought through spirit communications to confirm that belief. They obtained what they proclaimed to be communications from Apostles and prophets of the Bible. In 1849 James L. Scott, a Seventh Day Baptist minister of Brooklyn, joined this circle at Auburn, which now became known as the Apostolic Movement, and its spiritual leader was said to be the Apostle Paul. Scott was joined by the Rev. Thomas Lake Harris, and they established at Mountain Cove the religious community which attracted a strong following, until after some years their dupes became disillusioned and deserted their autocratic leaders.

This man, Thomas Lake Harris, is certainly one of the most curious personalities of whom we have any record, and it is hard to say whether Jekyll or Hyde predominated in his character. He was compounded of extremes, and everything which he did was outstanding for good or for evil. He was originally a Universalist minister, whence he derived the "Rev." which he long used as a prefix. He broke away from his associates, adopted the teachings of Andrew Jackson Davis, became a fanatical Spiritualist, and finally, as already stated, claimed to be one of the autocratic rulers of the souls and purses of the colonists of Mountain Cove. There came a time, however, when the said colonists concluded that they were quite capable of looking after their own affairs both spiritual and material, so Harris found his vocation gone. He then came to New York and threw himself violently into the Spiritualistic movement, preaching at Dodworth Hall, the head-quarters of the cult, and gaining a great and deserved reputation for remarkable eloquence. His megalomania—possibly an obsession—broke out once more, and he made extravagant claims which the sane and sober Spiritualists around him would not tolerate. There was one claim, however, which he could go to some length in making good, and that was inspiration from a very true and high poetic afflatus, though whether inborn or from without it is impossible to say. While at this stage of his career he, or some power through him, produced a series of poems, " A Lyric of the Golden Age," " The Morning Land," and others, which do occasionally touch the stars. Piqued by the refusal of the New York Spiritualists to admit his supernal claims, Harris then (1859) went to England, where he gained fame by his eloquence, shown in lectures which consisted of denunciations of his own former colleagues in New York. Each successive step in the man's life was accompanied by a defilement of the last step from which he had come.

In 1860, in London, Harris's life suddenly assumes a closer interest to Britons, especially to those who have literary affinities. Harris lectured at Steinway Hall, and while there Lady Oliphant listened to his wild eloquence, and was so affected by it that she brought the American preacher into touch with her son, Laurence Oliphant, one of the most brilliant men of his generation. It is difficult to see where the attraction lay, for the teaching of Harris at this stage had nothing uncommon in its matter, save that he seems to have adopted the Father-God and Mother-Nature idea which was thrown out by Davis. Oliphant placed Harris high as a poet, referring to him as " the greatest poet of the age as yet unknown to fame." Oliphant was no mean judge, and yet in an age which included Tennyson, Longfellow, Browning, and so many more, the phrase seems extravagant. The end of the whole episode was that, after delays and vacillations, both mother and son surrendered themselves entirely to Harris, and went forth to manual labour in a new colony at Brocton in New York, where they remained in a condition which was virtual slavery save that it was voluntary. Whether such self-abnegation is saintly or idiotic is a question for the angels. It certainly seems idiotic when we learn that Laurence Oliphant had the greatest difficulty in getting leave to marry, and expressed humble gratitude to the tyrant when he was at last allowed to do so. He was set free to report the Franco-German War of 1870, which he did in the brilliant manner that might be expected of him, and then he returned to his servitude once more, one of his duties being to sell strawberries in baskets to the passing trains, while he was arbitrarily separated from his young wife, she being sent to Southern California and he retained at Brocton. It was not until the year 1882, twenty years from his first entanglement, that Oliphant, his mother being then dead, broke these extraordinary bonds, and after a severe struggle, in the course of which Harris took steps to have him incarcerated in an asylum, rejoined his wife, recovered some of his property, and resumed his normal life. He drew the prophet Harris in his book " Masollam," written in his later years, and the result is so characteristic both of Oliphant's brilliant word-painting and of the extraordinary man whom he painted, that the reader will perhaps be glad to refer to it in the Appendix.

Such developments as Harris and others were only excrescences on the main Spiritualistic movement, which generally speaking was sane and progressive. The freaks stood in the way of its acceptance, however, as the communistic or free love sentiments of some of these wild sects were unscrupulously exploited by the opposition as being typical of the whole.

We have seen that though the spiritual manifestations obtained wide public notice through the Fox girls, they were known long before this. To the preceding testimony to this effect we may add that of Judge Edmonds, who says:* " It is about five years since the subject first attracted public attention, though we discover now that for the previous ten or twelve years there had been more or less of it in different parts of the country, but it had been kept concealed, either from fear of ridicule or from ignorance of what it was." This explains the surprising number of mediums who began to be heard of immediately after the publicity obtained through the Fox family. It was no new gift they exhibited, it was only that their courageous action in making it widely known made others come forward and confess that they possessed the same power. Also this universal gift of mediumistic faculties now for the first time began to be freely developed. The result was that mediums were heard of in ever-increasing numbers. In April, 1849, manifestations occurred in the family of the Rev. A. H. Jervis, the Methodist minister of Rochester, in that of Mr. Lyman Granger, also of Rochester, and in the home of Deacon Hale, in the neighbouring town of Greece. So, too, six families in the adjoining town of Auburn began to develop mediumship. In none of these cases had the Fox girls any connexion with what took place. So these leaders simply blazed the trail along which others followed.

* " Spiritualism," by John W. Edmonds and George T. Dexter, M.D., New York, 1853, p. 36.

Outstanding features of the next succeeding years were the rapid growth of mediums on every side, and the conversion to a belief in Spiritualism of great public men like Judge Edmonds, ex-Governor Tallmadge, Professor Robert Hare, and Professor Mapes. The public support of such well-known men gave enormous publicity to the subject, while at the same time it increased the virulence of the opposition, which now perceived it had to deal with more than a handful of silly, deluded people. Men such as these could command a hearing in the Press of the day. There was also a change in the character of the spiritual phenomena. In the years 1851-2 Mrs. Hayden and D. D. Home were instrumental in making many converts. We shall have more to say about these mediums in later chapters.

In a communication addressed " To the Public," published in the *New York Courier* and dated New York, August 1, 1853, Judge Edmonds, a man of high character and clear intellect, gave a convincing account of his own experience. It is a curious thing that the United States, which at that time gave conspicuous evidence of moral courage in its leading citizens, has seemed to fall behind in recent years in this respect, for the author in his recent journeys there found many who were aware of psychic truth and yet shrank in the face of a jeering Press from publishing their convictions.

Judge Edmonds, in the article alluded to, began by detailing the train of events which caused him to form his opinions. It is dwelt upon here in some detail, because it is very important as showing the basis on which a highly educated man received the new teaching :

It was January 1851 that my attention was first called to the subject of " spiritual intercourse." I was at the time withdrawn from general society ; I was labouring under great depression of spirits. I was occupying all my leisure in reading on the subject of death and man's existence after-ward. I had, in the course of my life, read and heard from the pulpit so many contradictory and conflicting doctrines on the subject, that I hardly knew what to believe. I could not, if I would, believe what I did not understand, and was anxiously seeking to know, if, after death, we should again meet with those whom we had loved here, and under what circumstances. I was invited by a friend to witness the " Rochester Knockings." I complied more to oblige her, and to while away a tedious hour. I thought a good deal on what I witnessed, and I determined to investigate the matter and find out what it was. If it was a deception, or a delusion, I thought that I could detect it. For about four months I devoted at least two evenings in a week and sometimes more to witnessing the phenomena in all its phases. I kept careful records of all I witnessed, and from time to time compared them with each other, to detect in-consistencies and contradictions. I read all I could lay my hands on on the subject, and especially all the professed " exposures of the humbug." I went from place to place, seeing different mediums, meeting with different parties of persons—often with persons whom I had never seen before, and sometimes where I was myself entirely un-known—sometimes in the dark and sometimes in the light—often with inveterate unbelievers, and more frequently with zealous believers.

In fine, I availed myself of every opportunity that was

afforded, thoroughly to sift the matter to the bottom. I was all this time an unbeliever, and tried the patience of believers sorely by my scepticism, my captiousness, and my obdurate refusal to yield my belief. I saw around me some who yielded a ready faith on one or two sittings only ; others again, under the same circumstances, avowing a determined unbelief ; and some who refused to witness it at all, and yet were confirmed unbelievers. I could not imitate either of these parties, and refused to yield unless upon most irrefragable testimony. At length the evidence came, and in such force that no sane man could withhold his faith.

It will thus be seen that this, the earliest outstanding convert to the new revelation, took the utmost pains before he allowed the evidence to convince him of the validity of the claims of the spirit. General experience shows that a facile acceptance of these claims is very rare among earnest thinkers, and that there is hardly any prominent Spiritualist whose course of study and reflection has not involved a noviciate of many years. This forms a striking contrast to those negative opinions which are founded upon initial prejudice and the biased or scandalous accounts of partisan authors.

Judge Edmonds, in the excellent summary of his position given in the article already quoted—an article which should have converted the whole American people had they been ready for assimilation—proceeds to show the solid basis of his beliefs. He points out that he was never alone when these manifestations occurred, and that he had many witnesses. He also shows the elaborate precautions which he took :

After depending upon my senses, as to these various phases of the phenomenon, I invoked the aid of science, and, with the assistance of an accomplished electrician and his machinery, and eight or ten intelligent, educated, shrewd persons, examined the matter. We pursued our inquiries many days, and established to our satisfaction two things : first, that the sounds were not produced by the agency of any person present or near us ; and, second, that they were not forthcoming at our will and pleasure.

He deals faithfully with the alleged " exposures " in newspapers, some of which at long intervals are true indictments of some villain, but which usually are greater deceptions, conscious or unconscious, of the public than the evils which they profess to attack. Thus:

While these things were going on, there appeared in the newspapers various explanations and " exposures of the humbug," as they were termed. I read them with care, in the expectation of being assisted in my researches, and I could not but smile at once at the rashness and the futility of the explanations. For instance, while certain learned professors in Buffalo were congratulating themselves on having detected it in the toe and knee joints, the manifestations in this city changed to ringing a bell placed under the table. They were like the solution lately given by a learned professor in England, who attributes the tipping of tables to a force in the hands which are laid upon them, overlooking the material fact that tables quite as frequently move when there is no hand upon them.

Having dealt with the objectivity of the phenomena, the Judge next touched upon the more important question of their source. He commented upon the fact that he had answers to mental questions and found that his own secret thoughts were revealed, and that purposes which he had privily entertained had been made manifest. He notes also that he had heard the mediums use Greek, Latin, Spanish, and French, when they were ignorant of these languages.

This drives him to the consideration of whether these things may not be explained as the reflection of the mind of some other living human being. These considerations have been exhausted by every inquirer in turn, for Spiritualists do not accept their creed in one bound, but make the journey step by step, with much timid testing of the path. Judge Edmonds's epitome of his course is but that which many others have followed. He gives the following reasons for negativing this question of other human minds :

Facts were communicated which were unknown then, but afterward found to be true ; like this, for instance : when I was absent last winter in Central America, my friends in town heard of my whereabouts and of the state of my health seven times ; and on my return, by comparing their information with the entries in my journal it was found to be invariably correct. So, in my recent visit to the West my whereabouts and my condition were told to a medium in this city, while I was travelling on the railroad between Cleveland and Toledo. So thoughts have been uttered on subjects not then in my mind, and utterly at variance with my own notions. This has often happened to me and to others, so as fully to establish the fact that it was not ou minds that gave birth to or affected the communication.

He then deals with the object of this marvellous development, and he points out its overwhelming religious significance on the general lines with which it is defined in a subsequent chapter of this work. Judge Edmonds's brain was indeed a remarkable one, and his judgment clear, for there is very little which we can add to his statement, and perhaps it has never been so well expressed in so small a compass. As we point to it one can claim that Spiritualism has been consistent from the first, and that the teachers and guides have not mixed their message. It is a strange and an amusing reflection that the arrogant science which endeavoured by its mere word and glare to crush this upstart knowledge in 1850 has been proved to be essentially wrong on its own ground. There are hardly any scientific axioms of that day, the finality of the element, the indivisibility of the atom, the separate origin of species, which have not been controverted, whereas the psychic knowledge which was so derided has steadily held its own, adding fresh facts but never contradicting those which were originally put forward.

Writing of the beneficent effects of this knowledge the Judge says :

There is that which comforts the mourner and binds up the broken-hearted; that which smooths the passage to the grave and robs death of its terrors; that which enlightens the atheist and cannot but reform the vicious; that which cheers and encourages the virtuous amid all the trials and vicissitudes of life ; and that which demonstrates to man his duty and his destiny, leaving it no longer vague and uncertain.

The matter has never been better summed up than that.

There is, however, one final passage in this remarkable document which causes some sadness. Speaking of the progress which the movement had made within four years in the United States, he says: " There are ten or twelve newspapers and periodicals devoted to the cause and the spiritual library embraces more than one hundred different publications, some of which have already attained a circulation of more than 10,000 copies. Besides the undistinguished multitude there are many men of high standing and talent ranked among them—doctors, lawyers, and clergymen in great numbers, a Protestant bishop, the learned and reverend president of a college, judges of our higher courts, members of Congress, foreign ambassadors and ex-members of the United States Senate." In four years the spirit force had done as much as this. How does the matter stand to-day ? The " undistinguished multitude " has carried bravely on and the hundred publications have grown into many more, but where are the men of light and leading who point the path ? Since the death of Professor Hyslop it is difficult to point to one man of eminence in the United States who is ready to stake his career and reputation upon the issue. Those who would have never feared the tyranny of man have shrank from the cat-calling of the public Press. The printing-machine has succeeded where the rack would have failed. The worldly loss in reputation and in business sustained by Judge Edmonds himself, who had to resign his seat upon the Supreme Court of New York, and by many others who testified to the truth, established a reign of terror which warns the intellectual classes from the subject. So the matter stands at present.

But the Press, for the moment, was well-disposed and Judge Edmonds's famous summing-up, perhaps the finest and most momentous that any judge has ever delivered, met with respect, if not with concurrence. The *New York Courier* wrote :

The letter from Judge Edmonds, published by us on Saturday, with regard to the so-called spiritual manifestations, coming as it did from an eminent jurist, a man remarkable for his clear common sense in the practical affairs of life, and a gentleman of irreproachable character, arrested the attention of the community, and is regarded by many persons as one of the most remarkable documents of the day.

The New York *Evening Mirror* said:

John W. Edmonds, the Chief Justice of the Supreme Court for this district, is an able lawyer, an industrious judge and a good citizen. For the last eight years occupying without interruption the highest judicial stations, whatever may be his faults no one can justly accuse him of lack of ability, industry, honesty or fearlessness. No one can doubt his general saneness, or can believe for a moment that the ordinary operations of his mind are not as rapid, accurate and reliable as ever. Both by the practitioners and suitors at his bar he is recognized as the head, in fact and in merit, of the Supreme Court for this District.

The experience of Dr. Robert Hare, Professor of Chemistry in the University of Pennsylvania, is also of interest, because he was one of the first eminent men of science who, setting out to expose the delusion of Spiritualism, became finally a firm believer. It was

in 1853 that, in his own words, he " felt called upon,
as an act of duty to his fellow creatures, to bring whatever influence he possessed to the attempt to stem the
tide of popular madness which, in defiance of reason
and science, was fast setting in favour of the gross
delusion called Spiritualism." A denunciatory letter
of his published in the newspapers of Philadelphia,
where he lived, was copied by other newspapers all
over the country, and it was made the text of numerous sermons. But, as with Sir William Crookes many
years later, the jubilation was premature. Professor
Hare, though a strong sceptic, was induced to experiment for himself, and after a period of careful testing
he became entirely convinced of the spiritual origin
of the manifestations. Like Crookes, he devised
apparatus for use with mediums. Mr. S. B. Brittan*
gives the following condensed account of some of
Hare's experiments :

First, to satisfy himself that the movements were not
the works of mortals, he took brass billiard balls, placed them
on zinc plates and placed the hands of the mediums on the
balls and, to his very great astonishment the tables *moved*.
He next arranged a table to slide backward and forward,
to which attachments were made, causing a disc to revolve
containing the alphabet, *hidden from the view of the mediums*.
The letters were variously arranged, out of their regular
consecutive order, and the spirit was required to place them
consecutively or in their regular places. And behold, it
was done ! Then followed intelligent sentences which the
medium could not see or know the import of till they were
told him.

* Editor of *The Spiritual Telegraph*.

Again he tried another capital test. The long end of a lever was placed on spiral scales with an index attached and the weight marked ; the medium's hand rested on the short end of the beam, where it was impossible to give pressure downward, but if pressed it would have a contrary effect and raise the long end ; and yet, most *astounding*, the weight was increased several pounds on the scale.

Professor Hare embodied his careful researches and his views on Spiritualism in an important book published in New York in 1855, entitled " Experimental Investigation of the Spirit Manifestations." In this (p. 55) he sums up the results of his early experiments as follows :

The evidence of the manifestations adduced in the foregoing narrative does not rest upon myself only, since there have been persons present when they were observed, and they have in my presence been repeated essentially under various modifications in many instances not specially alluded to.

The evidence may be contemplated under various phases ; first, those in which rappings or other noises have been made which could not be traced to any mortal agency ; secondly, those in which sounds were so made as to indicate letters forming grammatical, well-spelt sentences, affording proof that they were under the guidance of some rational being ; thirdly, those in which the nature of the communication has been such as to prove that the being causing them must, agreeably to accompanying allegations, be some known acquaintance, friend, or relative of the inquirer.

Again, cases in which movements have been made of ponderable bodies . . . of a nature to produce intellectual communications resembling those obtained, as above-mentioned, by sounds.

Although the apparatus by which these various proofs

were attained *with the greatest possible precaution and precision*, modified them as to the manner, essentially all the evidence which I have obtained tending to the conclusions above mentioned, has likewise been substantially obtained by a great number of observers. Many who never sought any spiritual communication and have not been induced to enrol themselves as Spiritualists, will nevertheless not only affirm the existence of the sounds and movements, but also admit their inscrutability.

Mr. James J. Mapes, LL.D., of New York, an agricultural chemist and member of various learned societies, commenced his investigation into Spiritualism in order to rescue, as he said, his friends, who were "running to imbecility" over the new craze. Through the mediumship of Mrs. Cora Hatch, afterwards Mrs. Richmond, he received what are described as marvellous scientific answers to his questions. He ended by becoming a thorough believer, and his wife, who had no artistic talent, became a drawing and painting medium. His daughter had, unknown to him, become a writing medium, and when she spoke to him about this development he asked her to give him an exhibition of her power. She took a pen and rapidly wrote what professed to be a message from Professor Mapes's father. The Professor asked for a proof of identity. His daughter's hand at once wrote: "You may recollect that I gave you, among other books, an Encyclopædia; look at page 120 of that book, and you will find my name written there, which you have never seen." The book referred to was stored with others at a warehouse. When Professor Mapes opened the case, which had been undisturbed for twenty-seven years, to his astonishment he found his father's name written on page 120. It was this incident which first led him to make a serious investigation, for, like his friend Professor Hare, he had up till that time been a strong materialist.

In April, 1854, the Hon. James Shields presented a memorial,* praying for inquiry, to the United States legislature, with thirteen thousand signatures attached, and with the name of Governor Tallmadge at the head of the list. After a frivolous discussion, in which Mr. Shields, who presented the petition, referred to the belief held by the petitioners as due to a delusion arising from defective education or deranged mental faculties, it was formally agreed that the petition should lie upon the table. Mr. E. W. Capron has this comment : †

It is not probable that any of the memorialists expected more favourable treatment than they received. The carpenters and fishermen of the world are the ones to investigate new truths and make Senates and Crowns believe and respect them. It is in vain to look for the reception or respect of new truths by men in high places.

The first regular Spiritualist organization was formed in New York on June 10, 1854. It was entitled the " Society for the Diffusion of Spiritual Knowledge," and included among its members such prominent people as Judge Edmonds and Governor Tallmadge, of Wisconsin.

Among the activities of the society was the estab-

---

* See Capron, " Modern Spiritualism," pp. 359–363.
† " Modern Spiritualism," p. 375.

lishment of a newspaper called *The Christian Spiritual-ist*, and the engagement of Miss Kate Fox to hold daily séances, to which the public were admitted free each morning from ten till one o'clock.

Writing in 1855 Capron* says :

It would be impossible to state particulars in regard to the spread of Spiritualism in New York up to the present time. It has become diffused throughout the city, and has almost ceased to be a curiosity or a wonder to any. Public meetings are regularly held, and the investigation is constantly going on, but the days of excitement on the subject have passed away, and all parties look upon it as, at least, something more than a mere trick. It is true that religious bigotry denounces it, but without disputing the occurrences, and occasionally a pretended exposé is made for purposes of speculation ; but the fact of spiritual intercourse has become an acknowledged fact in the Empire city.

Perhaps the most significant fa:t of the period we have been considering was the development of mediumship in prominent people, as, for instance, Judge Edmonds and Professor Hare. The latter writes : †

Having latterly acquired the powers of a medium in a sufficient degree to interchange ideas with my spirit friends, I am no longer under the necessity of defending media from the charge of falsehood and deception. It is now my own character only that can be in question.

Thus, dismissing the Fox girls from the field altogether, we have the *private* mediumship of Rev. A. H.

* "Modern Spiritualism," p. 197.
† "Experimental Investigation of the Spirit Manifestations," p. 54.

Jervis, Deacon Hale, Lyman Granger, Judge Edmonds, Professor Hare, Mrs. Mapes, Miss Mapes, and the public mediumship of Mrs. Tamlin, Mrs. Benedict, Mrs. Hayden, D. D. Home, and dozens of others.

It is not within the scope of this work to deal with the great number of individual cases of mediumship, some of them most dramatic and interesting, which occurred during this first period of demonstration. The reader is referred to Mrs. Hardinge Britten's two important compilations, " Modern American Spiritualism " and " Nineteenth Century Miracles," books which will always be a most valuable record of early days. The series of phenomenal cases was so great that Mrs. Britten has counted over five thousand separate instances recorded in the Press in the first few years, which probably represents some hundreds of thousands not so recorded. Religion so-called and Science so-called united for once in an unholy attempt to misrepresent and persecute the new truth and its supporters, while the Press unfortunately found that its interest lay in playing up to the prejudices of the majority of its subscribers. It was easy to do this, for naturally, in so vital and compelling a movement, there were some who became fanatical, some who threw discredit upon their opinions by their actions, and some who took advantage of the general interest to imitate, with more or less success, the real gifts of the spirit. These fraudulent rascals were sometimes mere cold-blooded swindlers, and sometimes seem to have been real mediums whose psychic power had for a time deserted them. There were scandals and exposures, some real and some pretended. These exposures were then, as now, due often to the Spiritualists themselves, who strongly objected to their sacred ceremonies being a screen for the hypocrisies and blasphemies of those villains who, like human hyenas, tried to make a fraudulent living out of the dead. The general result was to take the edge off the first fine enthusiasm, and to set back the acceptance of what was true by an eternal harping on what was false.

The brave report of Professor Hare led to a disgraceful persecution of that venerable savant, who was at that moment, with the exception of Agassiz, the best-known man of science in America. The professors of Harvard—a university which has a most unenviable record in psychic matters—passed a resolution denouncing him and his " insane adherence to a gigantic humbug." He could not lose his professorial chair at Pennsylvania University because that had been already resigned, but he suffered much in loss of reputation.

The crowning and most absurd instance of scientific intolerance—an intolerance which has always been as violent and unreasonable as that of the mediæval Church—was shown by the American Scientific Association. This learned body howled down Professor Hare when he attempted to address them, and put it on record that the subject was unworthy of their attention. It was remarked, however, by the Spiritualists, that the same society at the same session held an animated debate as to why cocks crow between twelve and one at night, coming finally to the conclusion that at that particular hour a wave of electricity passes over the earth from north to south, and that the fowls, disturbed out of their slumbers and " being naturally of a crowing disposition," register the event in this fashion. It had not then been learned—and perhaps it has hardly been learned yet—that a man, or a body of men, may be very wise upon those subjects on which they are experts, and yet show an extraordinary want of common sense when faced with a new proposition which calls for a complete readjustment of ideas. British science and, indeed, science the whole world over, have shown the same intolerance and want of elasticity which marked those early days in America.

These days have been drawn so fully by Mrs. Hardinge Britten, who herself played a large part in them, that those who are interested can always follow them in her pages. Some notes about Mrs. Britten herself may, however, be fitly introduced at this place, for no history of Spiritualism could be complete without an account of this remarkable woman who has been called the female St. Paul of the movement. She was a young Englishwoman who had gone to New York with a theatrical company, and had then, with her mother, remained in America. Being strictly Evangelical she was much repelled by what she considered the unorthodox views of Spiritualists, and fled in horror from her first séance. Later, in 1856, she was again brought into contact with the subject and received proofs which made it impossible for her to doubt its truth. She soon discovered that she was herself a powerful medium, and one of the best attested and most sensational cases in the early history of the movement was that in which she received intimation that the mail steamer *Pacific* had gone down in mid-Atlantic with all souls, and was threatened with prosecution by the owners of the boat for repeating what had been told her by the returning spirit of one of the crew. The information proved to be only too true, and the vessel was never heard of again.

Mrs. Emma Hardinge—who became, by a second marriage, Mrs. Hardinge Britten—threw her whole enthusiastic temperament into the young movement and left a mark upon it which is still visible. She was an ideal propagandist, for she combined every gift. She was a strong medium, an orator, a writer, a well-balanced thinker and a hardy traveller. Year after year she travelled the length and breadth of the United States proclaiming the new doctrine amid much opposition, for she was militant and anti-Christian in the views which she professed to get straight from her spirit guides. As these views were, however, that the morals of the Churches were far too lax and that a higher standard was called for, it is not likely that the Founder of Christianity would have been among her critics. These opinions of Mrs. Hardinge Britten had more to do with the broadly Unitarian view of the official Spiritualist bodies, which still exists, than any other cause.

In 1866 she returned to England, where she worked indefatigably, producing her two great chron-

icles, " Modern American Spiritualism " and, later,
" Nineteenth Century Miracles," both of which show
an amazing amount of research together with a very
clear and logical mind. In 1870 she married Dr.
Britten, as strong a Spiritualist as herself. The marriage seems to have been an ideally happy one. In
1878 they went together as missionaries for Spiritualism to Australia and New Zealand, and stayed there
for several years, founding various churches and
societies which the author found still holding their own
when he visited the Antipodes forty years later upon
the same errand. While in Australia she wrote her
" Faiths, Facts and Frauds of Religious History," a
book which still influences many minds. There was
at that time undoubtedly a close connexion between
the free thought movement and the new spirit revelation. The Hon. Robert Stout, Attorney-General of
New Zealand, was both President of the Free Thought
Association and an ardent Spiritualist. It is more
clearly understood now, however, that spirit intercourse and teaching are too wide to be fitted into any
system, whether negative or positive, and that it is
possible for a Spiritualist to profess any creed so long
as he has the essentials of reverence to the unseen and
unselfishness to those around him.

Among other monuments of her energy, Mrs.
Hardinge Britten founded *The Two Worlds* of Man-
chester, which has still as large a circulation as any
Spiritualistic paper in the world. She passed onwards
in 1899, having left her mark deep upon the religious
life of three continents.

This has been a long but necessary digression from the account of the early days of American progress. Those early days were marked by great enthusiasm, much success, and also considerable persecution. All the leaders who had anything to lose lost it. Mrs. Hardinge says :

Judge Edmonds was pointed at in the streets as a crazy Spiritualist. Wealthy merchants were compelled to assert their claims to be considered sane and maintain their commercial rights by the most firm and determined action. Professional men and tradesmen were reduced to the limits of ruin, and a relentless persecution, originated by the Press and maintained by the pulpit, directed the full flow of its evil tides against the cause and its representatives. Many of the houses where circles were being held were disturbed by crowds who would gather together after nightfall and with yells, cries, whistles and occasional breaking of windows try to molest the quiet investigators in their unholy work of " waking the dead," as one of the papers piously denominated the act of seeking for the " Ministry of Angels."

Passing the smaller ebb and flow of the movement, the rising of new true mediums, the exposure of occasional false ones, the committees of inquiry (negatived often by the want of perception of the inquirers that a psychic circle depends for success upon the psychic condition of *all* its members), the development of fresh phenomena and the conversion of new initiates, there are a few outstanding incidents of those early days which should be particularly noted. Prominent among them is the mediumship of D. D. Home, and of the two Davenport boys, which form such important episodes, and attracted public attention to such a degree and for so long a time, that they are treated in separate chapters. There are, however, certain lesser mediumships which call for a shorter notice.

One of these was that of Linton, the blacksmith, a man who was quite illiterate and yet, like A. J. Davis, wrote a remarkable book under alleged spirit control. This book of 530 pages, called " The Healing of the Nations," is certainly a remarkable production whatever its source, and it is obviously impossible that it could have been normally produced by such an author. It is adorned by a very long preface from the pen of Governor Tallmadge, which shows that the worthy senator was no mean student of antiquity. The case from the point of view of the classics and the early Church has seldom been better stated.

In 1857 Harvard University again made itself notorious by the persecution and expulsion of a student named Fred Willis, for the practice of mediumship. It would almost seem that the spirit of Cotton Mather and the old witch-finders of Salem had descended upon the great Boston seat of learning, for in those early days it was constantly at issue with those unseen forces which no one can hope to conquer. This matter began by an intemperate attempt upon the part of a Professor Eustis to prove that Willis was fraudulent, whereas all the evidence shows clearly that he was a true sensitive, who shrank greatly from any public use of his powers. The matter caused considerable excitement and scandal at the time. This and other cases of hard usage may be cited, but it must nevertheless be acknowledged that the hope of gain on the one hand, and the mental effervescence caused by so terrific a revelation on the other, did at this period lead to a degree of dishonesty in some so-called mediums, and to fanatical excesses and grotesque assertions in others, which held back that immediate success which the more sane and steady Spiritualists expected and deserved.

One curious phase of mediumship which attracted much attention was that of a farmer, Jonathan Koons and his family, living in a wild district of Ohio. The phenomena obtained by the Eddy brothers are discussed at some length in a subsequent chapter, and as those of the Koons family were much on the same lines they need not be treated in detail. The use of musical instruments came largely into the demonstrations of spirit force, and the Koons's log-house became celebrated through all the adjoining states—so celebrated that it was constantly crowded, although it was situated some seventy miles from the nearest town. It would appear to have been a case of true physical mediumship of a crude quality, as might be expected where a rude uncultured farmer was the physical centre of it. Many investigations were held, but the facts always remained untouched by criticism. Eventually, however, Koons and his family were driven from their home by the persecution of the ignorant people among whom they lived. The rude open-air life of the farmer seems to be particularly adapted to the development of strong physical mediumship. It was in an American farmer's household that it first developed, and Koons in Ohio, the Eddys in Vermont, Foss in Massachusetts, and many others, have shown the same powers.

We may fitly end this short review of the early days in America by an event where spirit intervention proved to be of importance in the world's history. This was the instance of the inspired messages which determined the action of Abraham Lincoln at the supreme moment of the Civil War. The facts are beyond dispute, and are given with the corroborative evidence in Mrs. Maynard's book on Abraham Lincoln. Mrs. Maynard's maiden name was Nettie Colburn, and she was herself the heroine of the story.

The young lady was a powerful trance medium, and she visited Washington in the winter of 1862 in order to see her brother who was in the hospital of the Federal Army. Mrs. Lincoln, the wife of the President, who was interested in Spiritualism, had a sitting with Miss Colburn, was enormously impressed by the result, and sent a carriage next day to bring the medium to see the President. She describes the kindly way in which the great man received her in the parlour of the White House, and mentions the names of those who were present. She sat down, passed into the usual trance, and remembered no more. She continued thus:

For more than an hour I was made to talk to him, and I learned from my friends afterwards that it was upon matters that he seemed fully to understand, while they com-

prehended very little until that portion was reached that
related to the forthcoming Emancipation Proclamation.
He was charged with the utmost solemnity and force of
manner not to abate the terms of its issue and not to delay
its enforcement as a law beyond the opening of the year;
and he was assured that it was to be the crowning event
of his administration and his life ; and that while he was
being counselled by strong parties to defer the enforcement of it, hoping to supplant it by other measures and to
delay action, he must in no wise heed such counsel, but
stand firm to his convictions and fearlessly perform the
work and fulfil the mission for which he had been raised up
by an overruling Providence. Those present declared
that they lost sight of the timid girl in the majesty of the
utterance, the strength and force of the language, and the
importance of that which was conveyed, and seemed to
realize that some strong masculine spirit force was giving
speech to almost divine commands.

I shall never forget the scene around me when I regained consciousness. I was standing in front of Mr.
Lincoln, and he was sitting back in his chair, with his arms
folded upon his breast, looking intently at me. I stepped
back, naturally confused at the situation—not remembering
at once where I was ; and glancing around the group where
perfect silence reigned. It took me a moment to remember
my whereabouts.

A gentleman present then said in a low tone, " Mr.
President, did you notice anything peculiar in the method
of address ? " Mr. Lincoln raised himself, as if shaking
off his spell. He glanced quickly at the full-length portrait of Daniel Webster that hung above the piano, and
replied: " Yes, and it is very singular, very! " with a marked
emphasis.

Mr. Somes said : " Mr. President, would it be improper
for me to inquire whether there has been any pressure

brought to bear upon you to defer the enforcement of the Proclamation ? " To which the President replied : " Under these circumstances that question is perfectly proper, as we are all friends." (Smiling upon the company). " It is taking all my nerve and strength to withstand such a pressure." At this point the gentlemen drew around him and spoke together in low tones, Mr. Lincoln saying least of all. At last he turned to me, and laying his hand upon my head, uttered these words in a manner I shall never forget. " My child, you possess a very singular gift, but that it is of God I have no doubt. I thank you for coming here to-night. It is more important than per- haps anyone present can understand. I must leave you all now, but I hope I shall see you again." He shook me kindly by the hand, bowed to the rest of the company, and was gone. We remained an hour longer, talking with Mrs. Lincoln and her friends, and then returned to Georgetown. Such was my first interview with Abraham Lincoln, and the memory of it is as clear and vivid as the evening on which it occurred.

This was one of the most important instances in the history of Spiritualism, and may also have been one of the most important in the history of the United States, as it not only strengthened the President in taking a step which raised the whole moral tone of the Northern armies and put something of the crusading spirit into the men, but a subsequent message urged Lincoln to visit the camps, which he did with the best effect upon the *moral* of the army. And yet the reader might, I fear, search every history of the great struggle and every life of the President without finding a mention of this vital episode. It is all part of that unfair treatment which Spiritualism has endured so long.

It is impossible that the United States, if it appreciated the truth, would allow the cult which proved its value at the darkest moment of its history to be persecuted and repressed by ignorant policemen and bigoted magistrates in the way which is now so common, or that the Press should continue to make mock of the movement which produced the Joan of Arc of their country.

CHAPTER VII

THE DAWN IN ENGLAND

THE early Spiritualists have frequently been compared with the early Christians, and there are indeed many points of resemblance. In one respect, however, the Spiritualists had an advantage. The women of the older dispensation did their part nobly, living as saints and dying as martyrs, but they did not figure as preachers and missionaries. Psychic power and psychic knowledge are, however, as great in one sex as in another, and therefore many of the great pioneers of the spiritual revelation were women. Especially may this be claimed for Emma Hardinge Britten, one whose name will grow more famous as the years roll by. There have, however, been several other women missionaries outstanding, and the most important of these from the British point of view is Mrs. Hayden, who first in the year 1852 brought the new phenomena to these shores. We had of old the Apostles of religious faith. Here at last was an apostle of religious fact.

Mrs. Hayden was a remarkable woman as well as an excellent medium. She was the wife of a respectable New England journalist who accompanied her in her mission, which had been organized by one Stone, who had some experience of her powers in America.

At the time of her visit she was described as being "young, intelligent, and at the same time simple and candid in her manners." Her British critic added:

She disarmed suspicion by the unaffected artlessness of her address, and many who came to amuse themselves at her expense were shamed into respect and even cordiality by the patience and good temper which she displayed. The impression invariably left by an interview with her was that if, as Mr. Dickens contended, the phenomena developed by her were attributed to art, she herself was the most perfect artist, as far as acting went, that had ever presented herself before the public.

The ignorant British Press treated Mrs. Hayden as a common American adventuress. Her real mental calibre, however, may be judged from the fact that some years later, after her return to the United States, Mrs. Hayden graduated as a doctor of medicine and practised for fifteen years. Dr. James Rodes Buchanan, the famous pioneer in psychometry, speaks of her as "one of the most skilful and successful physicians I have ever known." She was offered a medical professorship in an American college, and was employed by the Globe Insurance Company in protecting the company against losses in insurance on lives. A feature of her success was what Buchanan describes as her psychometric genius. He adds a unique tribute to the effect that her name was almost forgotten at the Board of Health because for years she had not a single death to report.

This sequel, however, was beyond the knowledge of the sceptics of 1852, and they cannot be blamed for insisting that these strange claims of other-world intervention should be tested with the utmost rigour before they could be admitted. No one could contest this critical attitude. But what does seem strange is that a proposition which, if true, would involve such glad tidings as the piercing of the wall of death and a true communion of the saints, should arouse not sober criticism, however exacting, but a storm of insult and abuse, inexcusable at any time, but particularly so when directed against a lady who was a visitor in our midst. Mrs. Hardinge Britten says that Mrs. Hayden no sooner appeared upon the scene than the leaders of the Press, pulpit and college levelled against her a storm of ribaldry, persecution and insult, alike disgraceful to themselves and humiliating to the boasted liberalism and scientific acumen of their age. She added that her gentle womanly spirit must have been deeply pained, and the harmony of mind so essential to the production of good psychological results constantly destroyed, by the cruel and insulting treatment she received at the hands of many of those who came, pretending to be investigators, but in reality burning to thwart her, and laying traps to falsify the truths of which Mrs. Hayden professed to be the instrument. Sensitively alive to the animus of her visitors, she could feel, and often writhed under the crushing force of the antagonism brought to bear upon her, without— at that time—knowing how to repel or resist it.

At the same time, the whole nation was not involved in this irrational hostility, which in a diluted form we still see around us. Brave men arose who were not afraid to imperil their worldly career, or even their reputation for sanity, by championing an unpopular cause with no possible motive save the love of truth and that sense of chivalry which revolted at the persecution of a woman. Dr. Ashburner, one of the Royal physicians, and Sir Charles Isham, were among those who defended the medium in the public Press.

Mrs. Hayden's mediumship seems, when judged by modern standards, to have been strictly limited in type. Save for the raps, we hear little of physical phenomena, nor is there any question of lights, materializations or Direct Voices. In harmonious company, however, the answers as furnished by raps were very accurate and convincing. Like all true mediums, she was sensitive to discord in her surroundings, with the result that the contemptible crew of practical jokers and ill-natured researchers who visited her found her a ready victim. Deceit is repaid by deceit and the fool is answered according to his folly, though the intelligence behind the words seems to care little for the fact that the passive instrument employed may be held accountable for the answer. These pseudo-researchers filled the Press with their humorous accounts of how they had deceived the spirits, when as a fact they had rather deceived themselves. George Henry Lewes, afterwards consort of George Eliot, was one of these cynical investigators. He recounts with glee how he had asked the control in writing: " Is Mrs. Hayden an impostor ? " to which the control rapped out: " Yes." Lewes was dishonest enough to quote this afterwards as being a confession of guilt from Mrs. Hayden. One would rather draw from it the inference that the raps were entirely independent of the medium, and also that questions asked in a spirit of pure frivolity met with no serious reply.

It is, however, by the positives and not by the negatives that such questions must be judged, and the author must here use quotations to a larger extent than is his custom, for in no other way can one bring home how those seeds were first planted in England which are destined to grow to such a goodly height. Allusion has already been made to the testimony of Dr. Ashburner, the famous physician, and it would be well perhaps to add some of his actual words. He says : *

Sex ought to have protected her from injury, if you gentlemen of the Press have no regard to the hospitable feelings due to one of your own cloth, for Mrs. Hayden is the wife of a former editor and proprietor of a journal in Boston having a most extensive circulation in New England. I declare to you that Mrs. Hayden is no impostor, and he who has the daring to come to an opposite conclusion must · do so at the peril of his character for truth.

Again, in a long letter to *The Reasoner*,† after admitting that he visited the medium in a thoroughly incredulous frame of mind, expecting to witness " the same class of transparent absurdities " he had previously encountered with other so-called mediums, Ashburner writes: " As for Mrs. Hayden, I have so strong a conviction of her perfect honesty that I marvel at anyone who could deliberately accuse her

* *The Leader*, March 14, 1853.   † June 1 and 8, 1853.

of fraud," and at the same time he gives detailed accounts of veridical communications he received.

Among the investigators was the celebrated mathematician and philosopher, Professor De Morgan. He gives some account of his experiences and conclusions in his long and masterly preface to his wife's book, " From Matter to Spirit," 1863, as follows:

Ten years ago Mrs. Hayden, the well-known American medium, came to my house *alone*. The sitting began immediately after her arrival. Eight or nine persons of all ages, and of all degrees of belief and unbelief in the whole thing being imposture, were present. The raps began in the usual way. They were to my ear clean, clear, faint sounds such as would be said to *ring*, had they lasted. I likened them at the time to the noise which the ends of knitting-needles would make, if dropped from a small distance upon a marble slab, and instantly checked by a damper of some kind ; and subsequent trial showed that my description was tolerably accurate. . . . At a late period in the evening, after nearly three hours of experiment, Mrs. Hayden having risen, and talking at another table while taking refreshment, a child suddenly called out, " Will all the spirits who have been here this evening rap together ? " The words were no sooner uttered than a hailstorm of knitting-needles was heard, crowded into certainly less than two seconds ; the big needle sounds of the men, and the little ones of the women and children, being clearly distinguishable, but perfectly disorderly in their arrival.

After a remark to the effect that for convenience he intends to speak of the raps as coming from spirits, Professor De Morgan goes on :

On being asked to put a question to the first spirit, I begged that I might be allowed to put my question mentally—that is, without speaking it, or writing it, or pointing it out to myself on an alphabet—and that Mrs. Hayden might hold both arms extended while the answer was in progress. Both demands were instantly granted by a couple of raps. I put the question and desired the answer might be in one word, which I assigned ; all mentally. I then took the printed alphabet, put a book upright before it, and, bending my eyes upon it, proceeded to point to the letters in the usual way. The word " chess " was given by a rap at each letter. I had now a reasonable certainty of the following alternative : either some *thought-reading* of a character wholly inexplicable, or such super-human acuteness on the part of Mrs. Hayden that she could detect the letter I wanted by my bearing, though she (seated six feet from the book which hid my alphabet) could see neither my hand nor my eye, nor at what rate I was going through the letters. I was fated to be driven out of the second alternative before the sitting was done.

As the next incident of the sitting, which he goes on to relate, is given with extra details in a letter written ten years earlier to the Rev. W. Heald, we quote this version published in his wife's " Memoir of Augustus De Morgan " (pp. 221-2):

Presently came *my father* (*ob.*, 1816), and after some conversation I went on as follows :

" Do you remember a periodical I have in my head ? " " Yes." " Do you remember the epithets therein applied to yourself ? " " Yes." " Will you give me the initials of them by the card ? " " Yes." I then began pointing to the alphabet, with a book to conceal the card, Mrs. H. being at the opposite side of a round table (large), and a bright lamp between us. I pointed letter by letter till I came to F, which I thought should be the first initial.

No rapping. The people round me said, "You have passed it ; there was a rapping at the beginning." I went back and heard the rapping distinctly at C. This puzzled me, but in a moment I saw what it was. The sentence was begun by the rapping agency earlier than I intended. I allowed C to pass, and then got D T F O C, being the initials of the consecutive words which I remembered to have been applied to my father in an old review published in 1817, which no one in the room had ever heard of but myself. C D T F O C was all right, and when I got so far I gave it up, perfectly satisfied that something, or somebody, or some spirit, was reading *my thoughts*. This and the like went on for nearly three hours, during a great part of which Mrs. H. was busy reading the " Key to Uncle Tom's Cabin," which she had never seen before, and I assure you she set to it with just as much avidity as you may suppose an American lady would who saw it for the first time, while we were amusing ourselves with the raps in our own way. All this I declare to be literally true. Since that time I have seen it in my house frequently, various persons presenting themselves. The answers are given mostly by the table, on which a hand or two is gently placed, tilting up at the letters. There is much which is confused in the answers, but every now and then comes something which surprises us. I have no theory about it, but in a year or two something curious may turn up. I am, however, satisfied of the reality of the phenomenon. A great many other persons are as cognizant of these phenomena in their own houses as myself. Make what you can of it if you are a philosopher.

When Professor De Morgan says that some spirit was reading his thoughts, he omits to observe that the incident of the first letter was evidence of something that was *not* in his mind. Also, from Mrs.

Hayden's attitude throughout the séance, it is clear that it was her atmosphere rather than her actual conscious personality which was concerned. Some further important evidence from the De Morgans is relegated to the Appendix.

Mrs. Fitzgerald, a well-known figure in the early days of Spiritualism in London, gives, in *The Spiritualist* of November 22, 1878, the following very striking experience with Mrs. Hayden :

My first introduction to Spiritualism commenced at the time of the first visit of the well-known medium, Mrs. Hayden, to this country nearly thirty years ago. I was invited to meet her at a party given by a friend in Wimpole Street, London. Having made a pre-engagement for that evening, which I could not avoid, I arrived late, after what appeared an extraordinary scene, of which they were all talking with great animation. My look of blank disappointment was noticed, and Mrs. Hayden, whom I then met for the first time, came most kindly forward, expressed her regrets, and suggested that I should sit at a small table by myself apart from the others, and she would ask the spirits if they would communicate with me. All this appeared so new and surprising I scarcely understood what she was talking about, or what I had to expect. She placed before me a printed alphabet, a pencil, and a piece of paper. Whilst she was in the act of doing this, I felt extraordinarily rappings all over the table, the vibrations from which I could feel on the sole of my foot as it rested against the table's leg. She then directed me to note down each letter at which I heard a distinct rap, and with this short explanation she left me to myself. I pointed as desired—a distinct rap came at the letter E—others followed, and a name that I could not fail to recognize was spelt out. The date of death was given, which I had not before known, and a message added which brought back to my memory the almost last dying words of an old friend—namely, " I shall watch over you." And then the recollection of the whole scene was brought vividly before me. I confess I was startled and somewhat awed.

I carried the paper upon which all this was written at the dictation of my spirit friend to his former legal adviser, and was assured by him that the dates, etc., were perfectly correct. They could not have been in my mind because I was not aware of them.

It is interesting to note that Mrs. Fitzgerald stated that she believed that Mrs. Hayden's first séance in England was held with Lady Combermere, her son, Major Cotton, and Mr. Henry Thompson, of York.

In the same volume of *The Spiritualist* (p. 264) there appears an account of a séance with Mrs. Hayden, taken from the life of Charles Young, the well-known tragedian, written by his son, the Rev. Julian Young :

1853, *April* 19*th.* I went up to London this day for the purpose of consulting my lawyers on a subject of some importance to myself, and having heard much of a Mrs. Hayden, an American lady, as a spiritual medium, I resolved, as I was in town, to discover her whereabouts, and judge of her gifts for myself. Accidentally meeting an old friend, Mr. H., I asked him if he could give me her address. He told me that it was 22, Queen Anne Street, Cavendish Square. As he had never been in her company, and had a great wish to see her, and yet was unwilling to pay his guinea for the treat, I offered to frank him, if he would go with me. He did so gladly. Spirit-rapping has been so common since 1853 that I should irritate my reader's patience by describing the conventional mode of communicating between the living and the dead. Since the above date I have seen very much of spirit-rapping ; and though my organs of wonder are largely developed, and I have a weakness for the mystic and supernatural, yet I cannot say that I have ever witnessed any spiritual phenomena which were not explicable on natural grounds, except in the instance I am about to give, in which collusion appeared to be out of the question, the friend who accompanied me never having seen Mrs. Hayden, and she knowing neither his name nor mine. The following dialogue took place between Mrs. H. and myself :

Mrs. H. : Have you, sir, any wish to communicate with the spirit of any departed friend ?

J. C. Y. : Yes.

Mrs. H. : Be pleased then to ask your questions in the manner prescribed by the formula, and I dare say you will get satisfactory replies.

J. C. Y. : (Addressing himself to one invisible yet supposed to be present) : Tell me the name of the person with whom I wish to communicate.

The letters written down according to the dictation of the taps when put together spelt " George William Young."

J. C. Y. : On whom are my thoughts now fixed ?

A. : Frederick William Young.

J. C. Y. : What is he suffering from ?

A. : Tic douloureux.

J. C. Y. : Can you prescribe anything for him ?

A. : Powerful mesmerism.

J. C. Y. : Who should be the administrator ?

A. : Someone who has strong sympathy with the patient.

J. C. Y. : Should I succeed ?

A. : No.

J. C. Y. : Who would ?

A. : Joseph Ries. (A gentleman whom my uncle much respected.)

J. C. Y. : Have I lost any friend lately ?

A. : Yes.

J. C. Y. : Who is it ? (I thinking of a Miss Young, a distant cousin.)

A. : Christiana Lane.

J. C. Y. : Can you tell me where I sleep to-night ?

A. : James B.'s, Esq., 9 Clarges Street.

J. C. Y. : Where do I sleep to-morrow ?

A. : Colonel Weymouth's, Upper Grosvenor Street.

I was so astounded by the correctness of the answers I received to my inquiries that I told the gentleman who was with me that I wanted particularly to ask a question to the nature of which I did not wish him to be privy, and that I should be obliged to him if he would go into the adjoining room for a few minutes. On his doing so I resumed my dialogue with Mrs. Hayden.

J. C. Y. : I have induced my friend to withdraw because I did not wish him to know the question I want to put, but I am equally anxious that you should not know it either, and yet, if I understand rightly, no answer can be transmitted to me except through you. What is to be done under these circumstances ?

Mrs. H. : Ask your question in such a form that the answer returned shall represent by one word the salient idea in your mind.

J. C. Y. : I will try. Will what I am threatened with take place ?

A. : No.

J. C. Y. : That is unsatisfactory. It is easy to say Yes or No, but the value of the affirmation or negation will depend on the conviction I have that you know what I am thinking of. Give me one word which shall show that you have the clue to my thoughts.

A. : Will.

Now, a will by which I had benefited was threatened to be disputed. I wished to know whether the threat would be carried out. The answer I received was correct.

It may be added that Mr. Young had no belief, before or after this séance, in spirit agency, which surely, after such an experience, is no credit to his intelligence or capacity for assimilating fresh knowledge.

The following letter in *The Spiritualist* from Mr. John Malcom, of Clifton, Bristol, mentions some well-known sitters. Discussing the question that had been raised as to where the first séance in England was held and who were the witnesses present at it, he says :

I do not remember the date ; but calling on my friend Mrs. Crowe, authoress of " The Night Side of Nature," she invited me to accompany her to a spiritual séance at the house of Mrs. Hayden in Queen Anne Street, Cavendish Square. She informed me that Mrs. Hayden had just arrived from America to exhibit the phenomena of Spiritualism to people in England who might feel interested in the subject. There were present Mrs. Crowe, Mrs. Milner Gibson, Mr. Colley Grattan (author of " High Ways and Bye Ways"), Mr. Robert Chambers, Dr. Daniels, Dr. Samuel Dickson, and several others whose names I did not hear. Some very remarkable manifestations occurred on that occasion. I afterwards had frequent opportunities of visiting Mrs. Hayden, and, though at first disposed to doubt the genuineness of the phenomena, such convincing evidence was given me of spirit communion that I became a firm believer in the truth of it.

The battle in the British Press raged furiously. In the columns of the London *Critic*, Mr. Henry

Spicer (author of " Sights and Sounds ") replied to
the critics in *Household Words*, the *Leader*, and
the *Zoist*. There followed in the same newspaper a
lengthy contribution from a Cambridge clergyman,
signing himself " M.A.," considered to be the Rev.
A. W. Hobson, of St. John's College, Cambridge.

This gentleman's description is graphic and powerful, but too long for complete transcription. The
matter is of some importance, as the writer is, so far as is
known, the first English clergyman who had gone into
the matter. It is strange, and perhaps characteristic
of the age, how little the religious implications appear
to have struck the various sitters, and how entirely
occupied they were by inquiries as to their grandmother's second name or the number of their uncles.
Even the more earnest seem to have been futile in their
questions, and no one shows the least sense of realiza-
tion of the real possibilities of such commerce, or that
a firm foundation for religious belief could at last be
laid. This clergyman did, however, in a purblind
way, see that there was a religious side to the matter.
He finishes his report with the paragraph:

I will conclude with a few words to the numerous
clerical readers of the *Critic*. Being myself a clergyman
of the Church of England, I consider that the subject
is one in which my brother clergy *must*, sooner or later,
take some interest, however reluctant they may be to have
anything to do with it. And my reasons are briefly as
follow : If such excitement become general in this country
as already exists in America—and what reason have we
to suppose that it will not ?—then the clergy throughout the
kingdom will be appealed to on all sides, will have to give

an opinion, and may probably be obliged, by their very
duties, to interfere and endeavour to prevent the delusions
to which, in many cases, this " mystery " has already led.
One of the most sensible and able writers on the subject
of these spirit manifestations in America, viz., Adin Ballou,
in his work has expressly cautioned his readers not to believe
all these spirits communicate, nor allow themselves to give
up their former opinions and religious creeds (as so many
thousands have done) at the bidding of these rappers.
The thing has scarcely begun in England as yet; but already,
within the few months since Mr. and Mrs. Hayden arrived
in London, it has spread like wild-fire, and I have good
reason for saying that the excitement is only commencing.
Persons who at first treated the whole affair as a contemptible imposture and humbug, on witnessing these strange
things for themselves, become first startled and astonished,
then rush blindly into all sorts of mad conclusions—as,
for instance, that it is all the work of the devil, or (in the
opposite degree) that it is a new revelation from Heaven.
I see scores of the most able and intelligent people whom I
know utterly and completely mystified by it ; and no one
knows what to make of it.   I am ready to confess, for my
own part, that I am equally mystified.   That it is not imposture, I feel perfectly and fully convinced.   In addition
to the tests, etc., above-named, I had a long conversation
in private with both Mr. and Mrs. Hayden separately,
and everything they said bore the marks of sincerity and
good faith.   Of course, this is no evidence to other people,
but it is to me.   If there is any deception, they are as much
deceived as any of their dupes.

It was not the clergy but the Free Thinkers who
perceived the real meaning of the message, and that
they must either fight against this proof of life eternal,
or must honestly confess, as so many of us have done

since, that their philosophy was shattered, and that they had been beaten on their own ground. These men had called for *proofs* in transcendent matters, and the more honest and earnest were forced to admit that they had had them. The noblest of them all was Robert Owen, as famous for his humanitarian works as for his sturdy independence in religious matters. This brave and honest man declared publicly that the first rays of this rising sun had struck him and had gilded the drab future which he had pictured. He said:

I have patiently traced the history of these manifestations, investigated the facts connected with them (testified to in innumerable instances by persons of high character), have had fourteen séances with the medium Mrs. Hayden, during which she gave me every opportunity to ascertain if it were possible there could be any deception on her part.

I am not only convinced that there is no deception with truthful media in these proceedings, but that they are destined to effect, at this period, the greatest moral revolution in the character and condition of the human race.

Mrs. Emma Hardinge Britten comments on the interest and astonishment created by the conversion of Robert Owen, the influence of whose purely materialistic belief was regarded as exerting an injurious effect on religion. She says that one of England's most prominent statesmen declared " that Mrs. Hayden deserved a monument, if only for the conversion of Robert Owen."

Shortly afterwards the famous Dr. Elliotson, who was the president of the Secular Society, was also con-

verted after, like St. Paul, violently assailing the new
revelation. He and Dr. Ashburner had been two of
the most prominent supporters of mesmerism in the
days when even that obvious phenomenon had to
fight for its existence, and when every medical man
who affirmed it was in danger of being called a quack.
It was painful to both of them, therefore, when Dr.
Ashburner threw himself into this higher subject with
enthusiasm, while his friend was constrained not only
to reject but actively to attack it. However, the
breach was healed by the complete conversion of
Elliotson, and Mrs. Hardinge Britten relates how in his
declining years he insisted upon her coming to him,
and how she found him a "warm adherent of Spiritualism, a faith which the venerable gentleman cherished
as the brightest revelation that had ever been vouchsafed to him, and one which finally smoothed the dark
passage to the life beyond, and made his transition a
scene of triumphant faith and joyful anticipation."

As might have been expected, it was not long
before the rapid growth of table phenomena compelled scientific sceptics to recognize their existence,
or at least to take steps to expose the delusion of those
who attributed to the movements an external origin.
Braid, Carpenter, and Faraday stated publicly that the
results obtained were due simply to unconscious muscular action. Faraday devised ingenious apparatus
which he considered conclusively proved his assertion.
But, like so many other critics, Faraday had had no
experience with a good medium, and the well-
attested fact of the movement of tables without con-

tact is sufficient to demolish his pretty theories. If
one could imagine a layman without a telescope contradicting with jeers and contempt the conclusions of
those astronomers who had used telescopes, it would
present some analogy to those people who have ven-
tured to criticize psychic matters without having had
any personal psychic experience.

The contemporary spirit is no doubt voiced by Sir
David Brewster. Speaking of an invitation from
Monckton Milnes to meet Mr. Galla, the African
traveller, " who assured him that Mrs. Hayden told
him the names of persons and places in Africa which
nobody but himself knew," Sir David comments,
" The world is obviously going mad."

Mrs. Hayden remained in England about a year,
returning to America towards the close of 1853.
Some day, when these matters have found their true
proportion to other events, her visit will be regarded
as historical and epoch-making. Two other American
mediums were in England during her visit—Mrs.
Roberts and Miss Jay—having followed shortly after,
but they appear to have had little influence on the
movement, and seem to have been very inferior in
psychic power.

A contemporary sidelight on those early days is
afforded by this extract from an article on Spiritualism in *The Yorkshireman* (October 25, 1856), a non-
Spiritualist journal :

The English public in general, we believe, are but
imperfectly acquainted with the nature of the Spiritualist
doctrines, and many of our readers are, doubtless, unpre-

pared to believe that they prevail to any extent in this country. The ordinary phenomena of table-moving, etc., are, it is true, familiar to most of us. Some two or three years ago there was not an evening party which did not essay the performance of a Spiritualist miracle. . . . In those days you were invited to " Tea and Table Moving " as a new excitement, and made to revolve with the family like mad round articles of furniture.

After declaring that Faraday's attack made " the spirits suddenly subside," so that for a time no more was heard of their doings, the journal continues :

We have ample evidence, however, that Spiritualism as a vital and active belief is not confined to the United States, but that it has found favour and acceptance among a considerable class of enthusiasts in our own country.

But the general attitude of the influential Press was much the same then as now—ridicule and denial of the facts, and the view that even if the facts were true, of what use were they ? *The Times*, for instance (a paper which has been very ill-informed and re-actionary in psychic matters), in a leading article of a little later date suggests :

It would be something to get one's hat off the peg by an effort of volition, without going to fetch it, or troubling a servant.

If table-power could be made to turn even a coffee-mill, it would be so much gained.

Let our mediums and clairvoyants, instead of finding out what somebody died of fifty years ago, find out what figure the Funds will be at this day three months.

When one reads such comments in a great paper

one wonders whether the movement was not really premature, and whether in so base and material an age the idea of outside intervention was not impossible to grasp. Much of this opposition was due, however, to the frivolity of inquirers who had not as yet realized the full significance of these signals from beyond, and used them, as the Yorkshire paper states, as a sort of social recreation and a new excitement for jaded worldlings.

But while in the eyes of the Press the death-blow had been given to a discredited movement, investigation went on quietly in many quarters. People of common sense, as Howitt points out, " were successfully testing those angels, under their own mode of advent, and finding them real," for, as he well says, " public mediums have never done more than inaugurate the movement."

If one were to judge from the public testimony of the time, Mrs. Hayden's influence might be considered to have been limited in extent. To the public at large she was only a nine days' wonder, but she scattered much seed which slowly grew. The fact is, she opened the subject up, and people, mostly in the humbler walks of life, began to experiment and to discover the truth for themselves, though, with a caution born of experience, they kept their discoveries for the most part to themselves. Mrs. Hayden, without doubt, fulfilled her ordained task.

The history of the movement may well be compared to an advancing sea with its successive crests and troughs, each crest gathering more volume than the last. With every trough the spectator has thought that the waves had ended, and then the great new billow gathered. The time between the leaving of Mrs. Hayden in 1853 until the advent of D. D. Home in 1855 represents the first lull in England. Superficial critics thought it was the end. But in a thousand homes throughout the land experiments were being carried on; many who had lost all faith in the things of the spirit, in what was perhaps the deadest and most material age in the world's history, had begun to examine the evidence and to understand with relief or with awe that the age of faith was passing and that the age of knowledge, which St. Peter has said to be better, was at hand. Devout students of the Scriptures remember the words of their Master: " I have yet many things to say unto you, but ye cannot bear them now," and wondered whether these strange stirrings of outside forces might not be part of that new knowledge which had been promised.

Whilst Mrs. Hayden had thus planted the first seeds in London, a second train of events had brought spiritual phenomena under the notice of the people of Yorkshire. This was due to a visit of a Mr. David Richmond, an American Shaker, to the town of Keighley, when he called upon Mr. David Weatherhead and interested him in the new development. Table manifestations were obtained and local mediums discovered, so that a flourishing centre was built up which still exists. From Yorkshire the movement spread over Lancashire, and it is an interesting link with the past that Mr. Wolstenholme, of Blackburn,

who died in 1925 at a venerable age, was able as
a boy to secrete himself under a table at one of
these early séances, where he witnessed, though we
will hope that he did not aid, the phenomena. A
paper, *The Yorkshire Spiritual Telegraph,* was started
at Keighley in 1855, this and other expenses being
borne by David Weatherhead, whose name should be
honoured as one who was the first to throw his whole
heart into the movement. Keighley is still an active
centre of psychic work and knowledge.

CHAPTER VIII

CONTINUED PROGRESS IN ENGLAND

MRS. DE MORGAN'S account of ten years' experience of Spiritualism covers the ground from 1853 to 1863. The appearance of this book, with the weighty preface by Professor De Morgan, was one of the first signs that the new movement was spreading upwards as well as among the masses. Then came the work of D. D. Home and of the Davenports, which is detailed elsewhere. The examination of the Dialectical Society began in 1869, which is also dealt with in a later chapter. The year 1870 was the date of the first researches of William Crookes, which he undertook after remarking upon the scandal caused by the refusal of scientific men " to investigate the existence and nature of facts asserted by so many competent and credible witnesses." In the same periodical, the *Quarterly Journal of Science*, he spoke of this belief being shared by millions, and added: " I wish to ascertain the laws governing the appearance of very remarkable phenomena, which, at the present time, are occurring to an almost incredible extent."

The story of his research was given in full in 1874, and caused such a tumult among the more fossilized men of science—those who may be said to have had

their minds subdued to that at which they worked—
that there was some talk of depriving him of his
Fellowship of the Royal Society. The storm blew
over, but Crookes was startled by its violence, and it
was noticeable that for many years, until his position
was impregnable, he was very cautious in any public
expression of his views. In 1872-73, the Rev. Stainton Moses appeared as a new factor, and his automatic
writings raised the subject to a more spiritual plane in
the judgment of many. The phenomenal side may
attract the curious, but when over-emphasized it is
likely to repel the judicious mind.

Public lectures and trance addresses became a
feature. Mrs. Emma Hardinge Britten, Mrs. Cora
L. V. Tappan, and Mr. J. J. Morse gave eloquent
orations, purporting to come from spirit influence, and
large gatherings were deeply interested. Mr. Gerald
Massey, the well-known poet and writer, and Dr.
George Sexton, also delivered public lectures. Altogether, Spiritualism had much publicity given to it.

The establishment of the British National Association of Spiritualists in 1873 gave the movement an
impetus, because many well-known public men and
women joined it. Among them may be mentioned
the Countess of Caithness, Mrs. Makdougall Gregory
(widow of Professor Gregory, of Edinburgh), Dr.
Stanhope Speer, Dr. Gully, Sir Charles Isham, Dr.
Maurice Davies, Mr. H. D. Jencken, Dr. George
Sexton, Mrs. Ross Church (Florence Marryat), Mr.
Newton Crosland, and Mr. Benjamin Coleman.

Mediumship of a high order in the department of

physical phenomena was supplied by Mrs. Jencken
(Kate Fox) and Miss Florence Cook. Dr. J. R. Newton, the famous healing medium from America,
arrived in 1870, and numbers of extraordinary cures
were registered at free treatments. From 1870 Mrs.
Everitt's wonderful mediumship exercised, like that
of D. D. Home, without charge, convinced many
influential people. Herne and Williams, Mrs. Guppy,
Eglinton, Slade, Lottie Fowler, and others, secured
many converts through their mediumship. In 1872
Hudson's spirit photographs created enormous interest, and in 1875 Dr. Alfred Russel Wallace published his famous book, " On Miracles and Modern
Spiritualism."

A good means of tracing the growth of Spiritualism at this period is to examine the statements of
worthy contemporary witnesses, especially those qualified by position and experience to give an opinion.
But before we glance at the period we are considering,
let us look at the situation in 1866, as viewed by Mr.
William Howitt in a few paragraphs which are so
admirable that the author is constrained to quote
them verbatim. He says:

The present position of Spiritualism in England,
were the Press, with all its influence, omnipotent, would be
hopeless. After having taken every possible means to
damage and sneer down Spiritualism ; after having opened
its columns to it, in the hope that its emptiness and folly
would be so apparent that its clever enemies would soon be
able to knock it on the head by invincible arguments, and
then finding that all the advantages of reason and fact were
on its side ; after having abused and maligned it to no pur-

pose, the whole Press as by one consent, or by one settled plan, has adopted the system of opening its columns and pages to any false or foolish story about it, and hermetically closing them to any explanation, refutation, or defence. It is, in fact, resolved, all other means of killing it having failed, to burke it. To clap a literary pitch-plaster on its mouth, and then let anyone that likes cut its throat if he can. By this means it hopes to stamp it out like the rinderpest. . . .

If anything could annihilate· Spiritualism, its present estimation by the English public, its treatment by the Press and the courts of law, its attempted suppression by all the powers of public intelligence, its hatred by the heroes of the pulpits of all churches and creeds, the simple acceptance of even the public folly and wickedness attributed to it by the Press, its own internal divisions—in a word, its pre-eminent unpopularity would put it out of existence. But does it ? On the contrary, it never was more firmly rooted into the mass of advanced minds ; its numbers never more rapidly increased ; its truths were never more earnestly and eloquently advocated ; the enquiries after it never more abundant or more anxious. The *soirées* in Harley Street have, through the whole time that Press and horsehair wig have been heaping every reproach and every scorn upon it, been crowded to excess by ladies and gentlemen of the middle and higher classes, who have listened in admiration to the eloquent and ever-varied addresses of Emma Hardinge. Meantime, the Davenports, a thousand times denounced as impostors, and exposed impostors, have a thousand times shown that their phenomena remain as unexplainable as ever on any but a spiritual theory.

What means all this ? What does it indicate ? That Press and pulpit, and magistrate and law courts, have all tried their powers, and have failed. They stand nonplussed before the thing which they themselves have protested is poor and foolish and false and unsubstantial. If it be so poor and foolish and false and unsubstantial, how is it that all their learning, their unscrupulous denunciation, their vast means of attack and their not less means of prevention of fair defence, their command of the ears and the opinions of the multitude—how happens it that all their wit and sarcasm and logic and eloquence cannot touch it ? So far from shaking and diminishing it, they do not even ruffle a hair on its head, or a fringe of its robe.

Is it not about time for these combined hosts of the great and wise, the scientific, the learned, the leaders of senates and colleges and courts of law, the eloquent favourites of Parliament, the magnates of the popular Press, furnished with all the intellectual artillery which a great national system of education, and great national system of Church and State and aristocracy, accustomed to proclaim what shall be held to be true and of honourable repute by all honourable men and women—is it not time, I say, that all this great and splendid world of wit and wisdom should begin to suspect that they have something solid to deal with ? That there is something vital in what they have treated as a phantom ?

I do not say to these great and world-commanding bodies, powers and agencies, open your eyes and see that your efforts are fruitless, and acknowledge your defeat, for probably they never will open their eyes and confess their shame ; but I say to the Spiritualists themselves, dark as the day may seem to you, never was it more cheering. Leagued as all the armies of public instructors and directors are against it, never was its bearing more anticipatory of ultimate victory. It has upon it the stamp of all the conquering influences of the age. It has all the legitimatism of history on its head. It is but fighting the battle that every great reform—social or moral or intellectual or religious—has fought and eventually won.

As showing the change that occurred after Mr. Howitt wrote in 1866, we find *The Times* of December 26, 1872, publishing an article entitled " Spiritualism and Science," occupying three and a half columns, in which the opinion is expressed that now " it is high time competent hands undertook the unravelling of this Gordian Knot," though why the existing hands of Crookes, Wallace or De Morgan were incompetent is not explained.

The writer, speaking of Lord Adare's little book (privately printed) on his experiences with D. D. Home, seems to be impressed by the social status of the various witnesses. Clumsy humour and snobbishness are the characteristics of the article:

A volume now lying before us may serve to show how this folly has spread throughout society. It was lent to us by a disinguished Spiritualist, under the solemn promise that we should not divulge a single name of those concerned. It consists of about 150 pages of reports of séances, and was privately printed by a noble Earl, who has lately passed beyond the House of Lords ; beyond also, we trust, the spirit-peopled chairs and tables which in his lifetime he loved, not wisely, but too well. In this book things more marvellous than any we have set down are circumstantially related, in a natural way, just as though they were ordinary, everyday matters of fact. We shall not fatigue the reader by quoting any of the accounts given, and no doubt he will take our word when we say that they range through every species of " manifestation," from prophesyings downwards.

What we more particularly wish to observe is, that the attestation of fifty respectable witnesses is placed before the title-page. Among them are a Dowager Duchess and other ladies of rank, a Captain in the Guards, a nobleman, a Baronet, a Member of Parliament, several officers of our scientific and other corps, a barrister, a merchant, and a doctor. Upper and upper middle-class society is represented in all its grades, and by persons who, to judge by the position they hold and the callings they follow, ought to be possessed of intelligence and ability.

Dr. Alfred Russel Wallace, the eminent naturalist, in the course of a letter to *The Times* (January 4, 1873), describing his visit to a public medium, said:

I consider it no exaggeration to say that the main facts are now as well established and as easily verifiable as any of the more exceptional phenomena of Nature which are not yet reduced to law. They have a most important bearing on the interpretation of history, which is full of narratives of similar facts, and on the nature of life and intellect, on which physical science throws a very feeble and uncertain light ; and it is my firm and deliberate belief that every branch of philosophy must suffer till they are honestly and seriously investigated, and dealt with as constituting an essential portion of the phenomena of human nature.

One becomes bemused by ectoplasm and laboratory experiments which lead the thoughts away from the essential. Wallace was one of the few whose great, sweeping, unprejudiced mind saw and accepted the truth in its wonderful completeness from the humble physical proofs of outside power to the highest mental teaching which that power could convey, teaching that far surpasses in beauty and in credibility any which the modern mind has known.

The public acceptance and sustained support of this great scientific man, one of the first brains of his age, were the more important since he had the wit to understand the complete religious revolution which lay at the back of these phenomena. It has been a curious fact that with some exceptions in these days, as of old, the wisdom has been given to the humble and withheld from the learned. Heart and intuition have won to the goal where brain has missed it. One would think that the proposition was a simple one. It may be expressed in a series of questions after the Socratic form: " Have we established connexion with the intelligence of those who have died ? " The Spiritualist says: " Yes." " Have they given us information of the new life in which they find themselves, and of how it has been affected by their earth life ? " Again " Yes." " Have they found it correspond to the account given by any religion upon earth ? " " No." Then if this be so, is it not clear that the new information is of vital religious import ? The humble Spiritualist sees this and adapts his worship to the facts.

Sir William (then Professor) Barrett brought the subject of Spiritualism before the British Association for the Advancement of Science in 1876. His paper was entitled " On Some Phenomena associated with Abnormal Conditions of Mind." He had difficulty in obtaining a hearing. The Biological Committee refused to accept the paper and passed it on to the Anthropological Sub-section, who only accepted it on the casting vote of the chairman, Dr. Alfred Russel Wallace. Colonel Lane Fox helped to overcome the opposition by asking why, as they had discussed ancient witchcraft the previous year, they should not examine modern witchcraft that year. The first part of Professor Barrett's paper dealt with mesmerism, but in the second part he related his experiences of Spiritualistic phenomena, and urged that further scientific examination should be given to the subject. He gave the convincing details of a remarkable experience he had had of raps occurring with a child.*

In the ensuing discussion Sir William Crookes spoke of the levitations he had witnessed with D. D. Home, and said of levitation: " The evidence in favour of it is stronger than the evidence in favour of almost any natural phenomenon the British Association could investigate." He also made the following remarks concerning his own method of psychic research :

I was asked to investigate when Dr. Slade first came over, and I mentioned my conditions. I have never investigated except under these conditions. It must be at my own house, and my own selection of friends and spectators, under my own conditions, and I may do whatever I like as regards apparatus. I have always tried, where it has been possible, to make the physical apparatus test the things themselves, and have not trusted more than is possible to my own senses. But when it is necessary to trust to my senses, I must entirely dissent from Mr. Barrett, when he says a trained physical inquirer is no match for a professional conjurer. I maintain a physical inquirer is more than a match.

An important contribution to the discussion was

* *The Spiritualist,* Sept. 22, 1876 (Vol. IX, pp. 87–88).

made by Lord Rayleigh, the distinguished mathematician, who said :

I think we are much indebted to Professor Barrett for his courage, for it requires some courage to come forward in this matter, and to give us the benefit of his careful experiments. My own interest in the subject dates back two years. I was first attracted to it by reading Mr. Crookes's investigations. Although my opportunities have not been so good as those enjoyed by Professor Barrett, I have seen enough to convince me that those are wrong who wish to prevent investigation by casting ridicule on those who may feel inclined to engage in it.

The next speaker, Mr. Groom Napier, was greeted with laughter when he described verified psychometric descriptions of people from their handwriting enclosed in sealed envelopes, and when he went on to describe spirit lights that he had seen, the uproar forced him to resume his seat. Professor Barrett, in replying to his critics, said:

It certainly shows the immense advance that this subject has made within the last few years, that a paper on the once laughed-at phenomena of so-called Spiritualism should have been admitted into the British Association, and should have been permitted to receive the full discussion it has had to-day.

The London *Spectator*, in an article entitled " The British Association on Professor Barrett's Paper," opened with the following broad-minded view :

Now that we have before us a full report of Professor Barrett's paper, and of the discussion upon it, we may be permitted to express our hope that the British Association will really take some action on the subject of the paper, in spite of the protests of the party which we may call the party of superstitious incredulity. We say superstitious incredulity because it is really a pure superstition, and nothing else, to assume that we are so fully acquainted with the laws of Nature, that even carefully-examined facts, attested by an experienced observer, ought to be cast aside as utterly unworthy of credit, only because they do not at first sight seem to be in keeping with what is most clearly known already.

Sir William Barrett's views steadily progressed until he accepted the Spiritualistic position in unequivocal terms before his lamented death in 1925. He lived to see the whole world ameliorate its antagonism to such subjects, though little difference perhaps could be observed in the British Association which remained as obscurantist as ever. Such a tendency, however, may not have been an unmixed evil, for, as Sir Oliver Lodge has remarked, if the great pressing material problems had been complicated by psychic issues, it is possible that they would not have been solved. It may be worth remarking that Sir William Barrett in conversation with the author recalled that of the four men who supported him upon that historical and difficult occasion, every one lived to receive the Order of Merit—the greatest honour which their country could bestow. The four were Lord Rayleigh, Crookes, Wallace and Huggins.

It was not to be expected that the rapid growth of Spiritualism would be without its less desirable features. These were of at least two kinds. First the cry of fraudulent mediumship was frequently heard.

In the light of our later, fuller knowledge we know that much that bears the appearance of fraud is not necessarily fraud at all. At the same time, the unbounded credulity of a section of Spiritualists undoubtedly provided an easy field for charlatans. In the course of a paper read before the Cambridge University Society for Psychological Investigation in 1879, the President of the Society, Mr. J. A. Campbell, said : *

Since the advent of Mr. Home, the number of media has increased yearly, and so has the folly and the imposture. Every spook has become, in the eyes of fools, a divine angel ; and not even every spook, but every rogue, dressed up in a sheet, who has chosen or shall choose to call himself a materialized " spirit." A so-called religion has been founded in which the honour of the most sacred names has been transferred to the ghosts of pickpockets. Of the characters of which divinities, and of the doctrines taught by them, I shall not insult you by speaking; so it ever is when folly and ignorance get into their hands the weapon of an eternal fact, abuse, distortion, crime itself ; such were ever the results of children playing with edged tools, but who but an ignoramus would cry, *naughty knife ?* Gradually the movement is clearing itself of such excretions, gradually is it becoming more sober and pure, and strong, and as sensible men and educated men study and pray and work, striving to make good use of their knowledge, will it become more so.

The second feature was the apparent increase of what may be termed anti-Christian, though not anti-religious, Spiritualism. This led to William Howitt

* *The Spiritualist,* April 11, 1879, p. 170.

and other stalwart supporters ceasing their connexion with the movement. Powerful articles against this tendency were contributed to the *Spiritual Magazine* by Howitt and others.

A suggestion of the need for caution and balance is afforded in the remarks of Mr. William Stainton Moses, who said in a paper read before the British National Association of Spiritualists on January 26, 1880 : *

We are emphatically in need of discipline and education. We have hardly yet settled down after our rapid growth. The child, born just thirty years ago, has increased in stature (if not in wisdom) at a very rapid rate. It has grown so fast that its education has been a little neglected. In the expressive phraseology of its native country, it has been " dragged up " rather promiscuously ; and its phenomenal growth has absorbed all other considerations. The time has now come when those who have regarded it as an ugly monster which was born by one of Nature's freaks only to die an early death, begin to recognize their mistake. The ugly brat means to live ; and beneath its ugliness the least sympathetic gaze detects a coherent purpose in its existence. It is the presentation of a principle inherent in man's nature, a principle which his wisdom has improved away until it is wellnigh eliminated altogether, but which crops out again and again in spite of him—the principle of Spirit as opposed to Matter, of Soul acting and existing independently of the body which enshrines it. Long years of denial of aught but the properties of matter have landed the chief lights of modern science in pure Materialism. To them, therefore, this Spiritualism is a portent and a problem. It is a return to superstition ; a survival of savagery ; a blot on nineteenth

* *The Psychological Review*, Vol. II, p. 546.

century intelligence. Laughed at, it laughs back ; scorned, it gives back scorn for scorn.

In 1881, *Light*, a high-class weekly Spiritualist newspaper, was begun, and 1882 saw the formation of the Society for Psychical Research.

Speaking generally, it may be said that the attitude of organized science during these thirty years was as unreasonable and unscientific as that of Galileo's cardinals, and that if there had been a Scientific Inquisition, it would have brought its terrors to bear upon the new knowledge. No serious attempt of any sort, up to the formation of the S.P.R. was made to understand or explain a matter which was engaging the attention of millions of minds. Faraday in 1853 put forward the theory that table-moving was caused by muscular pressure, which may be true enough in some cases, but bears no relation to the levitation of tables, and in any case applies only to the one limited class of psychic phenomena. The usual " scientific " objection was that nothing occurred at all, which neglected the testimony of thousands of credible witnesses. Others argued that what did happen was capable of being exposed by a conjurer, and any clumsy imitation such as Maskelyne's parody of the Davenports was eagerly hailed as an exposure, with no reference to the fact that the whole mental side of the question with its overwhelming evidence was untouched thereby.

The " religious " people, furious at being shaken out of their time-honoured ruts, were ready, like savages, to ascribe any new thing to the devil. Roman

Catholics and the Evangelical sects, alike, found themselves for once united in their opposition. That low spirits may be reached, and low, lying messages received, is beyond all doubt, since every class of spirit exists around us, and like attracts like; but the lofty, sustaining and philosophic teaching which comes to every serious and humble-minded inquirer shows that it is Angelism and not Diabolism which is within our reach. Dr. Carpenter put forward some complex theory, but seems to have been in a minority of one in its acceptance or even in its comprehension. The doctors had an explanation founded upon the cracking of joints, which is ludicrous to anyone who has had personal experience of those percussive sounds which vary in range from the tick of a watch to the blow of a sledge-hammer.

Further explanations, either then or later, included the Theosophic doctrine, which admitted the facts but depreciated the spirits, describing them as astral shells with a sort of dreamy half-consciousness, or possibly an attenuated conscience which made them sub-human in their intelligence or morality. Certainly the quality of spirit communion does vary greatly, but the highest is so high that we can hardly imagine that we are in touch with only a fraction of the speaker. As it is asserted, however, that even in this world our subliminal self is far superior to our normal workaday individuality, it would seem only fair that the spirit world should confront us with something less than its full powers.

Another theory postulates the *Anima Mundi*, a

huge reservoir or central bank of intelligence, with a clearing-house in which all inquiries are honoured. The sharp detail which we receive from the Other Side is incompatible with any vague grandiose idea of the sort. Finally, there is the one really formidable alternative, that man has an etheric body with many unknown gifts, among which a power of external manifestation in curious forms may be included. It is to this theory of Cryptesthesia that Richet and others have clung, and up to a point there is an argument in its favour. The author has satisfied himself that there is a preliminary and elementary stage in all psychic work which depends upon the innate and possibly unconscious power of the medium. The reading of concealed script, the production of raps upon demand, the description of scenes at a distance, the remarkable effects of psychometry, the first vibrations of the Direct Voice—each and all of these on different occasions have seemed to emanate from the medium's own power. Then in most cases there would appear an outside intelligence which was able to appropriate that force and use it for its own ends. An illustration might be given in the experiments of Bisson and Schrenck Notzing with Eva, where the ectoplasmic forms were at first undoubtedly reflections of newspaper illustrations, somewhat muddled by their passage through the medium's mind. Yet there came a later and deeper stage where an ectoplasmic form was evolved which was capable of movement and even of speech. Richet's great brain and close power of observation have been largely centred upon the physical phenomena, and he does not seem to have been brought much in contact with those personal mental and spiritual experiences which would probably have modified his views. It is fair to add, however, that those views have continually moved in the direction of the Spiritualistic explanation.

There only remains the hypothesis of complex personality, which may well influence certain cases, though it seems to the author that such cases might be explained equally well by obsession. These instances, however, can only touch the fringe of the subject, and ignore the whole phenomenal aspect, so that the matter need not be taken very seriously. It cannot be too often repeated, however, that the inquirer should exhaust every possible normal explanation to his own complete satisfaction before he adopts the Spiritualistic view. If he has done this his platform is stable—if he has not done it he can never be conscious of its solidity. The author can say truly, that year after year he clung on to every line of defence until he was finally compelled, if he were to preserve any claim to mental honesty, to abandon the materialistic position.

CHAPTER IX

THE CAREER OF D. D. HOME

DANIEL DUNGLAS HOME was born in 1833 at Currie, a village near Edinburgh. There was a mystery about his parentage, and it has been both asserted and denied that he was related in some fashion to the family of the Earl of Home. Certainly he was a man who inherited elegance of figure, delicacy of feature, sensitiveness of disposition and luxury in taste, from whatever source he sprang. But for his psychic powers, and for the earnestness which they introduced into his complex character, he might have been taken as the very type of the aristocratic younger son who inherits the tendencies, but not the wealth, of his forbears.

Home went from Scotland to New England, at the age of nine years, with his aunt who had adopted him, a mystery still surrounding his existence. When he was thirteen he began to show signs of the psychic faculties he had inherited, for his mother, who was descended from an old Highland family, had the characteristic second-sight of her race. His mystical trend had shown itself in a conversation with his boy friend, Edwin, about a short story where, as the result of a compact, a lover, after his death, manifested his presence to his lady-love. The two boys pledged themselves that whoever died first would come and show himself to the other. Home removed to another district some hundreds of miles distant, and about a month later, just after going to bed one night, he saw a vision of Edwin and announced to his aunt his death, news of which was received a day or two after. A second vision in 1850 concerned the death of his mother, who with her husband had gone to live in America. The boy was ill in bed at the time, and his mother away on a visit to friends at a distance. One evening he called loudly for help, and when his aunt came she found him in great distress. He said that his mother had died that day at twelve o'clock; that she had appeared to him and told him so. The vision proved to be only too true. Soon loud raps began to disturb the quiet household, and furniture to be moved by invisible agency. His aunt, a woman of a narrow religious type, declared the boy had brought the Devil into her house, and turned him out of doors.

He took refuge with friends, and in the next few years moved among them from town to town. His mediumship had become strongly developed, and at the houses where he stopped he gave frequent séances, sometimes as many as six or seven a day, for the limitations of power and the reactions between physical and psychic were little understood at that time. These proved a great drain on his strength, and he was frequently laid up with illness. People flocked from all directions to witness the marvels which occurred in Home's presence. Among those who investigated with him at this time was the American poet Bryant, who was accompanied by Professor Wells, of Harvard University. In New York he met many distinguished Americans, and three—Professor Hare, Professor Mapes, and Judge Edmonds, of the New York Supreme Court—had sittings with him. All three became, as already stated, convinced Spiritualists.

In these early years the charm of Home's personality, and the deep impression created by his powers, led to his receiving many offers. Professor George Bush invited him to stay with him and study for the Swedenborgian ministry; and Mr. and Mrs. Elmer, a rich and childless couple, who had grown to cherish a great affection for him, offered to adopt him and make him their heir on condition of his changing his name to Elmer.

His remarkable healing powers had excited wonder and, yielding to the persuasion of friends, he began to study for the medical profession. But his general delicate health, coupled with actual lung trouble, forced him to abandon this project and, acting under medical advice, he left New York for England.

He arrived in Liverpool on April 9, 1855, and has been described as a tall, slim youth with a marked elegance of bearing and a fastidious neatness of dress, but with a worn, hectic look upon his very expressive face which told of the ravages of disease. He was blue-eyed and auburn-haired, of a type which is peculiarly liable to the attack of tubercle, and the extreme emaciation of his frame showed how little power re-

mained with him by which he might resist it. An
acute physician watching him closely would probably
have gauged his life by months rather than years in
our humid climate, and of all the marvels which Home
wrought, the prolongation of his own life was perhaps
not the least. His character had already taken on
those emotional and religious traits which distinguished it, and he has recorded how, before landing,
he rushed down to his cabin and fell upon his knees
in prayer. When one considers the astonishing career
which lay before him, and the large part which he
played in establishing those physical foundations
which differentiate this religious development from
any other, it may well be claimed that this visitor was
among the most notable missionaries who has ever
visited our shores.

His position at that moment was a very singular
one. He had hardly a relation in the world. His
left lung was partly gone. His income was modest,
though sufficient. He had no trade or profession, his
education having been interrupted by his illness. In
character he was shy, gentle, sentimental, artistic,
affectionate, and deeply religious. He had a strong
tendency both to Art and the Drama, so that his
powers of sculpture were considerable, and as a reciter
he proved in later life that he had few living equals.
But on the top of all this, and of an unflinching honesty
which was so uncompromising that he often offended
his own allies, there was one gift so remarkable that it
threw everything else into insignificance. This lay in
those powers, quite independent of his own volition,

D. D. HOME

From a painting in the possession of the London Spiritualist Alliance

coming and going with disconcerting suddenness, but proving to all who would examine the proof, that there was something in this man's atmosphere which enabled forces outside himself and outside our ordinary apprehension to manifest themselves upon this plane of matter. In other words, he was a medium—the greatest in a physical sense that the modern world has ever seen.

A lesser man might have used his extraordinary powers to found some special sect of which he would have been the undisputed high priest, or to surround himself with a glamour of power and mystery. Certainly most people in his position would have been tempted to use it for the making of money. As to this latter point, let it be said at once that never in the course of the thirty years of his strange ministry did he touch one shilling as payment for his gifts. It is on sure record that as much as two thousand pounds was offered to him by the Union Club in Paris in the year 1857 for a single séance, and that he, a poor man and an invalid, utterly refused it. " I have been sent on a mission," he said. " That mission is to demonstrate immortality. I have never taken money for it and I never will." There were certain presents from Royalty which cannot be refused without boorishness: rings, scarf-pins, and the like—tokens of friendship rather than recompense; for before his premature death there were few monarchs in Europe with whom this shy youth from the Liverpool landing-stage was not upon terms of affectionate intimacy. Napoleon the Third provided for his only sister. The Emperor of Russia sponsored his marriage. What novelist would dare to invent such a career ?

But there are more subtle temptations than those of wealth. Home's uncompromising honesty was the best safeguard against those. Never for a moment did he lose his humility and his sense of proportion. " I have these powers," he would say ; " I shall be happy, up to the limit of my strength, to demonstrate them to you, if you approach me as one gentleman should approach another. I shall be glad if you can throw any further light upon them. I will lend myself to any reasonable experiment. I have no control over them. They use me, but I do not use them. They desert me for months and then come back in re-doubled force. I am a passive instrument—no more." Such was his unvarying attitude. He was always the easy, amiable man of the world, with nothing either of the mantle of the prophet or of the skull-cap of the magician. Like most truly great men, there was no touch of pose in his nature. An index of his fine feeling is that when confirmation was needed for his results he would never quote any names unless he was perfectly certain that the owners would not suffer in any way through being associated with an unpopular cult. Sometimes even after they had freely given leave he still withheld the names, lest he should un-wittingly injure a friend. When he published his first series of " Incidents in my Life," the *Saturday Review* waxed very sarcastic over the anonymous " evidence of Countess O——, Count B——, Count de K——, Princess de B—— and Mrs. S——," who were quoted as having witnessed manifestations. In his second volume, Home, having assured himself of the concurrence of his friends, filled the blanks with the names of the Countess Orsini, Count de Beaumont, Count de Komar, Princess de Beauveau, and the well-known American hostess, Mrs. Henry Senior. His Royal friends he never quoted at all, and yet it is notorious that the Emperor Napoleon, the Empress Eugénie, the Tsar Alexander, the Emperor William the First of Germany, and the Kings of Bavaria and Wurtemberg were all equally convinced by his extraordinary powers. Never once was Home convicted of any deception, either in word or in deed.

On first landing in England he took up his quarters at Cox's Hotel in Jermyn Street, and it is probable that he chose that hostelry because he had learned that through Mrs. Hayden's ministry the proprietor was already sympathetic to the cause. However that may be, Mr. Cox quickly discovered that his young guest was a most remarkable medium, and at his invitation some of the leading minds of the day were asked to consider those phenomena which Home could lay before them. Among others, Lord Brougham came to a séance and brought with him his scientific friend, Sir David Brewster. In full daylight they investigated the phenomena, and in his amazement at what happened Brewster is reported to have said: " This upsets the philosophy of fifty years." If he had said " fifteen hundred " he would have been within the mark. He described what took place in a letter written to his sister at the time, but published long after.* Those present were Lord Brougham, Sir David Brewster, Mr. Cox and the medium.

" We four," said Brewster, " sat down at a moderately-sized table, the structure of which we were invited to examine. In a short time the table struggled, and a tremulous motion ran up all our arms; at our bidding these motions ceased and returned. The most unaccountable rappings were produced in various parts of the table, and the table actually rose from the ground when no hand was upon it. A larger table was produced, and exhibited similar movements. . . .

" A small hand-bell was laid down with its mouth upon the carpet, and after lying for some time, it actually rang when nothing could have touched it." He adds that the bell came over to him and placed itself in his hand, and it did the same to Lord Brougham ; and concludes : " These were the principal experiments. We could give no explanation of them, and could not conjecture how they could be produced by any kind of mechanism."

The Earl of Dunraven states that he was induced to investigate the phenomena by what Brewster had told him. He describes meeting the latter, who said that the manifestations were quite inexplicable by fraud, or by any physical laws with which we were acquainted. Home sent an account of this sitting in a letter to a friend in America, where it was published with comments. When these were reproduced in the English Press, Brewster became greatly alarmed. It was one thing to hold certain views privately, it was quite another to face the inevitable loss of prestige

* " Home Life of Sir David Brewster," by Mrs. Gordon (his daughter), 1869.

that would occur in the scientific circles in which he moved. Sir David was not the stuff of which martyrs or pioneers are made. He wrote to the *Morning Advertiser*, stating that though he had seen several mechanical effects which he could not explain, yet he was satisfied that they could all be produced by human hands and feet. At the time it had, of course, never occurred to him that his letter to his sister, just quoted, would ever see the light.

When the whole correspondence came to be published, the *Spectator* remarked of Sir David Brewster :

It seems established by the clearest evidence that he felt and expressed, at and immediately after his séances with Mr. Home, a wonder and almost awe, which he afterwards wished to explain away. The hero of science does not acquit himself as one could wish or expect.

We have dwelt a little on this Brewster incident because it was typical of the scientific attitude of the day, and because its effect was to excite a wider public interest in ·Home and his phenomena, and to bring hundreds of fresh investigators. One may say that scientific men may be divided into three classes: those who have not examined the matter at all (which does not in the least prevent them from giving very violent opinions); those who know that it is true but are afraid to say so; and finally the gallant minority of the Lodges, the Crookes, the Barretts and the Lombrosos, who know it is true and who dare all in saying so.

From Jermyn Street, Home went to stay with the Rymer family in Ealing, where many séances were held. Here he was visited by Lord Lytton, the famous novelist, who, although he received striking evidence, never publicly avowed his belief in the medium's powers, though his private letters, and indeed his published novels, are evidence of his true feeling. This was the case with scores of well-known men and women. Among his early sitters were Robert Owen the Socialist, T. A. Trollope the author, and Dr. J. Garth Wilkinson the alienist.

In these days, when the facts of psychic phenomena are familiar to all save those who are wilfully ignorant, we can hardly realize the moral courage which was needed by Home in putting forward his powers and upholding them in public. To the average educated Briton in the material Victorian era a man who claimed to be able to produce results which upset Newton's law of gravity, and which showed invisible mind acting upon visible matter, was *prima facie* a scoundrel and an impostor. The view of Spiritualism pronounced by Vice-Chancellor Giffard at the conclusion of the Home-Lyon trial was that of the class to which he belonged. He knew nothing of the matter, but took it for granted that anything with such claims must be false. No doubt similar things were reported in far-off lands and ancient books, but that they could occur in prosaic, steady old England, the England of bank-rates and free imports, was too absurd for serious thought. It has been recorded that at this trial Lord Giffard turned to Home's counsel and said: " Do I understand you to state that your client claims that he has been levitated into the air ? " Counsel assented, on which the judge turned to the jury and made such a movement as the high priest may have made in ancient days when he rent his garments as a protest against blasphemy. In 1868 there were few of the jury who were sufficiently educated to check the judge's remarks, and it is just in that particular that we have made some progress in the fifty years between. Slow work—but Christianity took more than three hundred years to come into its own.

Take this question of levitation as a test of Home's powers. It is claimed that more than a hundred times in good light before reputable witnesses he floated in the air. Consider the evidence. In 1857, in a château near Bordeaux, he was lifted to the ceiling of a lofty room in the presence of Madame Ducos, widow of the Minister of Marine, and of the Count and Countess de Beaumont. In 1860 Robert Bell wrote an article, " Stranger than Fiction," in the *Cornhill*. " He rose from his chair," says Bell, " four or five feet from the ground. . . . We saw his figure pass from one side of the window to the other, feet foremost, lying horizontally in the air." Dr. Gully, of Malvern, a well-known medical man, and Robert Chambers, the author and publisher, were the other witnesses. Is it to be supposed that these men were lying confederates, or that they could not tell if a man were floating in the air or pretending to do so ? In the same year Home was raised at Mrs. Milner Gibson's house in the presence of Lord and Lady Clarence Paget, the former passing his hands underneath him to assure himself of the fact. A few months later Mr. Wason, a Liverpool solicitor, with seven others, saw the same phenomenon. " Mr. Home," he says, " crossed the table over the heads of the persons sitting around it." He added: " I reached his hand seven feet from the floor, and moved along five or six paces as he floated above me in the air." In 1861 Mrs. Parkes, of Cornwall Terrace, Regent's Park, tells how she was present with Bulwer Lytton and Mr. Hall when Home in her own drawing-room was raised till his hand was on the top of the door, and then floated horizontally forward. In 1866 Mr. and Mrs. Hall, Lady Dunsany, and Mrs. Senior, in Mr. Hall's house saw Home, his face transfigured and shining, twice rise to the ceiling, leaving a cross marked in pencil upon the second occasion, so as to assure the witnesses that they were not the victims of imagination.

In 1868 Lord Adare, Lord Lindsay, Captain Wynne, and Mr. Smith Barry saw Home levitate upon many occasions. A very minute account has been left by the first three witnesses of the occurrence of December 16* of this year, when at Ashley House Home, in a state of trance, floated out of the bedroom and into the sitting-room window, passing seventy feet above the street. After his arrival in the sitting-room he went back into the bedroom with Lord Adare, and upon the latter remarking that he could not understand how Home could have fitted through the window which was only partially raised, " he told me to stand a little distance off. He then went through the

* The almanac shows it to be Sunday the 13th.

open space head first quite rapidly, his body being nearly horizontal and apparently rigid. He came in again feet foremost." Such was the account given by Lords Adare and Lindsay. Upon its publication Dr. Carpenter, who earned an unenviable reputation by a perverse opposition to every fact which bore upon this question, wrote exultantly to point out that there had been a third witness who had not been heard from, assuming without the least justification that Captain Wynne's evidence would be contradictory. He went the length of saying " a single honest sceptic declares that Mr. Home was sitting in his chair all the time "— a statement which can only be described as false. Captain Wynne at once wrote corroborating the others and adding: " If you are not to believe the corroborative evidence of *three* unimpeached witnesses, there would be an end to all justice and courts of law."

To show how hard put to it the critics have been to find some loophole of escape from the obvious, they have made much of the fact that Lord Lindsay, writing some time after the event, declared that it was seen by moonlight; whereas the calendar shows that the moon was not at that time visible. Mr. Andrew Lang remarks: " Even in a fog, however, people in a room can see a man coming in by the window, and go out again, head first, with body rigid." * It would seem to most of us that if we saw so marvellous a sight we would have little time to spare to determine whether we viewed it by the light of the moon or by that of the street lamps. It must be admitted, however, that

* "Historical Mysteries," p. 236.

Lord Lindsay's account is clumsily worded—so clumsily that there is some excuse for Mr. Joseph McCabe's reading of it that the spectators looked not at the object itself and its shadow on the window-sill, but that they stood with their backs to it and viewed the shadow on the wall. When one considers, however, the standing of the three eye-witnesses who have testified to this, one may well ask whether in ancient or modern times any preternatural event has been more clearly proved.

So many are the other instances of Home's levitations that a long article might easily be written upon this single phase of his mediumship. Professor Crookes was again and again a witness to the phenomenon, and refers to fifty instances which had come within his knowledge. But is there any fair-minded person who has read the incident here recorded who will not say, with Professor Challis: " Either the facts must be admitted to be such as are reported, or the possibility of certifying facts by human testimony must be given up."

" Are we, then, back in the age of miracles ? " cries the reader. There is no miracle. Nothing on this plane is supernatural. What we see now, and what we have read of in ages past, is but the operation of law which has not yet been studied and defined. Already we realize something of its possibilities and of its limitations, which are as exact in their way as those of any purely physical power. We must hold the balance between those who would believe nothing and those who would believe too much. Gradually the mists will clear and we will chart the shadowy coast. When the needle first sprang up at the magnet it was not an infraction of the laws of gravity. It was that there had been the local intervention of another stronger force. Such is the case also when psychic powers act upon the plane of matter. Had Home's faith in this power faltered, or had his circle been unduly disturbed, he would have fallen. When Peter lost faith he sank into the waves. Across the centuries the same cause still produced the same effect. Spiritual power is ever with us if we do not avert our faces, and nothing has been vouchsafed to Judæa which is withheld from England.

It is in this respect, as a confirmation of the power of the unseen, and as a final answer to materialism as we now understand it, that Home's public career is of such supreme importance. He was an affirmative witness of the truth of those so-called " miracles " which have been the stumbling-block for so many earnest minds, and are now destined to be the strong solid proof of the accuracy of the original narrative. Millions of doubting souls in the agony of spiritual conflict had cried out for definite proof that all was not empty space around us, that there were powers beyond our grasp, that the ego was not a mere secretion of nervous tissue, and that the dead did really carry on their personal unbroken existence. All this was proved by this greatest of modern missionaries to anyone who could observe or reason. It is easy to poke superficial fun at rising tables and quivering walls, but they were the nearest and most natural objects which could record in material terms that power which was beyond our human ken. A mind which would be unmoved by an inspired sentence was struck into humility and into new paths of research in the presence of even the most homely of these inexplicable phenomena. It is easy to call them puerile, but they effected the purpose for which they were sent by shaking to its foundations the complaisance of those material men of science who were brought into actual contact with them. They are to be regarded not as ends in themselves, but as the elementary means by which the mind should be diverted into new channels of thought. And those channels of thought led straight to the recognition of the survival of the spirit. " You have conveyed incalculable joy and comfort to the hearts of many people," said Bishop Clark, of Rhode Island. " You have made dwelling-places light that were dark before." " Mademoiselle," said Home to the lady who was to be his wife, " I have a mission entrusted to me. It is a great and a holy one." The famous Dr. Elliotson, immortalized by Thackeray under the name of Dr. Goodenough, was one of the leaders of British materialism. He met Home, saw his powers, and was able soon to say that he had lived all his life in darkness and had thought there was nothing in existence but the material, but he now had a firm hope which he trusted he would hold while on earth.

Innumerable instances could be quoted of the spiritual value of Home's work, but it has never been better summed up than in a paragraph from Mrs.

Webster, of Florence, who saw much of his ministry. "He is the most marvellous missionary of modern times in the greatest of all causes, and the good that he has done cannot be reckoned. When Mr. Home passes he bestows around him the greatest of all blessings, the certainty of a future life."

Now that the details of his career can be read, it is to the whole wide world that he brings this most vital of all messages. His attitude as to his own mission was expressed in a lecture given in London in Willis's Rooms on February 15, 1866. He said: " I believe in my heart that this power is being spread more and more every day to draw us nearer to God. You ask if it makes us purer? My only answer is that we are but mortals, and as such liable to err; but it does teach that the pure in heart shall see God. It teaches us that He is love, and that there is no death. To the aged it comes as a solace, when the storms of life are nearly over and rest cometh. To the young it speaks of the duty we owe to each other, and that as we sow so shall we reap. To all it teaches resignation. It comes to roll away the clouds of error, and bring the bright morning of a never-ending day."

It is curious to see how his message affected those of his own generation. Reading the account of his life written by his widow—a most convincing document, since she of all living mortals must have known the real man—it would appear that his most utterly whole-hearted support and appreciation came from those aristocrats of France and Russia with whom he was brought into contact. The warm glow of personal admiration and even reverence in their letters is such as can hardly be matched in any biography. In England he had a close circle of ardent supporters, a few of the upper classes, with the Halls, the Howitts, Robert Chambers, Mrs. Milner Gibson, Professor Crookes, and others. But there was a sad lack of courage among those who admitted the facts in private and stood aloof in public. Lord Brougham and Bulwer Lytton were of the type of Nicodemus, the novelist being the worst offender. " Intelligentzia " on the whole came badly out of the matter, and many an honoured name suffers in the story. Faraday and Tyndall were fantastically unscientific in their methods of prejudging a question first, and offering to examine it afterwards on the condition that their prejudgment was accepted. Sir David Brewster, as already shown, said some honest things, and then in a panic denied that he had said them, forgetting that the evidence was on actual record. Browning wrote a long poem—if such doggerel can be called poetry—to describe an exposure which had never taken place. Carpenter earned an unenviable notoriety as an unscrupulous opponent, while proclaiming some strange Spiritualistic thesis of his own. The secretaries of the Royal Society refused to take a cab-drive in order to see Crookes's demonstration of the physical phenomena, while they pronounced roundly against them. Lord Giffard inveighed from the Bench against a subject the first elements of which he did not understand.

As to the clergy, such an order might not have existed during the thirty years that this, the most marvellous spiritual outpouring of many centuries, was before the public. One cannot recall the name of one British clergyman who showed any intelligent interest; and when in 1872 a full account of the St. Petersburg séances began to appear in *The Times*, it was cut short, according to Mr. H. T. Humphreys, " on account of strong remonstrances to Mr. Delane, the editor, by certain of the higher clergy of the Church of England." Such was the contribution of our official spiritual guides. Dr. Elliotson the Rationalist, was far more alive than they. The rather bitter comment of Mrs. Home is: " The verdict of his own generation was that of the blind and deaf upon the man who could hear and see."

Home's charity was among his more beautiful characteristics. Like all true charity it was secret, and only comes out indirectly and by chance. One of his numerous traducers declared that he had allowed a bill for £50 to be sent in to his friend, Mr. Rymer. In self-defence it came out that it was not a bill but a cheque most generously sent by Home to help this friend in a crisis. Considering his constant poverty, fifty pounds probably represented a good part of his bank balance. His widow dwells with pardonable pride upon the many evidences found in his letters after his death. " Now it is an unknown artist for whose brush Home's generous efforts had found employment; now a distressed worker writes of his sick wife's life saved by comforts that Home provided; now a mother thanks him for a start in life for her son. How much time and thought he devoted to helping others when the circumstance of his own life would have led most men to think only of their own needs and cares."

" Send me a word from the heart that has known so often how to cheer a friend ! " cries one of his protégés.

" Shall I ever prove worthy of all the good you have done me ? " says another letter.

We find him roaming the battlefields round Paris, often under fire, with his pockets full of cigars for the wounded. A German officer writes affectionately to remind him how he saved him from bleeding to death, and carried him on his own weak back out of the place of danger. Truly Mrs. Browning was a better judge of character than her spouse, and Sir Galahad a better name than Sludge.

At the same time, it would be absurd to depict Home as a man of flawless character. He had the weakness of his temperament, and something feminine in his disposition which showed itself in many ways. The author, while in Australia, came across a correspondence dating from 1856 between Home and the elder son of the Rymer family. They had travelled together in Italy, and Home had deserted his friend under circumstances which showed inconstancy and ingratitude. It is only fair to add that his health was so broken at the time that he could hardly be called normal. " He had the defects of an emotional character," said Lord Dunraven, " with vanity highly developed, perhaps wisely to enable him to hold his own against the ridicule that was then poured out on

Spiritualism and everything connected with it. He was liable to fits of great depression and to nervous crises difficult to understand, but he was withal of a simple, kindly, humorous, loving disposition that appealed to me. . . . My friendship remained without change or diminution to the end."

There are few of the varied gifts which we call " mediumistic " and St. Paul " of the spirit " which Home did not possess—indeed, the characteristic of his psychic power was its unusual versatility. We speak usually of a Direct Voice medium, of a trance speaker, of a clairvoyant or of a physical medium, but Home was all four. So far as can be traced, he had little experience of the powers of other mediums, and was not immune from that psychic jealousy which is a common trait of these sensitives. Mrs. Jencken, formerly Miss Kate Fox, was the only other medium with whom he was upon terms of friendship. He bitterly resented any form of deception, and carried this excellent trait rather too far by looking with eyes of suspicion upon all forms of manifestations which did not exactly correspond with his own. This opinion, expressed in an uncompromising manner in his last book, " Lights and Shadows of Spiritualism," gave natural offence to other mediums who claimed to be as honest as himself. A wider acquaintance with phenomena would have made him more charitable. Thus he protested strongly against any séance being held in the dark, but this is certainly a counsel of perfection, for experiments upon the ectoplasm which is the physical basis of all materializations show that it is usually affected by light unless the light is tinted red. Home had no large experience of complete material- izations such as were obtained in those days by Miss Florence Cook, or Madame d'Esperance, or in our own time, by Madame Bisson's medium, and therefore he could dispense with complete darkness in his own ministry. Thus, his opinion was unjust to others. Again, Home declared roundly that matter could not pass through matter, because his own phenomena did not take that form; and yet the evidence that matter can in certain cases be passed through matter seems to be overwhelming. Even birds of rare varieties have been brought into séance rooms under circum- stances which seem to preclude fraud, and the experi- ments of passing wood through wood, as shown before Zöllner and the other Leipzig professors, were quite final as set forth in the famous physicist's account in " Transcendental Physics " of his experiences with Slade. Thus, it may count as a small flaw in Home's character that he decried and doubted the powers which he himself did not happen to possess.

Some also might count it as a failing that he carried his message rather to the leaders of society and of life than to the vast toiling masses. It is probable that Home had, in fact, the weakness as well as the graces of the artistic nature and that he was most at ease and happiest in an atmosphere of elegance and refinement, with a personal repulsion from all that was sordid and ill-favoured. If there were no other reason the pre- carious state of his health unfitted him for any sterner mission, and he was driven by repeated hæmorrhages to seek the pleasant and refined life of Italy, Switzerland and the Riviera. But for the prosecution of his mission, as apart from personal self-sacrifice, there can be no doubt that his message carried to the laboratory of a Crookes or to the Court of a Napoleon was more useful than if it were laid before the crowd. The assent of science and of character was needed before the public could gain assurance that such things were true. If it was not fully gained the fault lies assuredly with the hidebound men of science and thinkers of the day, and by no means with Home, who played his part of actual demonstration to perfection, leaving it to other and less gifted men to analyse and to make public that which he had shown them. He did not profess to be a man of science, but he was the raw material of science, willing and anxious that others should learn from him all that he could convey to the world, so that science should itself testify to religion while religion should be buttressed upon science. When Home's message has been fully learned an unbelieving man will not stand convicted of impiety, but of ignorance.

There was something pathetic in Home's efforts to find some creed in which he could satisfy his own gregarious instinct—for he had no claims to be a strong-minded individualist—and at the same time find a niche into which he could fit his own precious packet of assured truth. His pilgrimage vindicates the assertion of some Spiritualists that a man may belong to any creed and carry with him the spiritual knowledge, but it also bears out those who reply that perfect harmony with that spiritual knowledge can only be found, as matters now stand, in a special Spiritualist community. Alas! that it should be so, for it is too big a thing to sink into a sect, however great that sect might become. Home began in his youth as a Wesleyan, but soon left them for the more liberal atmosphere of Congregationalism. In Italy the artistic atmosphere of the Roman Catholic Church, and possibly its record of so many phenomena akin to his own, caused him to become a convert with an intention of joining a monastic Order—an intention which his common sense caused him to abandon. The change of religion was at a period when his psychic powers had deserted him for a year, and his confessor assured him that as they were of evil origin they would certainly never be heard of again now that he was a son of the true Church. None the less, on the very day that the year expired they came back in renewed strength. From that time Home seems to have been only nominally a Catholic, if at all, and after his second marriage—both his marriages were to Russian ladies—he was strongly drawn towards the Greek Church, and it was under their ritual that he was at last laid to rest at St. Germain in 1886. " To another discerning of Spirits " (1 Cor. xii. 10) is the short inscription upon that grave, of which the world has not yet heard the last.

If proof were needed of the blamelessness of Home's life, it could not be better shown than by the fact that his numerous enemies, spying ever for some opening to attack, could get nothing in his whole

career upon which to comment save the wholly innocent affair which is known as the Home-Lyon case.
Any impartial judge reading the depositions in this
case—they are to be found verbatim in the second
series of " Incidents in My Life "—would agree that
it is not blame but commiseration which was owing
to Home. One could desire no higher proof of the
nobility of his character than his dealings with this
unpleasant freakish woman, who first insisted upon
settling a large sum of money upon him, and then,
her whim having changed and her expectations of an
immediate introduction into high society being dis-
appointed, stuck at nothing in order to get it back
again. Had she merely asked for it back there is
little doubt that Home's delicate feelings would have
led him to return it, even though he had been put to
much trouble and expense over the matter, which had
entailed a change of his name to Home-Lyon, to meet
the woman's desire that he should be her adopted son.
Her request, however, was so framed that he could not
honourably agree to it, as it would have implied an
admission that he had done wrong in accepting the
gift. If one consults the original letters—which few
of those who comment upon the case seem to have
done—one finds that Home, S. C. Hall as his representative and Mr. Wilkinson as his solicitor, implored
the woman to moderate the unreasonable benevolence
which was to change so rapidly into even more unreasonable malevolence. She was absolutely determined that Home should have the money and be her
heir. A less mercenary man never lived, and he

begged her again and again to think of her relatives, to which she answered that the money was her own to do what she pleased with, and that no relatives were dependent upon it. From the time that he accepted the new situation he acted and wrote as a dutiful son, and it is not uncharitable to suppose that this entirely filial attitude may not have been that which this elderly lady had planned out in her scheming brain. At any rate, she soon tired of her fad and reclaimed her money upon the excuse—a monstrous one to anyone who will read the letters and consider the dates—that spirit messages had caused her to take the action she had done.

The case was tried in the Court of Chancery, and the judge alluded to Mrs. Lyon's " innumerable misstatements on many important particulars—misstatements upon oath so perversely untrue that they have embarrassed the Court to a great degree and quite discredited the plaintiff's testimony." In spite of this caustic comment, and in spite also of elementary justice, the verdict was against Home on the general ground that British law put the burden of disproof upon the defendant in such a case, and complete disproof is impossible when assertion is met by counter-assertion. Lord Giffard might, no doubt, have risen superior to the mere letter of the law had it not been that he was deeply prejudiced against all claims to psychic power, which were from his point of view manifestly absurd and yet were persisted in by the defendant under his nose in his own Court of Chancery. Even Home's worst enemies were forced to admit that the fact that he had retained the money in England and had not lodged it where it would have been beyond recovery proved his honest intentions in this the most unfortunate episode of his life. Of all the men of honour who called him friend, it is not recorded that he lost one through the successful machinations of Mrs. Lyon. Her own motives were perfectly obvious. As all the documents were in order, her only possible way of getting the money back was to charge Home with having extorted it from her by misrepresentation, and she was cunning enough to know what chance a medium—even an amateur unpaid medium—would have in the ignorant and material atmosphere of a mid-Victorian court of law. Alas ! that we can omit the " mid-Victorian " and the statement still holds good.

The powers of Home have been attested by so many famous observers, and were shown under such frank conditions, that no reasonable man can possibly doubt them. Crookes's evidence alone is conclusive.* There is also the remarkable book, reprinted at a recent date, in which Lord Dunraven gives the story of his youthful connexion with Home. But apart from these, among those in England who investigated in the first few years and whose public testimony or letters to Home show they were not only convinced of the genuineness of the phenomena, but also of their spiritual origin, may be mentioned the Duchess of Sutherland, Lady Shelley, Lady

* " Researches in the Phenomena of Spiritualism," and S.P.R. *Proceedings*, VI., p. 98.

Gomm, Dr. Robert Chambers, Lady Otway, Miss
Catherine Sinclair, Mrs. Milner Gibson, Mr. and
Mrs. William Howitt, Mrs. De Burgh, Dr. Gully
(of Malvern), Sir Charles Nicholson, Lady Dunsany,
Sir Daniel Cooper, Mrs. Adelaide Senior, Mr. and
Mrs. S. C. Hall, Mrs. Makdougall Gregory, Mr.
Pickersgill, R.A., Mr. E. L. Blanchard, and Mr.
Robert Bell.

Others who went so far as to admit that the theory
of imposture was insufficient to account for the phenomena were: Mr. Ruskin, Mr. Thackeray (then editor
of the *Cornhill Magazine*), Mr. John Bright, Lord
Dufferin, Sir Edwin Arnold, Mr. Heaphy, Mr.
Durham (sculptor), Mr. Nassau Senior, Lord Lynd-
hurst, Mr. J. Hutchinson (ex-Chairman of the Stock
Exchange), and Dr. Lockhart Robertson.

Such were his witnesses and such his works. And
yet, when his most useful and unselfish life had come
to an end, it must be recorded to the eternal disgrace
of our British Press that there was hardly a paper
which did not allude to him as an impostor and a
charlatan. The time is coming, however, when he
will be recognized for what he was, one of the pioneers
in the slow and arduous advance of Humanity into
that jungle of ignorance which has encompassed it
so long.

CHAPTER X

THE DAVENPORT BROTHERS

IN order to present a consecutive story the career of D. D. Home has been traced in its entirety. It is necessary now to return to earlier days in America and consider the development of the two Davenports. Home and the Davenports both played an international part, and their history helps to cover the movement both in England and in the States. The Davenports worked upon a far lower level than Home, making a profession of their remarkable gifts, and yet by their crude methods they got their results across to the multitude in a way which a more refined mediumship could not have done. If one considers this whole train of events as having been engineered by a wise but by no means infallible or omnipotent force upon the Other Side, one observes how each occasion is met by the appropriate instrument, and how as one demonstration fails to impress some other one is substituted.

The Davenports have been fortunate in their chroniclers. Two writers have published books*

* "A Biography of the Brothers Davenport." By T. L. Nichols, M.D., London, 1864. "Supramundane Facts in the Life of Rev. J. B. Ferguson, LL.D." By T. L. Nichols, M.D., London, 1865. "Spiritual Experiences : Including Seven Months with the Brothers Davenport." By Robert Cooper, London, 1867.

describing the events of their life, and the periodical literature of the time is full of their exploits.

Ira Erastus Davenport and William Henry Davenport were born at Buffalo in the State of New York, the former on September 17, 1839, and the latter on February 1, 1841. Their father, who was descended from the early English settlers in America, occupied a position in the police department of Buffalo. Their mother was born in Kent, England, and went to America when a child. Some indications of psychic gifts were observed in the mother's life. In 1846 the family were disturbed in the middle of the night by what they described as " raps, thumps, loud noises, snaps, crackling noises." This was two years before the outbreak in the Fox family. But it was the Fox manifestations which, in this case as in so many others, led them to investigate and discover their mediumistic powers.

The two Davenport boys and their sister Elizabeth, the youngest of the three, experimented by placing their hands on a table. Loud and violent noises were heard and messages were spelt out. The news leaked abroad, and as with the Fox girls, hundreds of curious and incredulous people flocked to the house. Ira developed automatic writing, and handed to those present messages written with extraordinary rapidity and containing information he could not have known. Levitation quickly followed, and the boy was floated in the air above the heads of those in the room at a distance of nine feet from the floor. Next, the brother and sister were influenced in the same way, and the three children floated high up in the room. Hundreds of respectable citizens of Buffalo are reported to have seen these occurrences. Once when the family was at breakfast the knives, forks, and dishes danced about and the table was raised in the air. At a sitting soon after this a lead pencil was seen to write in broad daylight, with no human contact. Séances were now held regularly, lights began to appear, and musical instruments floated and played above the heads of the company. The Direct Voice and other extraordinary manifestations too numerous to mention followed. Yielding to requests from the communicating intelligences, the brothers started journeying to various places and holding public séances. Among strangers, tests were insisted upon. At first the boys were held by persons selected from those present, but this being found unsatisfactory because it was thought that those holding them were confederates, the plan of tying them with ropes was adopted. To read the list of ingenious tests successively proposed, and put into operation without interfering with the manifestations, shows how almost impossible it is to convince resolute sceptics. As soon as one test succeeded another was proposed, and so on. The professors of Harvard University in 1857 conducted an examination of the boys and their phenomena. Their biographer writes : *

The professors exercised their ingenuity in proposing tests. Would they submit to be handcuffed ? Yes.

* "'A Biography of the Brothers Davenport." By T. L. Nichols, M.D., pp. 87–88.

Would they allow men to hold them ? Yes. A dozen propositions were made, accepted, and then rejected by those who made them. If any test was adopted by the brothers, that was reason enough for not trying it. They were supposed to be prepared for that, so some other must be found.

Finally, the professors bought five hundred feet of new rope, bored with holes the cabinet set up in one of their rooms, and trussed the boys in what is described as a brutal manner. All the knots in the rope were tied with linen thread, and one of their number, Professor Pierce, took his place in the cabinet between the two brothers. At once a phantom hand was shown, instruments were rattled and were felt by the professor about his head and face. At every movement he felt for the boys with his hands, only to find them still securely bound. The unseen operators at last released the boys from their bindings, and when the cabinet was opened the ropes were found twisted round the neck of the professor ! After all this, the Harvard professors *made no report.* It is instructive also to read the account of the really ingenious test-apparatus consisting of what may be described as wooden sleeves and trousers, securely fastened, devised by a man named Darling, in Bangor (U.S.A.). Like other tests, it proved incapable of preventing instant manifestations. It is to be remembered that many of these tests were applied at a time when the brothers were mere boys, too young to have learned any elaborate means of deception.

It is not strange to read that the phenomena

raised violent opposition almost everywhere, and the brothers were frequently denounced as jugglers and humbugs. It was after ten years of public work in the largest cities and towns in the United States that the Davenport Brothers came to England. They had submitted successfully to every test that human ingenuity could devise, and no one had been able to say how their results were obtained. They had won for themselves a great reputation. Now they had to begin all over again.

The two brothers, Ira and William, at this time were aged twenty-five and twenty-three years respectively. The New York *World* thus describes them:

They looked remarkably like each other in almost every particular, both quite handsome with rather long, curly black hair, broad, but not high foreheads, dark keen eyes, heavy eyebrows, moustache and " goatee," firm-set lips, muscular though well-proportioned frame. They were dressed in black with dress-coats, one wearing a watchchain.

Dr. Nichols, their biographer, gives this first impression of them :

The young men, with whom I have had but a brief personal acquaintance, and whom I never saw until their arrival in London, appear to me to be in intellect and character above the average of their young countrymen, they are not remarkable for cleverness, though of fair abilities, and Ira has some artistic talent. . . . The young men seem entirely honest, and singularly disinterested and unmercenary—far more anxious to have people satisfied of their integrity and the reality of their manifestations than to make money. They have an ambition, without doubt, which is gratified in their having been selected as the instruments of what they believe will be some great good to mankind.

They were accompanied to England by the Rev. Dr. Ferguson, formerly pastor of a large church at Nashville, Tennessee, at which Abraham Lincoln attended, Mr. D. Palmer, a well-known operatic manager, who acted as secretary, and Mr. William M. Fay, who was also a medium.

Mr. P. B. Randall, in his biography of the Davenports (Boston 1869, published anonymously), points out that their mission to England was " to meet on its own low ground and conquer, by appropriate means, the hard materialism and scepticism of England." The first step to knowledge, he says, is to be convinced of ignorance, and adds :

If the manifestations given by the aid of the Brothers Davenport can prove to the intellectual and scientific classes that there are forces—and intelligent forces, or powerful intelligences—beyond the range of their philosophies, and that what they consider physical impossibilities are readily accomplished by invisible, and to them unknown, intelligences, a new universe will be open to human thought and investigation.

There is little doubt that the mediums had this effect on many minds.

The manifestations of Mrs. Hayden's mediumship were quiet and unobtrusive, and while those of D. D. Home were more remarkable, they were confined entirely to exclusive sets of people to whom no fees

were charged. Now these two brothers hired public
halls and challenged the world at large to come and
witness phenomena which passed the bounds of all
ordinary belief. It needed no foresight to predict for
them a strenuous time of opposition, and so it proved.
But they attained the end which the unseen directors
undoubtedly had in view. They roused public attention as it had never been roused before in England on
this subject. No better testimony in proof of that
could be had than that of their strongest opponent,
Mr. J. N. Maskelyne, the celebrated conjurer. He
writes : * " Certain it is, England was completely
taken aback for a time by the wonders presented by
these jugglers." He further adds :

> The Brothers did more than all other men to familiarize
> England with the so-called Spiritualism, and before crowded
> audiences and under varied conditions, they produced really
> wonderful feats. The hole-and-corner séances of other
> media, where with darkness or semi-darkness, and a pliant,
> or frequently a devoted assembly, manifestations are occa-
> sionally *said* to occur, cannot be compared with the Daven-
> port exhibitions in their effect upon the public mind.

Their first séance in London, a private one, was
held on September 28, 1864, at the residence in
Regent Street of Mr. Dion Boucicault, the famous
actor and author, in the presence of leading newspaper
men and distinguished men of science. The Press
reports of the séance were remarkably full and, for a
wonder, fair.

The account in the *Morning Post* the next day

* " Modern Spiritualism," p. 65.

says that the guests were invited to make the most critical examination and to take all needful precautions against fraud or deception, and continues:

The party invited to witness the manifestations last night consisted of some twelve or fourteen individuals, all of whom are admitted to be of considerable distinction in the various professions with which they are connected. The majority have never previously witnessed anything of the kind. All, however, were determined to detect and if possible expose any attempt at deception. The Brothers Davenport are slightly built, gentleman-like in appearance, and about the last persons in the world from whom any great muscular performances might be expected. Mr. Fay is apparently a few years older, and of more robust constitution.

After describing what occurred, the writer goes on:

All that can be asserted is, that the displays to which we have referred took place on the present occasion under conditions and circumstances that preclude the presumption of fraud.

The Times, the *Daily Telegraph*, and other newspapers published long and honest reports. We omit quotations from them because the following important statement from Mr. Dion Boucicault, which appeared in the *Daily News* as well as in many other London journals, covers all the facts. It describes a later séance at Mr. Boucicault's house on October 11, 1864, at which were present, among others Viscount Bury, M.P., Sir Charles Wyke, Sir Charles Nicholson, the Chancellor of the University of Sydney, Mr. Robert

Chambers, Charles Reade, the novelist, and Captain
Inglefield, the Arctic explorer.

SIR,

A séance by the Brothers Davenport and Mr. W. Fay
took place in my house yesterday in the presence of . . .
(here he mentions twenty-four names including all those
already quoted). . . .

At three o'clock our party was fully assembled. . . .
We sent to a neighbouring music-seller for six guitars and
two tambourines, so that the implements to be used should
not be those with which the operators were familiar.

At half-past three the Davenport Brothers and Mr.
Fay arrived, and found that we had altered their arrange-
ments by changing the room which they had previously
selected for their manifestations.

The séance then began by an examination of the dress
and persons of the Brothers Davenport, and it was certified
that no apparatus or other contrivance was concealed on or
about their persons. They entered the cabinet, and sat
facing each other. Captain Inglefield then, with a new rope
provided by ourselves, tied Mr. W. Davenport hand and
foot, with his hands behind his back, and then bound him
firmly to the seat where he sat. Lord Bury, in like manner,
secured Mr. I. Davenport. The knots on these ligatures
were then fastened with sealing-wax, and a seal was affixed.
A guitar, violin, tambourine, two bells, and a brass trumpet
were placed on the floor of the cabinet. The doors were
then closed, and a sufficient light was permitted in the room
to enable us to see what followed.

I shall omit any detailed account of the babel of sounds
which arose in the cabinet, and the violence with which the
doors were repeatedly burst open and the instruments
expelled ; the hands appearing, as usual, at a lozenge-
shaped orifice in the centre door of the cabinet. The
following incidents seem to us particularly worthy of note :

While Lord Bury was stooping inside the cabinet, the door being open and the two operators seen to be sealed and bound, a detached hand was clearly observed to descend upon him, and he started back, remarking that a hand had struck him. Again, in the full light of the gas chandelier and during an interval in the séance, the doors of the cabinet being open, and while the ligatures of the Brothers Davenport were being examined, a very white, thin, female hand and wrist quivered for several seconds in the air above. This appearance drew a general exclamation from all the party.

Sir Charles Wyke now entered the cabinet and sat between the two young men—his hands being right and left on each, and secured to them. The doors were then closed, and the babel of sounds recommenced. Several hands appeared at the orifice—among them the hand of a child. After a space, Sir Charles returned amongst us and stated that while he held the two brothers, several hands touched his face and pulled his hair ; the instruments at his feet crept up, played round his body and over his head —one of them lodging eventually on his shoulders. During the foregoing incidents the hands which appeared were touched and grasped by Captain Inglefield, and he stated that to the touch they were apparently human hands, though they passed away from his grasp.

I omit mentioning other phenomena, an account of which has already been rendered elsewhere.

The next part of the séance was performed in the dark. One of the Messrs. Davenport and Mr. Fay seated themselves amongst us. Two ropes were thrown at their feet, and in two minutes and a half they were tied hand and foot, their hands behind their backs bound tightly to their chairs, and their chairs bound to an adjacent table. While this process was going on, the guitar rose from the table and swung or floated round the room and over the heads of the party, and slightly touching some. Now a phosphoric light shot from side to side over our heads; the laps and hands and shoulders of several were simultaneously touched, struck, or pawed by hands, the guitar meanwhile sailing round the room, now near the ceiling, and then scuffling on the head and shoulders of some luckless wight. The bells whisked here and there, and a light thrumming was maintained on the violin. The two tambourines seemed to roll hither and thither on the floor, now shaking violently, and now visiting the knees and hands of our circle—all these foregoing actions, audible or tangible, being simultaneous. Mr. Rideout, holding a tambourine, requested it might be plucked from his hand ; it was almost instantaneously taken from him. At the same time, Lord Bury made a similar request, and a forcible attempt to pluck a tambourine from his grasp was made which he resisted. Mr. Fay then asked that his coat should be removed. We heard instantly a violent twitch, and here occurred the most remarkable fact. A light was struck before the coat had quite left Mr. Fay's person, and it was seen quitting him, plucked off him upwards. It flew up to the chandelier, where it hung for a moment and then fell to the ground. Mr. Fay was seen meanwhile bound hand and foot as before. One of our party now divested himself of his coat, and it was placed on the table. The light was extinguished and this coat was rushed on to Mr. Fay's back with equal rapidity. During the above occurrences in the dark, we placed a sheet of paper under the feet of these two operators, and drew with a pencil an outline around them, to the end that if they moved it might be detected. They of their own accord offered to have their hands filled with flour, or any other similar substance, to prove they made no use of them, but this precaution was deemed unnecessary ; we required them, however, to count from one to twelve repeatedly, that their voices constantly heard might certify to us that they were in the places where they were tied. Each of our own party held his neighbour firmly, so that no one could move without two adjacent neighbours being aware of it.

At the termination of this séance, a general conversation took place on the subject of what we had heard and witnessed. Lord Bury suggested that the general opinion seemed to be that we should assure the Brothers Davenport and Mr. W. Fay that after a very stringent trial and strict scrutiny of their proceedings, the gentlemen present could arrive at no other conclusion than that there was no trace of trickery in any form, and certainly there were neither confederates nor machinery, and that all those who had witnessed the results would freely state in the society in which they moved that, so far as their investigations enabled them to form an opinion, the phenomena which had taken place in their presence were not the product of legerdemain. This suggestion was promptly acceded to by all present.

There is a concluding paragraph in which Mr. Dion Boucicault states that he is not a Spiritualist, and at the close of the report his name and the date are affixed.

This wonderfully full and lucid account is given without abbreviation because it supplies the answer to many objections, and because the character of the narrator and the witnesses cannot be questioned. It surely must be accepted as quite final so far as honesty is concerned. All subsequent objections are mere ignorance of the facts.

In October, 1864, the Davenports began to give public séances at the Queen's Concert Rooms, Hanover Square. Committees were appointed from the audience, and every effort made to detect how it was all done, but without avail. These séances, interspersed with private ones, were continued almost nightly until the close of the year. The daily Press was full of accounts of them, and the brothers' names were on everyone's lips. Early in 1865 they toured the English provinces, and in Liverpool, Huddersfield, and Leeds they suffered violence at the hands of excited mobs. At Liverpool, in February, two members of the audience tied their hands so brutally that blood flowed, and Mr. Ferguson cut the rope and released them. The Davenports refused to continue, and the mob rushed the platform and smashed up the cabinet. The same tactics were resorted to at Huddersfield on February 21, and then at Leeds with increased violence, the result of organized opposition. These riots led to the Davenports cancelling any other engagements in England. They next went to Paris, where they received a summons to appear at the Palace of St. Cloud, where the Emperor and Empress and a party of about forty witnessed a séance. While in Paris, Hamilton, the successor of the celebrated conjurer, Robert Houdin, visited them, and in a letter to a Paris newspaper, he said: " The phenomena surpassed my expectations, and the experiments are full of interest for me. I consider it my duty to add they are inexplicable." After a return visit to London, Ireland was visited at the beginning of 1866. In Dublin they had many influential sitters, including the editor of the *Irish Times* and the Rev. Dr. Tisdal, who publicly proclaimed his belief in the manifestations.

In April of the same year the Davenports went to Hamburg and then to Berlin, but the expected war (which their guides told them would come about) made the trip unremunerative. Theatre managers offered them liberal terms for exhibitions, but, heeding the advice of their ever-present spirit monitor, who said that their manifestations, being supernatural, should be kept above the level of theatrical entertainments, they declined, though much against the wish of their business manager. During their month's stay in Berlin they were visited by members of the Royal family. After three weeks in Hamburg they proceeded to Belgium, where considerable success was attained in Brussels, and all the principal towns. They next went to Russia, arriving in St. Petersburg on December 27, 1866. On January 7, 1867, they gave their first public séance to an audience numbering one thousand. The next séance was at the residence of the French Ambassador to a gathering of about fifty people, including officers of the Imperial Court, and on January 9 they gave a séance in the Winter Palace to the Emperor and the Imperial family. They afterwards visited Poland and Sweden. On April 11, 1868, they reappeared in London at the Hanover Square Rooms, and received an enthusiastic, welcome from a crowded audience. Mr. Benjamin Coleman, a prominent Spiritualist, who arranged their first public séances in London, writing at this time of their stay of close on four years in Europe, says : *

* *Spiritual Magazine*, 1868, p. 321.

THE DAVENPORT BROTHERS

I desire to convey to those of my friends in America who introduced them to me, the assurance of my conviction that the Brothers' mission to Europe has been of great service to Spiritualism ; that their public conduct as mediums—in which relation I alone know them—has been steady and unexceptionable.

He adds that he knows no form of mediumship better adapted for a large audience than theirs. After this visit to London the Davenports returned home to America. The brothers visited Australia in 1876, and on August 24 gave their first public séance in Melbourne. William died in Sydney in July, 1877.

Throughout their career the Davenport Brothers excited the deep envy and malice of the conjuring fraternity. Maskelyne, with amazing effrontery, pretended to have exposed them in England. His claims in this direction have been well answered by Dr. George Sexton, a former editor of the *Spiritual Magazine*, who described in public, in the presence of Mr. Maskelyne, how his tricks were done, and comparing them with the results achieved by the Davenports, said : " The two bear about as much resemblance to each other as the productions of the poet Close to the sublime and glorious dramas of the immortal bard of Avon." * Still the conjurers made more noise in public than the Spiritualists, and with the Press to support them they made the general public believe that the Davenport Brothers had been exposed.

In announcing the death in America of Ira Davenport in 1911, *Light* comments on the outpouring of

* Address at Cavendish Rooms, London, June 15, 1873.

journalistic ignorance for which it furnished the opportunity. The *Daily News* is quoted as saying of the brothers : " They made the mistake of appearing as sorcerers instead of as honest conjurers. If, like their conqueror, Maskelyne, they had thought of saying, ' It's so simple,' the brethren might have achieved not only fortune but respectability." In reply to this, *Light* asks why, if they were mere conjurers and not honest believers in their mediumship, did the Davenport Brothers endure hardships, insults, and injuries, and suffer the indignities that were put upon them, when by renouncing their claims to mediumship they might have been " respectable " and rich ?

An inevitable remark on the part of those who are not able to detect trickery is to ask what elevating purpose can be furthered by phenomena such as those observed with the Davenports. The well-known author and sturdy Spiritualist, William Howitt, has given a good answer :

Are these who play tricks and fling about instruments spirits from Heaven ? Can God really send such ? Yes, God sends them, to teach us this, if nothing more : that He has servants of all grades and tastes ready to do all kinds of work, and He has here sent what you call low and harlequin spirits to a low and very sensual age. Had He sent anything higher it would have gone right over the heads of their audiences. As it is, nine-tenths cannot take in what they see.

It is a sad reflection that the Davenports—probably the greatest mediums of their kind that the world has ever seen—suffered throughout their lives from brutal opposition and even persecution. Many times they were in danger of their lives.

One is forced to think that there could be no clearer evidence of the influence of the dark forces of evil than the prevailing hostility to all spiritual manifestations.

Touching this aspect, Mr. Randall says : *

There seems to be a sort of chronic dislike, almost hatred, in the minds of some persons toward any and every thing spiritual. It seems as if it were a vapour floating, in the air—a kind of mental spore flowing through the spaces, and breathed in by the great multitude of humankind, which kindles a rankly poisonous fire in their hearts against all those whose mission it is to bring peace on earth and good will to men. The future men and women of the world will marvel greatly at those now living, when they shall, as they will, read that the Davenports, and all other mediums, were forced to encounter the most inveterate hostility ; that they, and the writer among them, were compelled to endure horrors baffling description, for no other offence than trying to convince the multitude that they were not beasts that perish and leave no sign, but immortal, deathless, grave-surviving souls.

Mediums *alone* are capable of *demonstrating* the fact of man's continued existence after death; and yet (strange inconsistency of human nature !) the very people who persecute these, their truest and best friends, and fairly hound them to premature death or despair, are the very ones who freely lavish all that wealth can give upon those whose office it is merely to *guess* at human immortality.

In discussing the claims of various professional magicians to have exposed or imitated the Davenports, Sir Richard Burton said:

* Biography, p. 82.

I have spent a great part of my life in Oriental lands, and have seen their many magicians. Lately I have been permitted to see and be present at the performances of Messrs. Anderson and Tolmaque. The latter showed, as they profess, clever conjuring, but they do not even attempt what the Messrs. Davenport and Fay succeed in doing : for instance, the beautiful management of the musical instruments. Finally, I have read and listened to every explanation of the Davenport " tricks " hitherto placed before the English public, and, believe me, if anything would make me take that tremendous jump " from matter to spirit," it is the utter and complete unreason of the reasons by which the " manifestations " are explained.

It is to be remarked that the Davenports themselves, as contrasted with their friends and travelling companions, never claimed any preternatural origin for their results. The reason for this may have been that as an entertainment it was more piquant and less provocative when every member of the audience could form his own solution. Writing to the American conjurer Houdini, Ira Davenport said in his old age, " We never *in public* affirmed our belief in Spiritualism. That we regarded as no business of the public, nor did we offer our entertainment as the result of sleight-of-hand, or, on the other hand, as Spiritualism. We let our friends and foes settle that as best they could between themselves, but, unfortunately, we were often the victims of their disagreements."

Houdini further claimed that Davenport admitted that his results were normally effected, but Houdini has himself stuffed so many errors of fact into his book, " A Magician Among the Spirits," and has shown such extraordinary bias on the whole question, that his statement carries no weight. The letter which he produces makes no such admission. A further statement quoted as being made by Ira Davenport is demonstrably false. It is that the instruments never left the cabinet. As a matter of fact, *The Times* representative was severely struck in the face by a floating guitar, his brow being cut, and on several occasions when a light was struck instruments dropped all over the room. If Houdini has completely misunderstood this latter statement, it is not likely that he is very accurate upon the former (*vide* Appendix).

It may be urged, and has been urged, by Spiritualists as well as by sceptics that such mountebank psychic exhibitions are undignified and unworthy. There are many of us who think so, and yet there are many others who would echo these words of Mr. P. B. Randall :

The fault lies not with the immortals, but in us ; for, as is the demand, so is the supply. If we cannot be reached in one way, we must be, and are, reached in another ; and the wisdom of the eternal world gives the blind race just as much as it can bear and no more. If we are intellectual babes, we must put up with mental pap till our digestive capacities warrant and demand stronger food ; and, if people can best be convinced of immortality by spiritual pranks and antics, the ends resorted to justify the means. The sight of a spectral arm in an audience of three thousand persons will appeal to more hearts, make a deeper impression, and convert more people to a belief in their hereafter, in ten minutes, than a whole regiment of preachers, no matter how eloquent, could in five years.

CHAPTER XI

THE RESEARCHES OF SIR WILLIAM CROOKES
(1870-1874)

THE research into the phenomena of Spiritualism by Sir William Crookes—or Professor Crookes, as he then was—during the years from 1870 to 1874 is one of the outstanding incidents in the history of the movement. It is notable on account of the high scientific standing of the inquirer, the stern and yet just spirit in which the inquiry was conducted, the extraordinary results, and the uncompromising declaration of faith which followed them. It has been a favourite device of the opponents of the movement to attribute some physical weakness or growing senility to each fresh witness to psychic truth, but none can deny that these researches were carried out by a man at the very zenith of his mental development, and that the famous career which followed was a sufficient proof of his intellectual stability. It is to be remarked that the result was to prove the integrity not only of the medium Florence Cook with whom the more sensational results were obtained, but also that of D. D. Home and of Miss Kate Fox, who were also severely tested.

Sir William Crookes, who was born in 1832 and died in 1919, was pre-eminent in the world of science.

SIR WILLIAM CROOKES

From the painting by P. Ludovici in the National Portrait Gallery

Elected a Fellow of the Royal Society in 1863, he received from this body in 1875 a Royal Gold Medal for his various chemical and physical researches, the Davy Medal in 1888, and the Sir Joseph Copley Medal in 1904. He was knighted by Queen Victoria in 1897, and was awarded the Order of Merit in 1910. He occupied the position of President at different times of the Royal Society, the Chemical Society, the Institution of Electrical Engineers, the British Association, and the Society for Psychical Research. His discovery of the new chemical element which he named "Thallium," his inventions of the radiometer, the spinthariscope, and the "Crookes' tube," only represent a slight part of his great research. He founded in 1859 the *Chemical News*, which he edited, and in 1864 he became editor of the *Quarterly Journal of Science*. In 1880 the French Academy of Sciences awarded him a gold medal and a prize of 3,000 francs in recognition of his important work.

Crookes confesses that he began his investigations into psychical phenomena believing that the whole matter might prove to be a trick. His scientific brethren held the same view, and were delighted at the course he had adopted. Profound satisfaction was expressed because the subject was to be investigated by a man so thoroughly qualified. They had little doubt that what were considered to be the sham pretensions of Spiritualism would now be exposed. One writer said, "If men like Mr. Crookes grapple with the subject . . . we shall soon know how much to believe." Dr. (afterwards Professor) Balfour Stewart, in a communication to *Nature*, commended the boldness and honesty which had led Mr. Crookes to take this step. Crookes himself took the view that it was the duty of scientists to make such investigation. He writes : " It argues ill for the boasted freedom of opinion among scientific men that they have so long refused to institute a scientific investigation into the existence and nature of facts asserted by so many competent and credible witnesses, and which they are freely invited to examine when and where they please. For my own part, I too much value the pursuit of truth, and the discovery of any new fact in Nature, to avoid inquiry because it appears to clash with prevailing opinions." In this spirit he began his inquiry.

It should be stated, however, that though Professor Crookes was sternly critical as to the physical phenomena, already he had had acquaintance with the mental phenomena, and would appear to have accepted them. Possibly this sympathetic spiritual attitude may have aided him in obtaining his remarkable results, for it cannot be too often repeated—because it is too often forgotten—that psychic research of the best sort is really " psychic," and depends upon spiritual conditions. It is not the bumptious self-opinionated man, sitting with a ludicrous want of proportion as a judge upon spiritual matters, who attains results; but it is he who appreciates that the strict use of reason and observation is not incompatible with humility of mind, and that courteous gentleness of demeanour which makes for harmony and sympathy between the inquirer and his subject.

Crookes's less material inquiries seem to have begun in the summer of 1869. In July of that year he had sittings with the well-known medium, Mrs. Marshall, and in December with another famous medium, J. J. Morse. In July, 1869, D. D. Home who had been giving séances in St. Petersburg, returned to London with a letter of introduction to Crookes from Professor Butlerof.

An interesting fact emerges from a private diary kept by Crookes during his voyage to Spain in December, 1870, with the Eclipse Expedition. Under the date December 31, he writes : *

> I cannot help reverting in thought to this time last year. Nelly (his wife) and I were then sitting together in communion with dear departed friends, and as twelve o'clock struck they wished us many happy New Years. I feel that they are looking on now, and as space is no obstacle to them, they are, I believe, looking over my dear Nelly at the same time. Over us both I know there is one whom we all—spirits as well as mortals—bow down to as Father and Master, and it is my humble prayer to Him —the Great Good as the mandarin calls Him—that He will continue His merciful protection to Nelly and me and our dear little family. . . . May He also allow us to continue to receive spiritual communications from my brother who passed over the boundary when in a ship at sea more than three years ago.

He further adds New Year loving greetings to his wife and children, and concludes :

* " Life of Sir William Crookes." By E. E. Fournier d'Albe, 1923.

And when the earthly years have ended may we continue to spend still happier ones in the spirit land, glimpses of which I am occasionally getting.

Miss Florence Cook, with whom Crookes undertook his classical series of experiments, was a young girl of fifteen who was asserted to possess strong psychic powers, taking the rare shape of complete materialization. It would appear to have been a family characteristic, for her sister, Miss Kate Cook, was not less famous. There had been some squabble with an alleged exposure in which a Mr. Volckman had taken sides against Miss Cook, and in her desire for vindication she placed herself entirely under the protection of Mrs. Crookes, declaring that her husband might make any experiments upon her powers under his own conditions, and asking for no reward save that he should clear her character as a medium by giving his exact conclusions to the world. Fortunately, she was dealing with a man of unswerving intellectual honesty. We have had experience in these latter days of mediums giving themselves up in the same unreserved way to scientific investigation and being betrayed by the investigators, who had not the moral courage to admit those results which would have entailed their own public acceptance of the spiritual interpretation.

Professor Crookes published a full account of his methods in the *Quarterly Journal of Science*, of which he was then editor. In his house at Mornington Road a small study opened into the chemical laboratory, a door with a curtain separating the two rooms. Miss

Cook lay entranced upon a couch in the inner room. In the outer in subdued light sat Crookes, with such other observers as he invited. At the end of a period which varied from twenty minutes to an hour the materialized figure was built up from the ectoplasm of the medium. The existence of this substance and its method of production were unknown at that date, but subsequent research has thrown much light upon it, an account of which has been embodied in the chapter on ectoplasm. The actual effect was that the curtain was opened, and there emerged into the laboratory a female who was usually as different from the medium as two people could be. This apparition, which could move, talk, and act in all ways as an independent entity, is known by the name which she herself claimed as her own, " Katie King."

The natural explanation of the sceptic is that the two women were really the same woman, and that Katie was a clever impersonation of Florence. The objector could strengthen his case by the observation made not only by Crookes but by Miss Marryat and others, that there were times when Katie was very like Florence.

Herein lies one of the mysteries of materialization which call for careful consideration rather than sneers. The author, sitting with Miss Besinnet, the famous American medium, has remarked the same thing, the psychic faces beginning when the power was weak by resembling those of the medium, and later becoming utterly unlike. Some speculators have imagined that the etheric form of the medium, her spiritual body, has been liberated by the trance, and is the basis upon which the other manifesting entities build up their own simulacra. However that may be, the fact has to be admitted ; and it is paralleled by Direct Voice phenomena, where the voice often resembles that of the medium at first and then takes an entirely different tone, or divides into two voices speaking at the same time.

However, the student has certainly the right to claim that Florence Cook and Katie King were the same individual until convincing evidence is laid before him that this is impossible. Such evidence Professor Crookes is very careful to give.

The points of difference which he observed between Miss Cook and Katie are thus described :

Katie's height varies ; in my house I have seen her six inches taller than Miss Cook. Last night, with bare feet and not tip-toeing, she was four and a half inches taller than Miss Cook. Katie's neck was bare last night ; the skin was perfectly smooth both to touch and sight, whilst on Miss Cook's neck is a large blister, which under similar circumstances is distinctly visible and rough to the touch. Katie's ears are unpierced, whilst Miss Cook habitually wears ear-rings. Katie's complexion is very fair, while that of Miss Cook is very dark. Katie's fingers are much longer than Miss Cook's, and her face is also larger. In manners and ways of expression there are also many decided differences.

In a later contribution, he adds :

Having seen so much of Katie lately, when she has been illuminated by the electric light, I am enabled to add to the points of difference between her and her medium which I mentioned in a former article. I have the most absolute certainty that Miss Cook and Katie are two separate individuals so far as their bodies are concerned. Several little marks on Miss Cook's face are absent on Katie's. Miss Cook's hair is so dark a brown as almost to appear black ; a lock of Katie's, which is now before me, and which she allowed me to cut from her luxuriant tresses, having first traced it up to the scalp and satisfied myself that it actually grew there, is a rich golden auburn.

On one evening I timed Katie's pulse. It beat steadily at 75, whilst Miss Cook's pulse a little time after was going at its usual rate of 90. On applying my ear to Katie's chest, I could hear a heart beating rhythmically inside, and pulsating even more steadily than did Miss Cook's heart when she allowed me to try a similar experiment after the séance. Tested in the same way, Katie's lungs were found to be sounder than her medium's, for at the time I tried my experiment Miss Cook was under medical treatment for a severe cough.

Crookes took forty-four photographs of Katie King by the aid of electric light. Writing in *The Spiritualist* (1874, p. 270), he describes the methods he adopted :

During the week before Katie took her departure, she gave séances at my house almost nightly, to enable me to photograph her by artificial light. Five complete sets of photographic apparatus were accordingly fitted up for the purpose, consisting of five cameras, one of the whole-plate size, one half-plate, one quarter-plate, and two binocular stereoscopic cameras, which were all brought to bear upon Katie at the same time on each occasion on which she stood for her portrait. Five sensitizing and fixing baths were used, and plenty of plates were cleaned ready for use in advance, so that there might be no hitch or delay during the photographing operations, which were performed by myself, aided by one assistant.

My library was used as a dark cabinet. It has folding doors opening into the laboratory ; one of these doors was taken off its hinges, and a curtain suspended in its place to enable Katie to pass in and out easily. Those of our friends who were present were seated in the laboratory facing the curtain, and the cameras were placed a little behind them, ready to photograph Katie when she came outside, and to photograph anything also inside the cabinet, whenever the curtain was withdrawn for the purpose. Each evening there were three or four exposures of plates in the five cameras, giving at least fifteen separate pictures at each séance ; some of these were spoilt in the developing, and some in regulating the amount of light. Altogether I have forty-four negatives, some inferior, some indifferent, and some excellent.

Some of these photographs are in the author's possession, and surely there is no more wonderful impression upon any plate than that which shows Crookes at the height of his manhood, with this angel —for such in truth she was—leaning upon his arm. The word " angel " may seem an exaggeration, but when an other-world spirit submits herself to the discomforts of temporary and artificial existence in order to convey the lesson of survival to a material and worldly generation, there is no more fitting term.

Some controversy has arisen as to whether Crookes ever saw the medium and Katie at the same moment. Crookes says in the course of his report that he frequently followed Katie into the cabinet, " and have sometimes seen her and her medium together, but most generally I have found nobody but the entranced

PROFESSOR CROOKES'S TEST TO SHOW THAT THE MEDIUM AND
THE SPIRIT WERE SEPARATE ENTITIES

From a drawing by S. Drigin

medium lying on the floor, Katie and her white robes having instantaneously disappeared."

Much more direct testimony, however, is given by Crookes in a letter to the *Banner of Light* (U.S.A.), which is reproduced in *The Spiritualist* (London) of July 17, 1874, p. 29. He writes :

In reply to your request, I beg to state that I saw Miss Cook and Katie together at the same moment, by the light of a phosphorus lamp, which was quite sufficient to enable me to see distinctly all I described. The human eye will naturally take in a wide angle, and thus the two figures were included in my field of vision at the same time, but the light being dim, and the two faces being several feet apart, I naturally turned the lamp and my eyes alternately from one to the other, when I desired to bring either Miss Cook's or Katie's face to that portion of my field of view where vision is most distinct. Since the occurrence here referred to took place, Katie and Miss Cook have been seen together by myself and eight other persons, in my own house, illuminated by the full blaze of the electric light. On this occasion Miss Cook's face was not visible, as her head had to be closely bound up in a thick shawl, but I specially satisfied myself that she was there. An attempt to throw the light direct on to her uncovered face, when entranced, was attended with serious consequences.

The camera, too, emphasizes the points of difference between the medium and the form. He says :

One of the most interesting of the pictures is one in which I am standing by the side of Katie ; she has her bare foot upon a particular part of the floor. Afterwards I dressed Miss Cook like Katie, placed her and myself in exactly the same position, and we were photographed by the same cameras, placed exactly as in the other experiment, and illuminated by the same light. When these two pictures are placed over each other, the two photographs of myself coincide exactly as regards stature, etc., but Katie is half a head taller than Miss Cook, and looks a big woman in comparison with her. In the breadth of her face, in many of the pictures, she differs essentially in size from her medium, and the photographs show several other points of difference.

Crookes pays a high tribute to the medium, Florence Cook :

The almost daily séances with which Miss Cook has lately favoured me have proved a severe tax upon her strength, and I wish to make the most public acknowledgment of the obligations I am under to her for her readiness to assist me in my experiments. Every test that I have proposed she has at once agreed to submit to with the utmost willingness ; she is open and straightforward in speech, and I have never seen anything approaching the slightest symptom of a wish to deceive. Indeed, I do not believe she could carry on a deception if she were to try, and if she did she would certainly be found out very quickly, for such a line of action is altogether foreign to her nature. And to imagine that an innocent schoolgirl of fifteen should be able to conceive and then successfully carry out for three years so gigantic an imposture as this, and in that time should submit to any test which might be imposed upon her, should bear the strictest scrutiny, should be willing to be searched at any time, either before or after a séance, and should meet with even better success in my own house than at that of her parents, knowing that she visited me with the express object of submitting to strict scientific tests—to imagine, I say, the Katie King of the last three years to be the result of imposture, does more violence to one's reason and common sense than to believe her to be what she herself affirms.*

* " Researches in the Phenomena of Spiritualism."

Granting that a temporary form was built up from the ectoplasm of Florence Cook, and that this form was then occupied and used by an independent being who called herself " Katie King," we are still faced with the question, " Who was Katie King ? " To this we can only give the answer which she gave herself, while admitting that we have no proof of it. She declared that she was the daughter of John King, who had long been known among Spiritualists as the presiding spirit at séances held for material phenomena. His personality is discussed later in the chapter upon the Eddy brothers and Mrs. Holmes, to which the reader is referred. Her earth name had been Morgan, and King was rather the general title of a certain class of spirits than an ordinary name. Her life had been spent two hundred years before, in the reign of Charles the Second, in the island of Jamaica. Whether this be true or not, she undoubtedly conformed to the part, and her general conversation was consistent with her account. One of the daughters of Professor Crookes wrote to the author and described her vivid recollection of tales of the Spanish Main told by this kindly spirit to the children of the family. She made herself beloved by all. Mrs. Crookes wrote :

At a séance with Miss Cook in our own house when one of our sons was an infant of three weeks old, Katie King, a materialized spirit, expressed the liveliest interest in him and asked to be allowed to see the baby. The infant was accordingly brought into the séance room and placed in the arms of Katie, who, after holding him in the most natural way for a short time, smilingly gave him back again.

Professor Crookes has left it on record that her beauty and charm were unique in his experience.

The reader may reasonably think that the subdued light which has been alluded to goes far to vitiate the results by preventing exact observation. Professor Crookes has assured us, however, that as the series of séances proceeded toleration was established, and the figure was able to bear a far greater degree of light. This toleration had its limits, however, which were never passed by Professor Crookes, but which were tested to the full in a daring experiment described by Miss Florence Marryat (Mrs. Ross-Church). It should be stated that Professor Crookes was not present at this experience, nor did Miss Marryat ever claim that he was. She mentions, however, the name of Mr. Carter Hall as being one of the company present. Katie had very good-humouredly consented to testing what the effect would be if a full light were turned upon her image :

She took up her station against the drawing-room wall, with her arms extended as if she were crucified. Then three gas-burners were turned on to their full extent in a room about sixteen feet square. The effect upon Katie King was marvellous. She looked like herself for the space of a second only, then she began gradually to melt away. I can compare the dematerialization of her form to nothing but a wax doll melting before a hot fire. First the features became blurred and indistinct ; they seemed to run into each other. The eyes sunk in the sockets, the nose disappeared, the frontal bone fell in. Next the limbs appeared to give way under her, and she sank lower and lower on the carpet, like a crumbling edifice. At last there was *nothing but her head* left above the ground—then a heap of white drapery only, which disappeared with a whisk, as if a hand had pulled it after her—and we were left staring by the light of three gas-burners at the spot on which Katie King had stood.*

Miss Marryat adds the interesting detail that at some of these séances Miss Cook's hair was nailed to the ground, which did not in the least interfere with the subsequent emergence of Katie from the cabinet.

The results obtained in his own home were honestly and fearlessly reported by Professor Crookes in his *Journal,* and caused the greatest possible commotion in the scientific world. A few of the larger spirits, men like Russel Wallace, Lord Rayleigh, the young and rising physicist William Barrett, Cromwell Varley, and others, had their former views confirmed, or were encouraged to advance upon a new path of knowledge. There was a fiercely intolerant party, however, headed by Carpenter the physiologist, who derided the matter and were ready to impute anything from lunacy to fraud to their illustrious colleague. Organized science came badly out of the matter. In his published account Crookes gave the letters in which he asked Stokes, the secretary of the Royal Society, to come down and see these things with his own eyes. By his refusal to do so, Stokes placed himself in exactly the same position as those cardinals who would not look at the moons of Jupiter through Galileo's telescope. Material science, when faced with a new problem, showed itself to be just as bigoted as mediæval theology.

* " There Is No Death," p. 143.

Before quitting the subject of Katie King one should say a few words as to the future of the great medium from whom she had her physical being. Miss Cook became Mrs. Corner, but continued to exhibit her remarkable powers. The author is only aware of one occasion upon which the honesty of her mediumship was called in question, and that was when she was seized by Sir George Sitwell and accused of personating a spirit. The author is of opinion that a materializing medium should always be secured so that she cannot wander around—and this as a protection against herself. It is unlikely that she will move in deep trance, but in the half-trance condition there is nothing to prevent her unconsciously, or semi-consciously, or in obedience to suggestion from the expectations of the circle, wandering out of the cabinet into the room. It is a reflection of our own ignorance that a lifetime of proof should be clouded by a single episode of this nature. It is worthy of remark, however, that upon this occasion the observers agreed that the figure was white, whereas when Mrs. Corner was seized no white was to be seen. An experienced investigator would probably have concluded that this was not a materialization, but a transfiguration, which means that the ectoplasm, being insufficient to build up a complete figure, has been used to drape the medium so that she herself may carry the simulacrum. Commenting upon such cases, the great German investigator, Dr. Schrenck Notzing, says : *

This (a photograph) is interesting as throwing a light on

* " Phenomena of Materialization " (English Translation).

the genesis of the so-called transfiguration, i.e. . . . . the medium takes upon herself the part of the spirit, endeavouring to dramatize the character of the person in question by clothing herself in the materialized fabrics. This transition stage is found in nearly all materialization mediums. The literature of the subject records a large number of attempts at exposure of mediums thus impersonating " spirits," e.g. that of the medium Bastian by the Crown Prince Rudolph, that of Crookes's medium, Miss Cook, that of Madame d'Esperance, etc. In all these cases the medium was seized, but the fabrics used for masking immediately disappeared, and were not afterwards found.

It would appear, then, that the true reproach in such cases lies with the negligent sitters rather than with the unconscious medium.

The sensational nature of Professor Crookes's experiments with Miss Cook, and the fact, no doubt, that they seemed more vulnerable to attack, have tended to obscure his very positive results with Home and with Miss Fox, which have established the powers of those mediums upon a solid basis. Crookes soon found the usual difficulties which researchers encounter, but he had sense enough to realize that in an entirely new subject one has to adapt oneself to the conditions, and not abandon the study in disgust because the conditions refuse to adapt themselves to our own preconceived ideas. Thus, in speaking of Home, he says :

The experiments I have tried have been very numerous, but owing to our imperfect knowledge of the conditions which favour or oppose the manifestations of this force, to the apparently capricious manner in which it is exerted, and to the fact that Mr. Home himself is subject to unaccountable ebbs and flows of the force, it has but seldom happened that a result obtained on one occasion could be subsequently confirmed and tested with apparatus specially contrived for the purpose.*

The most marked of these results was the alteration in the weight of objects, which was afterwards so completely confirmed by Dr. Crawford working with the Goligher circle, and also in the course of the " Margery " investigation at Boston. Heavy objects could be made light, and light ones heavy, by the action of some unseen force which appeared to be under the influence of an independent intelligence. The checks by which all possible fraud was eliminated are very fully set out in the record of the experiments, and must convince any unprejudiced reader. Dr. Huggins, the well-known authority on the spectroscope, and Serjeant Cox, the eminent lawyer, together with several other spectators, witnessed the experiments. As already recorded, however, Crookes found it impossible to get some of the official heads of science to give the matter one hour of their attention.

The playing upon musical instruments, especially an accordion, under circumstances when it was impossible to reach the notes, was another of the phenomena which was very thoroughly examined and then certified by Crookes and his distinguished assistants. Granting that the medium has himself the knowledge which would enable him to play the instrument, the author is not prepared to admit that such a pheno-

* " Researches in the Phenomena of Spiritualism," p. 10.

menon is an absolute proof of independent intelligence. When once the existence of an etheric body is granted, with limbs which correspond with our own, there is no obvious reason why a partial detachment should not take place, and why the etheric fingers should not be placed upon the keys while the material ones remain upon the medium's lap. The problem resolves itself, then, into the simpler proposition that the medium's brain can command his etheric fingers, and that those fingers can be supplied with sufficient force to press down the keys. Very many psychic phenomena, the reading with blindfolded eyes, the touching of distant objects, and so forth, may, in the opinion of the author, be referred to the etheric body and may be classed rather under a higher and subtler materialism than under Spiritualism. They are in a class quite distinct from those mental phenomena such as evidential messages from the dead, which form the true centre of the spiritual movement. In speaking of Miss Kate Fox, Professor Crookes says : " I have observed many circumstances which appear to show that the will and intelligence of the medium have much to do with the phenomena." He adds that this is not in any conscious or dishonest way, and continues, " I have observed some circumstances which seem conclusively to point to the agency of an outside intelligence not belonging to any human being in the room." * This is the point which the author has attempted to make as expressed by an authority far higher than his own.

* " Researches in the Phenomena of Spiritualism," p. 95.

The phenomena which were chiefly established in the investigation of Miss Kate Fox were the movement of objects at a distance, and the production of percussive sounds—or raps. The latter covered a great range of sound, "delicate ticks . . . sharp sounds as from an induction coil in full work, detonations in the air, sharp metallic taps, a crackling like that heard when a frictional machine is at work, sounds like scratching, the twittering as of a bird, etc." * All of us who have had experience of these sounds have been compelled to ask ourselves how far they are under the control of the medium. The author has come to the conclusion, as already stated, that up to a point they *are* under the control of the medium, and that beyond that point they are not. He cannot easily forget the distress and embarrassment of a great North-country medium when in the author's presence loud raps, sounding like the snapping of fingers, broke out round his head in the coffee-room of a Doncaster hotel. If he had any doubts that raps were independent of the medium they were finally set at rest upon that occasion. As to the objectivity of these noises, Crookes says of Miss Kate Fox :

It seems only necessary for her to place her hand on any substance for loud thuds to be heard in it, like a triple pulsation, sometimes loud enough to be heard several rooms off. In this manner I have heard them in a living tree—on a sheet of glass—on a stretched iron wire—on a stretched membrane—a tambourine—on the roof of a cab—and on the floor of a theatre. Moreover, actual contact is not always necessary. I have had these sounds proceed-

* "Researches in the Phenomena of Spiritualism," p. 86.

ing from the floor, walls, etc., when the medium's hands and feet were held—when she was standing on a chair—when she was suspended in a swing from the ceiling—when she was enclosed in a wire cage—and when she had fallen fainting on a sofa. I have heard them on a glass harmonicon—I have felt them on my own shoulder and under my own hands. I have heard them on a sheet of paper, held between the fingers by a piece of thread passed through one corner. With a full knowledge of the numerous theories which have been started, chiefly in America, to explain these sounds, I have tested them in every way that I could devise, until there has been no escape from the conviction that they were true objective occurrences not produced by trickery or mechanical means.

So finishes the legend of cracking toe-joints, dropping apples, and all the other absurd explanations which have been put forward to explain away the facts. It is only fair to say, however, that the painful incidents connected with the latter days of the Fox sisters go some way to justify those who, without knowing the real evidence, have had their attention drawn to that single episode—which is treated elsewhere.

It has sometimes been supposed that Crookes modified or withdrew his opinions upon psychic subjects as expressed in 1874. It may at least be said that the violence of the opposition, and the timidity of those who might have supported him, did alarm him and that he felt his scientific position to be in danger. Without going the length of subterfuge, he did unquestionably shirk the question. He refused to have his articles upon the subject republished, and he would not circulate the wonderful photographs in which the materialized Katie King stood arm-in-arm with himself. He was exceedingly cautious also in defining his position. In a letter quoted by Professor Angelo Brofferio, he says : *

All that I am concerned in is that invisible and intelligent beings exist who say that they are the spirits of dead persons. But proof that they really are the individuals they assume to be, which I require in order to believe it, I have never received, though I am disposed to admit that many of my friends assert that they have actually obtained the desired proofs, and I myself have already frequently been many times on the verge of this conviction.

As he grew older, however, this conviction hardened, or perhaps he became more conscious of the moral responsibilities which such exceptional experiences must entail.

In his presidential address before the British Association at Bristol in 1898, Sir William briefly referred to his earlier researches. He said:

Upon one other interest I have not yet touched—to me the weightiest and farthest-reaching of all. No incident in my scientific career is more widely known than the part I took many years ago in certain psychic researches. Thirty years have passed since I published an account of experiments tending to show that outside our scientific knowledge there exists a Force exercised by intelligence differing from the ordinary intelligence common to mortals. . . . I have nothing to retract. I adhere to my already published statements. Indeed, I might add much thereto.

* " Fur den Spiritismus," Leipzig, 1894, p. 319.

Nearly twenty years later his belief was stronger than ever. In the course of an interview, he said :*

I have never had any occasion to change my mind on the subject. I am perfectly satisfied with what I have said in earlier days. It is quite true that a connexion has been set up between this world and the next.

In reply to the question whether Spiritualism had not killed the old materialism of the scientists, he added:

I think it has. It has at least convinced the great majority of people, who know anything about the subject, of the existence of the next world.

The author has had an opportunity lately, through the courtesy of Mr. Thomas Blyton, of seeing the letter of condolence written by Sir William Crookes on the occasion of the death of Mrs. Corner. It is dated April 24, 1904, and in it he says: " Convey Lady Crookes's and my own sincerest sympathy to the family in their irreparable loss. We trust that the certain belief that our loved ones, when they have passed over, are still watching over us—a belief which owes so much of its certainty to the mediumship of Mrs. Corner (or Florence Cook, as she will always be in our memory)—will strengthen and console those who are left behind." The daughter in announcing the death said, " She died in deep peace and happiness."

* *The International Psychic Gazette*, December, 1917, pp. 61–2.

CHAPTER XII

THE EDDY BROTHERS AND THE HOLMESES

IT is difficult within any reasonable compass to follow the rise of various mediums in the United States, and a study of one or two outstanding cases must typify the whole. The years 1874 and 1875 were years of great psychic activity, bringing conviction to some and scandal to others. On the whole the scandal seems to have predominated, but whether rightly or not is a question which may well be debated. The opponents of psychic truth having upon their side the clergy of the various churches, organized science, and the huge inert bulk of material mankind, had the lay Press at their command, with the result that everything that was in its favour was suppressed or contorted, and everything which could tell against it was given the widest publicity. Hence, a constant checking of past episodes and reassessment of old values are necessary. Even at the present day the air is charged with prejudice. If any man of standing at the present instant were to enter a London newspaper office and say that he had detected a medium in fraud, the matter would be seized upon eagerly and broadcast over the country; while if the same man proclaimed that he had beyond all question satisfied himself that the phenomena were true, it is doubtful if he would get a paragraph. The scale is always heavily weighted. In America, where there is practically no Libel Act, and where the Press is often violent and sensational, this state of things was—and possibly is—even more in evidence.

The first outstanding incident was the mediumship of the Eddy brothers, which has probably never been excelled in the matter of materialization, or, as we may now call them, ectoplasmic forms. The difficulty at that date in accepting such phenomena lay in the fact that they seemed to be regulated by no known law, and to be isolated from all our experiences of Nature. The labours of Geley, Crawford, Madame Bisson, Schrenck Notzing and others have removed this, and have given us, what is at the lowest, a complete scientific hypothesis, sustained by prolonged and careful investigations, so that we can bring some order into the matter. This did not exist in 1874, and we can well sympathize with the doubt of even the most honest and candid minds, when they were asked to believe that two rude farmers, unmannered and uneducated, could produce results which were denied to the rest of the world and utterly inexplicable to science.

The Eddy brothers, Horatio and William, were primitive folk farming a small holding at the hamlet of Chittenden, near Rutland, in the State of Vermont. An observer has described them as " sensitive, distant and curt with strangers, look more like hard-working rough farmers than prophets or priests of a new dispensation, have dark complexions, black hair and eyes, stiff joints, a clumsy carriage, shrink from advances, and make new-comers ill at ease and unwelcome. They are at feud with some of their neighbours and not liked. . . . They are, in fact, under the ban of a public opinion that is not prepared or desirous to study the phenomena as either scientific marvels or revelations from another world."

The rumours of the strange doings which occurred in the Eddy homestead had got abroad, and raised an excitement similar to that caused by the Koons's music-room in earlier days. Folk came from all parts to investigate. The Eddys seem to have had ample, if rude, accommodation for their guests, and to have boarded them in a great room with the plaster stripping off the walls and the food as simple as the surroundings. For this board, of course, they charged at a low rate, but they do not seem to have made any profit out of their psychic demonstrations.

A good deal of curiosity had been aroused in Boston and New York by the reports of what was happening, and a New York paper, the *Daily Graphic*, sent up Colonel Olcott as investigator. Olcott was not at that time identified with any psychic movement —indeed, his mind was prejudiced against it, and he approached his task rather in the spirit of an " exposer." He was a man of clear brain and outstanding ability, with a high sense of honour. No one can read the very full and intimate details of his own life which are contained in his " Old Diary Leaves " without feeling a respect for the man—loyal to a fault, unselfish, and with that rare moral courage which will follow truth and accept results even when they oppose

one's expectations and desires. He was no mystic
dreamer but a very practical man of affairs, and some
of his psychic research observations have met with far
less attention than they deserve.

Olcott remained for ten weeks in the Vermont
atmosphere, which must in itself have been a feat of
considerable endurance, with plain fare, hard living
and uncongenial hosts. He came away with something very near to personal dislike for his morose
entertainers, and at the same time with absolute confidence in their psychic powers. Like every wise investigator, he refuses to give blank certificates of
character, and will not answer for occasions upon which
he was not present, nor for the future conduct of those
whom he is judging. He confines himself to his
actual experience, and in fifteen remarkable articles
which appeared in the *New York Daily Graphic* in
October and November, 1874, he gave his full results
and the steps which he had taken to check them.
Reading these, it is difficult to suggest any precaution
which he had omitted.

His first care was to examine the Eddy history.
It was a good but not a spotless record. It cannot be
too often insisted upon that the medium is a mere
instrument and that the gift has no relation to character. This applies to physical phenomena, but not
to mental, for no high teaching could ever come
through a low channel. There was nothing wrong
in the record of the brothers, but they had once
admittedly given a fake mediumistic show, announcing it as such and exposing tricks. This was probably

done to raise the wind and also to conciliate their bigoted neighbours, who were incensed against the real phenomena. Whatever the cause or motive, it naturally led Olcott to be very circumspect in his dealings, since it showed an intimate knowledge of tricks.

The ancestry was most interesting, for not only was there an unbroken record of psychic power extending over several generations, but their grandmother four times removed had been burned as a witch—or at least had been sentenced to that fate in the famous Salem trials of 1692. There are many living now who would be just as ready to take this short way with our mediums as ever Cotton Mather was, but police prosecutions are the modern equivalent. The father of the Eddys was unhappily one of those narrow persecuting fanatics. Olcott declares that the children were marked for life by the blows which he gave them in order to discourage what he chose to look upon as diabolical powers. The mother, who was herself strongly psychic, knew how unjustly this " religious " brute was acting, and the homestead must have become a hell upon earth. There was no refuge for the children outside, for the psychic phenomena used to follow them even into the schoolroom, and excite the revilings of the ignorant young barbarians around them. At home, when young Eddy fell into a trance, the father and a neighbour poured boiling water over him and placed a red-hot coal on his head, leaving an indelible scar. The lad fortunately slept on. Is it to be wondered at that after such a childhood the children should have grown into morose and secretive men ?

As they grew older the wretched father tried to make some money out of the powers which he had so brutally discouraged, and hired the children out as mediums. No one has ever yet adequately described the sufferings which public mediums used to undergo at the hands of idiotic investigators and cruel sceptics. Olcott testifies that the hands and arms of the sisters as well as the brothers were grooved with the marks of ligatures and scarred with burning sealing wax, while two of the girls had pieces of flesh pinched out by handcuffs. They were ridden on rails, beaten, fired at, stoned and chased while their cabinet was repeatedly broken to pieces. The blood oozed from their finger-nails from the compression of arteries. These were the early days in America, but Great Britain has little to boast of when one recalls the Davenport brothers and the ignorant violence of the Liverpool mob.

The Eddys seem to have covered about the whole range of physical mediumship. Olcott gives the list thus—rappings, movement of objects, painting in oils and water-colours under influence, prophecy, speaking strange tongues, healing, discernment of spirits, levitation, writing of messages, psychometry, clairvoyance, and finally the production of materialized forms. Since St. Paul first enumerated the gifts of the spirit no more comprehensive list has ever been given.

The method of the séances was that the medium

should sit in a cabinet at one end of the room, and that his audience should occupy rows of benches in front of him. The inquirer will probably ask why there should be a cabinet at all, and extended experience has shown that it can, as a matter of fact, be dispensed with save in this particular crowning phenomenon of materialization. Home never used a cabinet, and it is seldom used by our chief British mediums of to-day. There is, however, a very definite reason for its presence. Without being too didactic upon a subject which is still under examination, it may at least be stated, as a working hypothesis with a great deal to recommend it, that the ectoplasmic vapour which solidifies into the plasmic substance from which the forms are constructed can be more easily condensed in a limited space. It has been found, however, that the presence of the medium within that space is not needful. At the greatest materialization séance which the author has ever attended, where some twenty forms of various ages and sizes appeared in one evening, the medium sat outside the door of the cabinet from which the shapes emerged. Presumably, according to the hypothesis, his ectoplasmic vapour was conducted into the confined space, irrespective of the position of his physical body. This had not been recognized at the date of this investigation, so the cabinet was employed.

It is obvious, however, that the cabinet offered a means for fraud and impersonation, so it had to be carefully examined. It was on the second floor, with one small window. Olcott had the window netted

with a mosquito curtain fastened on the outside. The
rest of the cabinet was solid wood and unapproachable
save by the room in which the spectators were sitting.
There seems to have been no possible opening for
fraud. Olcott had it examined by an expert, whose
certificate is given in the book.

Under these circumstances Olcott related in his
newspaper articles, and afterwards in his remarkable
book, " People from the Other World," that he saw
in the course of ten weeks no fewer than four hundred
apparitions appear out of this cabinet, of all sorts,
sizes, sexes and races, clad in the most marvellous
garments, babies in arms, Indian warriors, gentlemen
in evening dress, a Kurd with a nine-foot lance,
squaws who smoked tobacco, ladies in fine costumes.
Such was Olcott's evidence, and there was not a statement he made for which he was not prepared to produce the evidence of a roomful of people. His story
was received with incredulity then, and will excite
little less incredulity now. Olcott, full of his subject
and knowing his own precautions, chafed, as all of us
chafe, at the criticism of those who had not been present, and who chose to assume that those who *were*
present were dupes and simpletons. He says: " If
one tells them of babies being carried in from the
cabinet by women, of young girls with lithe forms,
yellow hair and short stature, of old women and men
standing in full sight and speaking to us, of half-
grown children seen, two at a time, simultaneously
with another form, of costumes of different makes,
of bald heads, grey hair, black shocky heads of hair,

curly hair, of ghosts instantly recognized by friends, and ghosts speaking audibly in a foreign language of which the medium is ignorant—their equanimity is not disturbed. . . . The credulity of some scientific men, too, is boundless—they would rather believe that a baby could lift a mountain without levers, than that a spirit could lift an ounce."

But apart from the extreme sceptic, whom nothing will convince and who would label the Angel Gabriel at the last day as an optical delusion, there are some very natural objections which an honest novice is bound to make, and an honest believer to answer. What about these costumes? Whence come they? Can we accept a nine-foot lance as being a spiritual object? The answer lies, so far as we understand it, in the amazing properties of ectoplasm. It is the most protean substance, capable of being moulded instantly into any shape, and the moulding power is spirit will, either in or out of the body. *Anything* may in an instant be fashioned from it if the predominating intelligence so decides. At all such séances there appears to be present one controlling spiritual being who marshals the figures and arranges the whole programme. Sometimes he speaks and openly directs. Sometimes he is silent and manifests only by his actions. As already stated, such controls are very often Red Indians who appear in their spiritual life to have some special affinity with physical phenomena.

William Eddy, the chief medium for these phenomena, does not appear to have suffered in health or strength from that which is usually a most exhausting process. Crookes has testified how Home would " lie in an almost fainting condition on the floor, pale and speechless." Home, however, was not a rude open-air farmer, but a sensitive artistic invalid. Eddy seems to have eaten little, but smoked incessantly. Music and singing were employed at the séances, for it has long been observed that there is a close connexion between musical vibrations and psychic results. White light also has been found to prohibit results, and this is now explained from the devastating effects which light has been shown to exert upon ectoplasm. Many colours have been tried in order to prevent total darkness, but if you can trust your medium the latter is the most conducive to results, especially to those results of phosphorescent and flashing lights which are among the most beautiful of the phenomena. If a light is used, red is the colour which is best tolerated. In the Eddy séances there was a subdued illumination from a shaded lamp.

It would be wearisome to the reader to enter into details as to the various types which appeared in these remarkable gatherings. Madame Blavatsky, who was then an unknown woman in New York, had come up to see the sights. At that time she had not yet developed the theosophical line of thought, and was an ardent Spiritualist. Colonel Olcott and she met for the first time in the Vermont farm-house, and there began a friendship which was destined in the future to lead to strange developments. In her honour apparently a whole train of Russian images appeared, who carried on conversations in that language with the lady. The chief apparitions, however, were a giant Indian named Santum and an Indian squaw named Honto, who materialized so completely and so often that the audience may well have been excused if they forgot sometimes that they were dealing with spirits at all. So close was the contact that Olcott measured Honto on a painted scale beside the cabinet door. She was five feet three. On one occasion she exposed her woman's breast and asked a lady present to feel the beating of her heart. Honto was a light-hearted person, fond of dancing, of singing, of smoking, and of exhibiting her wealth of dark hair to the audience. Santum, on the other hand, was a taciturn warrior, six feet three in height. The height of the medium was five feet nine.

It is worth noting that the Indian always wore a powder-horn, which had been actually given him by a visitor to the circle. This was hung up in the cabinet and was donned by him when he materialized. Some of the Eddy spirits could speak and others could not, while the amount of fluency varied greatly. This was in accordance with the author's experience at similar séances. It seems that the returning soul has much to learn when it handles this simulacrum of itself, and that here, as elsewhere, practice goes for much. In speaking, these figures move their lips exactly as human beings would do. It has been shown also that their breath in lime water produces the characteristic reaction of carbon dioxide. Olcott says: " The spirits themselves say that they have to learn the art of self-

materialization, as one would any other art." At first
they could only make tangible hands as in the cases of
the Davenports, the Foxes, and others. Many
mediums never get beyond this stage.

Among the numerous visitors to the Vermont
homestead there were naturally some who took up a
hostile attitude. None of these, however, seems to
have gone into the matter with any thoroughness.
The one who attracted most attention was a Dr.
Beard, of New York, a medical man, who on the
strength of a single sitting contended that the figures
were all impersonations by William Eddy himself.
No evidence, and only his own individual impression
is put forward to sustain this view, and he declared
that he could produce all the effects with " three
dollars' worth of theatrical properties." Such an
opinion might well be honestly formed upon a single
performance, especially if it should have been a more
or less unsuccessful one. But it becomes perfectly
untenable when it is compared with the experiences
of those who attended a number of sittings. Thus,
Dr. Hodgson, of Stoneham, Mass., together with four
other witnesses, signed a document: " We certify
. . . that Santum was out on the platform when
another Indian of almost as great a stature came out,
and the two passed and re-passed each other as they
walked up and down. At the same time a conversation was being carried on between George Dix, May-
flower, old Mr. Morse, and Mrs. Eaton inside the
cabinet. We recognized the familiar voice of each."
There are many such testimonies, apart from Olcott,

and they put the theory of impersonation quite out of
court. It should be added that many of the forms
were little children and babies in arms. Olcott
measured one child two feet four in height. It
should, in fairness, be added that the one thing which
clouds the reader occasionally is Olcott's own hesitation and reservations. He was new to the subject, and
every now and then a wave of fear and doubt would
pass over his mind, and he would feel that he had committed himself too far and that he must hedge in case,
in some inexplicable way, he should be shown to be
in the wrong. Thus, he says: " The forms I saw at
Chittenden, while apparently defying any other explanation than that they are of super-sensual origin,
are still as a scientific fact to be regarded as ' not
proven.' " Elsewhere he talks about not having
" test conditions."

This expression " test conditions " has become a
sort of shibboleth which loses all meaning. Thus,
when you say that you have beyond all question or
doubt seen your own dead mother's face before you,
the objector replies: " Ah, but was it under test conditions ? " The test lies in the phenomenon itself.
When one considers that Olcott was permitted for ten
weeks to examine the little wooden enclosure which
served as cabinet, to occlude the window, to search
the medium, to measure and to weigh the ectoplasmic
forms, one wonders what else he would demand in
order to make assurance complete. The fact is, that
while Olcott was writing his account there came the
alleged exposure of Mrs. Holmes, and the partial

recantation of Mr. Dale Owen, and that this caused him to take these precautions.

It was William Eddy whose mediumship took the form of materializations. Horatio Eddy gave séances of quite a different character. In his case a sort of cloth screen was fixed up, in front of which he used to sit in good light with one of his audience beside him holding his hand. Behind the screen was placed a guitar and other instruments, which presently began to play, apparently of their own accord, while materialized hands showed themselves over the edge of the screen. The general effect of the performance was much the same as that of the Davenport brothers, but it was more impressive, inasmuch as the medium was in full view, and was under control by a spectator. The hypothesis of modern psychic science, founded upon many experiments, especially those of Dr. Crawford, of Belfast, is that invisible bands of ectoplasm, which are rather conductors of force than forcible in themselves, are evolved from the body of the medium and connect up with the object to be manipulated, where they are used to raise it, or to play it, as the unseen power may desire—that unseen power being, according to the present views of Professor Charles Richet, some extension of the personality of the medium, and according to the more advanced school some independent entity. Of this nothing was known at the time of the Eddys, and the phenomena presented the questionable appearance of a whole series of effects without any cause. As to the reality of the fact, it is impossible to read Olcott's very detailed description without being convinced that there could be no error in that. This movement of objects at a distance from the medium, or *Telekinesis*, to use the modern phrase, is now a rare phenomenon in light, but on one occasion at an amateur circle of experienced Spiritualists the author has seen a large platter-shaped circle of wood in the full light of a candle, rising up on edge and flapping code answers to questions when no one was within six feet of it.

In Horatio Eddy's dark séances, where the complete absence of light gave the psychic power full scope, Olcott has testified that there were mad Indian war dances with the thudding of a dozen feet, and the wild playing of every instrument simultaneously, accompanied by yells and whoops. " As an exhibition of pure brute force," he says, " this Indian dance is probably unsurpassed in the annals of such manifestations." A light turned on would find all the instruments littered about the floor, and Horatio in a deep slumber, without a trace of perspiration, lying unconscious in his chair. Olcott assures us that he and other gentlemen present, whose names he gives, were permitted to sit on the medium, but that within a minute or two all the instruments were playing once again. After such an experiment all further experiences—and there were very many—seem to be beside the point. Short of wholesale and senseless lying on the part of Olcott and the other spectators, there can be no doubt that Horatio Eddy was exercising powers of which science was, and still is, very imperfectly acquainted.

Some of Olcott's experiments were so definite, and are narrated so frankly and so clearly, that they deserve respectful consideration, and antedate the work of many of our modern researchers. For example, he brought from New York a balance which was duly tested as correct with a published certificate to that effect. He then persuaded one of the forms, the squaw Honto, to stand upon it, the actual weights being recorded by a third person, Mr. Pritchard, who was a reputable citizen and disinterested in the matter. Olcott gives his account of the results, and adds the certificate of Pritchard as sworn to before a magistrate. Honto was weighed four times, standing upon the platform so that she could not ease her weight in any way. She was a woman five feet three in height, and might be expected to register about 135 lb. The four results were actually 88, 58, 58, and 65 lb., all on the same evening. This seems to show that her body was a mere simulacrum which could vary in density from minute to minute. It showed also what was clearly brought out afterwards by Crawford, that the whole weight of the simulacrum cannot be derived from the medium. It is inconceivable that Eddy, who weighed 179 lb., was able to give up 88 of them. The whole circle, according to their capacity, which varies greatly, are called upon to contribute, and other elements may in all probability be drawn from the atmosphere. The highest actual loss of weight ever shown by Miss Goligher in the Crawford experiments was 52 lb., but each member of the circle was shown by the dials on the weighing chairs to have contributed some substance to the building of the ectoplasmic formations.

Colonel Olcott also prepared two spring balances and tested the pulling power of the spirit hands, while those of the medium were held by one of the audience. A left hand pulled with a force of forty lb., and the right hand with fifty in a light which was so good that Olcott could clearly see that the right hand was one finger short. He was already familiar with the assertion of the spirit in question that he had been a sailor and had lost a finger in his lifetime. When one reads of such things the complaint of Olcott that his results were not final, and that he had not perfect test conditions, becomes more and more hard to comprehend. He winds up his conclusions, however, with the words: " No matter how many sceptics came battering against these granitic facts, no matter what array of ' exposers ' might blow their tin horns and penny trumpets, that Jericho would stand."

One observation which Olcott made was that these ectoplasmic forms were quick to obey any mental order from a strong-minded sitter, coming and going as they were willed to do. Other observers in various séances have noted the same fact, and it may be taken as one of the fixed points in this baffling problem.

There is one other curious point which probably escaped Olcott's notice. The mediums and the spirits who had been fairly amiable to him during his long visit turned suddenly very acid and repellent. This change seems to have occurred just after the arrival of Madame Blavatsky, with whom Olcott had struck up a close comradeship. Madame was, as stated, an ardent Spiritualist at the time, but it is at least possible that the spirits may have had foresight, and that they sensed danger from this Russian lady. Her theosophical teachings which were put forward in a year or two were to take the shape that, although the phenomena were real, the spirits were empty astral shells, and had no true life of their own. Whatever the true explanation, the change in the spirits was remarkable. " So far from the importance of my labour being recognized and all reasonable facilities afforded, I was kept constantly at a distance, as though I were an enemy instead of an unprejudiced observer."

Colonel Olcott narrates many cases where the sitters have recognized spirits, but too much stress should not be laid upon this, as with a dim light and an emotional condition it is easy for an honest observer to be mistaken. The author has had the opportunity of gazing into the faces of at least a hundred of these images, and he can only recall two cases in which he was absolutely certain in his recognition. In both these cases the faces were self-illuminated, and he had not to depend upon the red lamp. There were two other occasions when, with the red lamp, he was morally certain, but in the vast majority of cases it was possible, if one allowed one's imagination to work, to read anything into the vague moulds which rose before one. It is likely that this occurred in the Eddy circle—indeed, C. C. Massey, a very competent judge, sitting with the Eddys in 1875, complained of the fact. The real miracle consisted not in the recognition but in the presence of the figure at all.

There can be no doubt that the interest aroused by the Press accounts of the Eddy phenomena might have caused a more serious treatment of psychic science, and possibly advanced the cause of truth by a generation. Unhappily, at the very moment when the public attention was strongly drawn to the subject there came the real or imaginary scandal of the Holmeses at Philadelphia, which was vigorously exploited by the materialists, helped by the exaggerated honesty of Robert Dale Owen. The facts were as follows:

Two mediums in Philadelphia, Mr. and Mrs. Nelson Holmes, had given a series of séances at which an alleged spirit had continually appeared, which took the name of Katie King, and professed to be the same as that with which Professor Crookes had experimented in London. On the face of it the assertion seemed most doubtful since the original Katie King had clearly stated that her mission was ended. However, apart from the identity of the spirit, there seemed to be good evidence that the phenomenon was genuine and not fraudulent, for it was most fully endorsed by Mr. Dale Owen, General Lippitt, and a number of other observers, who quoted personal experiences which were entirely beyond the reach of imposture.

There was in Philadelphia at the time a Dr. Child, who plays a very ambiguous part in the obscure events which followed. Child had vouched for the genuine character of these phenomena in the most pronounced way. He had gone so far as to state in a pamphlet published in 1874 that the same John and Katie King, whom he had seen in the séance room, had come to him in his own private offices and had there dictated particulars of their earth life which he duly published. Such a statement must raise grave doubts in the mind of any psychic student, for a spirit form can only manifest from a medium, and there is no indication that Child was one. In any case one would imagine that, after such an assertion, Child was the last man in the world who could declare that the séances were fraudulent.

Great public interest had been aroused in the séances by an article by General Lippitt in the *Galaxy* of December, 1874, and another by Dale Owen in the *Atlantic Monthly* of January, 1875. Then suddenly came the crash. It was heralded by a notice from Dale Owen, dated January 5, to the effect that evidence had been laid before him which compelled him to withdraw his previous expressions of confidence in the Holmeses. A similar card was issued by Dr. Child. Writing to Olcott, who after his Eddy investigation was recognized as an authority, Dale Owen said: " I believe they have been latterly playing us false, which *may* be only supplementing the genuine with the spurious, but it does cast a doubt on last summer's manifestations, so that I shall probably not use them in my next book on Spiritualism. It is a loss, but you and Mr. Crookes have amply made it up."

Dale Owen's position is clear enough, since he was a man of sensitive honour, who was horrified at the idea that he could for one instant have certified an imposture to be a truth. His error seems to have lain in acting upon the first breath of suspicion instead of waiting until the facts were clear. Dr. Child's position is, however, more questionable, for if the manifestations were indeed fraudulent, how could he possibly have had interviews with the same spirits alone in his own private room?

It was asserted now that a woman, whose name was not given, had been impersonating Katie King at these séances, that she had allowed her photograph to be taken and sold as Katie King, that she could produce the robes and ornaments worn by Katie King at the séances, and that she was prepared to make a full confession. Nothing could appear to be more damning and more complete. It was at this point that Olcott took up the investigation, and he seems to have been quite prepared to find that the general verdict was correct.

His investigation soon revealed some facts, however, which threw fresh lights upon the matter and proved that psychic research in order to be accurate should examine " exposures " with the same critical care that it does phenomena. The name of the person who confessed that she had personated Katie King was revealed as Eliza White. In an account of the matter which she published, without giving the name, she declared that she had been born in 1851, which would make her twenty-three years of age. She had married at fifteen and had one child eight years old. Her husband had died in 1872, and she had to keep herself and child. The Holmeses had come to lodge with her in March, 1874. In May they engaged her to personate a spirit. The cabinet had a false panel at the back through which she could slip, clad in a muslin robe. Mr. Dale Owen was invited to the séances and was completely taken in. All this caused violent twinges of her own conscience which did not prevent her from going to greater lengths and learning to fade away or re-form by the help of black cloths, and finally, of being photographed as Katie King.

One day, according to her account, there came to her performance a man named Leslie, a railroad contractor. This gentleman showed his suspicions, and at a subsequent interview taxed her with her deceit, offering her pecuniary aid if she would confess to it. This she accepted, and then showed Leslie the methods of her impersonation. On December 5, a mock séance was held at which she rehearsed her part as played in the real séances, and this so impressed Dale Owen and also Dr. Child, both of whom were present, that they issued the notices in which they recanted their former belief—a recantation which was a staggering blow to those who had accepted Dale Owen's previous assurances, and who now claimed that he should have made some thorough investigation before issuing such a document. It was the more painful as Dale Owen was seventy-three years of age, and had been one of the most eloquent and painstaking of all the disciples of the new dispensation.

Olcott's first task was to sift the record already given, and to get past the anonymity of the authoress. He soon discovered that she was, as already stated, Mrs.

Eliza White, and that, though in Philadelphia, she refused to see him. The Holmeses, on the other hand, acted in a very open manner towards him and offered him every facility for examining their phenomena with such reasonable test conditions as he might desire. An examination of the past life of Eliza White showed that her statement, so far as it concerned her own story, was a tissue of lies. She was very much older than stated—not less than thirty-five—and it was doubtful whether she had ever been married to White at all. For years she had been a vocalist in a travelling show. White was still alive, so there was no question of widowhood. Olcott published the certificate of the Chief of the Police to that effect.

Among other documents put forward by Colonel Olcott was one from a Mr. Allen, Justice of the Peace of New Jersey, given under oath. Eliza White, according to this witness, was " so untruthful that those to whom she spoke never knew when to believe her, and her moral reputation was as bad as bad could be." Judge Allen was able, however, to give some testimony which bore more directly upon the matter under discussion. He deposed that he had visited the Holmeses in Philadelphia, and had assisted Dr. Child to put up the cabinet, that it was solidly constructed, and that there was no possibility of any entrance being effected from behind, as alleged by Mrs. White. Further, that he was at a séance at which Katie King appeared, and that the proceedings had been disturbed by the singing of Mrs. White in another room, so that it was quite impossible that Mrs. White could, as she claimed, have acted an impersonation of the spirit. This being a sworn deposition by a Justice of the Peace would seem to be a weighty piece of evidence.

This cabinet seems to have been made in June, for General Lippitt, an excellent witness, described quite another arrangement on the occasion when he experimented. He says that two doors folded backwards, so as to touch each other, and the cabinet was simply the recess between these doors with a board over the top. " The first two or three evenings I made a careful examination, and once with a professional magician, who was perfectly satisfied that there was no chance of any trick." This was in May, so the two descriptions are not contradictory, save to Eliza White's claim that she could pass into the cabinet.

In addition to these reasons for caution in forming an opinion, the Holmeses were able to produce letters written to them from Mrs. White in August, 1874, which were quite incompatible with there being any guilty secret between them. On the other hand, one of these letters did relate that efforts had been made to bribe her into a confession that she had been Katie King. Later in the year Mrs. White seems to have assumed a more threatening tone, as is sworn by the Holmeses in a formal affidavit, when she declared that unless they paid a rent which she claimed, there were a number of gentlemen of wealth, including members of the Young Men's Christian Association, who were ready to pay her a large sum of money, and she need not trouble the Holmeses any more. A thousand dollars was the exact sum which Eliza White was to get if she would consent to admit that she impersonated Katie King. It must surely be conceded that this statement, taken in conjunction with the woman's record, makes it very essential to demand corroboration for every assertion she might make.

One culminating fact remains. At the very hour that the bogus séance was being held at which Mrs. White was showing how Katie King was impersonated, the Holmeses held a real séance, attended by twenty people, at which the spirit appeared the same as ever. Colonel Olcott collected several affidavits from those who were present on this occasion, and there can be no doubt about the fact. That of Dr. Adolphus Fellger is short, and may be given almost in full. He says under oath that " he has seen the spirit known as Katie King in all perhaps eighty times, is perfectly familiar with her features, and cannot mistake as to the identity of the Katie King who appeared upon the evening of December 5, for while the said spirit scarcely ever appeared of exactly the same height or features two evenings in succession, her voice was always the same, and the expression of her eyes, and the topics of her conversation enabled him to be still more certain of her being the same person." This Fellger was a well-known and highly respected Philadelphia physician, whose simple word, says Olcott, would outweigh " a score of affidavits of your Eliza Whites."

It was also clearly shown that Katie King appeared constantly when Mrs. Holmes was at Blissfield and Mrs. White was in Philadelphia, and that Mrs. Holmes had written to Mrs. White describing their successful appearances, which seems a final proof that the latter was not a confederate.

By this time one must admit that Mrs. White's anonymous confession is shot through and through with so many holes that it is in a sinking condition. But there is one part which, it seems to the author, will still float. That is the question of the photograph. It was asserted by the Holmeses in an interview with General Lippitt—whose word is a solid patch in this general quagmire—that Eliza White was hired by Dr. Child to pose in a photograph as Katie King. Child seems to have played a dubious part all through this business, making affirmations at different times which were quite contradictory, and having apparently some pecuniary interest in the matter. One is inclined, therefore, to look seriously into this charge, and to believe that the Holmeses may have been party to the fraud. Granting that the Katie King image was real, they may well have doubted whether it could be photographed, since dim light was necessary for its production. On the other hand, there was clearly a source of revenue if photographs at half a dollar each could be sold to the numerous sitters. Colonel Olcott in his book produces a photograph of Mrs. White alongside of the one which was supposed to be Katie King, and claims that there is no resemblance. It is clear, however, that the photographer would be asked to touch up the negative so as to conceal the resemblance, otherwise the fraud would be obvious. The author has the impression, though not the certainty, that the two faces *are* the same with just such changes as manipulation would produce. Therefore he thinks that the photograph may well be a fraud, but that this by no means corroborates the rest of Mrs. White's narrative, though it would shake our faith in the character of Mr. and Mrs. Holmes as well as of Dr. Child. But the character of physical mediums has really only an indirect bearing upon the question of the reality of their psychic powers, which should be tested upon their own merits whether the individual be saint or sinner.

Colonel Olcott's wise conclusion was that, as the evidence was so conflicting, he would put it all to one side and test the mediums in his own way without reference to what was past. This he did in a very convincing way, and it is impossible for anyone who reads his investigation ("People From the Other World," p. 460 and onwards) to deny that he took every possible precaution against fraud. The cabinet was netted at the sides so that no one could enter as Mrs. White claimed to have done. Mrs. Holmes was herself put into a bag which tied round the neck and, as her husband was away, she was confined to her own resources. Under these circumstances numerous heads were formed, some of which were semi-materialized, presenting a somewhat terrible appearance. This may have been done as a test, or it may have been that the long contention had impaired the powers of the medium. The faces were made to appear at a level which the medium could in no case have reached. Dale Owen was present at this demonstration and must have already begun to regret his premature declaration.

Further séances with similar results were then held in Olcott's own rooms, so as to preclude the possibility of some ingenious mechanism under the control of the medium. On one occasion, when the head of John King, the presiding spirit, appeared in the air, Olcott, remembering Eliza White's assertion that these faces were merely ten cent masks, asked and obtained permission to pass his stick all round it, and so satisfied himself that it was not supported. This experiment seems so final that the reader who desires even more evidence may be referred to the book where he will find much. It was perfectly clear that whatever part Eliza White may have played in the photograph, there was not a shadow of a doubt that Mrs. Holmes was a genuine and powerful medium for material phenomena. It should be added that the Katie King head was repeatedly seen by the investigators, though the whole form appears only once to have been materialized. General Lippitt was present at these experiments and associated himself publicly (*Banner of Light*, February 6, 1875) with Olcott's conclusions.

The author has dwelt at some length upon this case, as it is very typical of the way in which the public has been misled over Spiritualism. The papers are full of an " exposure." It is investigated and is shown to be either quite false or very partially true. This is not reported, and the public is left with the original impression uncorrected. Even now, when one mentions Katie King, one hears some critic say: " Oh,

she was shown to be a fraud in Philadelphia," and by
a natural confusion of thought this has even been
brought as an argument against Crookes's classical
experiments. The affair—especially the temporary
weakening of Dale Owen—set the cause of Spiritualism back by many years in America.

Mention has been made of John King, the presiding spirit at the Holmes séances. This strange
entity would appear to have been the chief controller
of *all* physical phenomena in the early days of the
movement, and is still occasionally to be seen and
heard. His name is associated with the Koons's
music saloon, with the Davenport brothers, with
Williams in London, with Mrs. Holmes, and many
others. In person when materialized he presents the
appearance of a tall, swarthy man with a noble head
and a full black beard. His voice is loud and deep,
while his rap has a decisive character of its own. He
is master of all languages, having been tested in the
most out-of-the-way tongues, such as Georgian, and
never having been found wanting. This formidable
person controls the bands of lesser primitive spirits,
Red Indians and others, who assist at such phenomena.
He claims that Katie King is his daughter, and that
he was himself when in life Henry Morgan, the buc-
caneer who was pardoned and knighted by Charles II
and ended as Governor of Jamaica. If so, he has
been a most cruel ruffian and has much to expiate.
The author is bound to state, however, that he has in
his possession a contemporary picture of Henry Morgan (it will be found in Howard Pyle's " Buccaneers,"

p. 178), and that if reliable it has no resemblance to John King. All these questions of earthly identity are very obscure.*

Before closing the account of Olcott's experiences at this stage of his evolution, some notice should be taken of the so-called Compton transfiguration case, which shows what deep waters we are in when we attempt psychic research. These particular waters have not been plumbed yet, nor in any way charted. Nothing can be clearer than the facts, or more satisfactory than the evidence. The medium Mrs. Compton was shut up in her small cabinet, and thread passed through the bored holes in her ears and fastened to the back of her chair. Presently a slim white figure emerged from the cabinet. Olcott had a weighing platform provided, and on it the spirit figure stood. Twice it was weighed, the records being 77 lb. and 59 lb. Olcott then, as prearranged, went into the cabinet leaving the figure outside. *The medium was gone.* The chair was there, but there was no sign of the woman. Olcott then turned back and again weighed the apparition, who this time scaled 52 lb. The spirit then returned into the cabinet from which other figures emerged. Finally, Olcott says :

I went inside with a lamp and found the medium just as I left her at the beginning of the séance, with every

* As the author has given a point against the identity of John King with Morgan, it is only fair that he should give one which supports it and comes to him almost first-hand from a reliable source. The daughter of a recent Governor of Jamaica was at a séance in London lately, and was confronted with John King. The King spirit said to her, " You have brought back from Jamaica something which was mine." She said, " What was it ? " He answered, " My will." It was a fact, quite unknown to the company, that her father had brought back this document.

thread unbroken and every seal undisturbed ! She sat there, with her head leaning against the wall, her flesh as pale and as cold as marble, her eyeballs turned up beneath the lids, her forehead covered with a death-like damp, no breath coming from her lungs and no pulse at her wrist. When every person had examined the threads and seals, I cut the flimsy bonds with a pair of scissors, and, lifting the chair by its back and seat, carried the cataleptic woman out into the open air of the chamber.

She lay thus inanimate for eighteen minutes ; life gradually coming back to her body, until respiration and pulse and the temperature of her skin became normal . . . I then put her upon the scale. . . . She weighed one hundred and twenty-one pounds !

What are we to make of such a result as that ? There were eleven witnesses besides Olcott himself. The facts seem to be beyond dispute. But what are we to deduce from such facts ? The author has seen a photograph, taken in the presence of an amateur medium, where every detail of the room has come out but the sitter has vanished. Is the disappearance of the medium in some way analogous to that ? If the ectoplasmic figure weighed only 77 lb. and the medium 121 lb., then it is clear that only 44 lb. of her were left when the phantom was out. If 44 lb. were not enough to continue the processes of life, may not her guardians have used their subtle occult chemistry in order to dematerialize her and so save her from all danger until the return of the phantom would enable her to reassemble ? It is a strange supposition, but it seems to meet the facts—which cannot be done by mere blank, unreasoning incredulity.

CHAPTER XIII

HENRY SLADE AND DR. MONCK

IT is impossible to record the many mediums of various shades of power, and occasionally of honesty, who have demonstrated the effects which outside intelligences can produce when the material conditions are such as to enable them to manifest upon this plane. There are a few, however, who have been so pre-eminent and so involved in public polemics that no history of the movement can disregard them, even if their careers have not been in all ways above suspicion. We shall deal in this chapter with the histories of Slade and Monck, both of whom played a prominent part in their days.

Henry Slade, the celebrated slate-writing medium, had been before the public in America for fifteen years before he arrived in London on July 13, 1876. Colonel H. S. Olcott, a former president of the Theosophical Society, states that he and Madame Blavatsky were responsible for Slade's visit to England. It appears that the Grand Duke Constantine of Russia, desiring to make a scientific investigation of Spiritualism, a committee of professors of the Imperial University of St. Petersburg requested Colonel Olcott and Madame Blavatsky to select out of the best American mediums one whom they could recommend for tests

They chose Slade, after submitting him to exacting tests for several weeks before a committee of sceptics, who in their report certified that " messages were written inside double slates, sometimes tied and sealed together, while they either lay upon the table in full view of all, or were laid upon the heads of members of the committee, or held flat against the under surface of the table-top, or held in a committeeman's hand without the medium touching it." It was *en route* to Russia that Slade came to England.

A representative of the London *World*, who had a sitting with Slade soon after his arrival, thus describes him: " A highly-wrought, nervous temperament, a dreamy, mystical face, regular features, eyes luminous with expression, a rather sad smile, and a certain melancholy grace of manner, were the impressions conveyed by the tall, lithe figure introduced to me as Dr. Slade. He is the sort of man you would pick out of a roomful as an enthusiast." The Seybert Commission Report says, " he is probably six feet in height, with a figure of unusual symmetry," and that " his face would attract notice anywhere for its uncommon beauty," and sums him up as " a noteworthy man in every respect."

Directly after his arrival in London Slade began to give sittings at his lodgings in 8 Upper Bedford Place, Russell Square, and his success was immediate and pronounced. Not only was writing obtained of an evidential nature, under test conditions, with the sitter's own slates, but the levitation of objects and materialized hands were observed in strong sunlight.

The editor of *The Spiritual Magazine*, the soberest and most high-class of the Spiritualist periodicals of the time, wrote: " We have no hesitation in saying that Dr. Slade is the most remarkable medium of modern times."

Mr. J. Enmore Jones, a well-known psychic researcher of that day, who afterwards edited *The Spiritual Magazine*, said that Slade was taking the place vacated by D. D. Home. His account of his first sitting indicates the business-like method of procedure: " In Mr. Home's case, he refused to take fees, and as a rule the sittings were in the evening in the quiet of domestic life; but in Dr. Slade's case it was any time during the day, in one of the rooms he occupies at a boarding-house. The fee of twenty shillings is charged, and he prefers that only one person be present in the large room he uses. No time is lost; as soon as the visitor sits down the incidents commence, are continued, and in, say, fifteen minutes are ended." Stainton Moses, who was afterwards the first president of the London Spiritualist Alliance, conveys the same idea with regard to Slade. He wrote: " In his presence phenomena occur with a regularity and precision, with an absence of regard for ' conditions,' and with a facility for observation which satisfy my desires entirely. It is impossible to conceive circumstances more favourable to minute investigation than those under which I witnessed the phenomena which occur in his presence with such startling rapidity. . . . There was no hesitation, no tentative experiments. All was short, sharp, and decisive. The invisible operators knew exactly what they were going to do, and did it with promptitude and precision." *

Slade's first séance in England was given on July 15, 1876, to Mr. Charles Blackburn, a prominent Spiritualist, and Mr. W. H. Harrison, editor of *The Spiritualist*. In strong sunlight the medium and the two sitters occupied three sides of an ordinary table about four feet square. A vacant chair was placed at the fourth side. Slade put a tiny piece of pencil, about the size of a grain of wheat, upon a slate, and held the slate by one corner with one hand under the table flat against the leaf. Writing was heard on the slate, and on examination a short message was found to have been written. While this was taking place the four hands of the sitters and Slade's disengaged hand were clasped in the centre of the table. Mr. Blackburn's chair was moved four or five inches while he was sitting upon it, and no one but himself was touching it. The unoccupied chair at the fourth side of the table once jumped in the air, striking its seat against the under edge of the table. Twice a life-like hand passed in front of Mr. Blackburn while both Slade's hands were under observation. The medium held an accordion under the table, and while his other hand was in clear view on the table " Home, Sweet Home " was played. Mr. Blackburn then held the accordion in the same way, when the instrument was drawn out strongly and one note sounded. While this occurred Slade's hands were on the table. Finally,

* *The Spiritualist*, Vol. IX, p. 2.

the three present raised their hands a foot above the table, and it rose until it touched their hands. At another sitting on the same day a chair rose about four feet, when no one was touching it, and when Slade rested one hand on the top of Miss Blackburn's chair, she and the chair were raised about half a yard from the floor.

Mr. Stainton Moses thus describes an early sitting which he had with Slade:

A midday sun, hot enough to roast one, was pouring into the room ; the table was uncovered ; the medium sat with the whole of his body in full view ; there was no human being present save myself and him. What conditions could be better ? The raps were instantaneous and loud, as if made by the clenched fist of a powerful man. The slate-writing occurred under any suggested condition. It came on a slate held by Dr. Slade and myself ; on one held by myself alone in the corner of the table farthest from the medium ; on a slate which I had myself brought with me, and which I held myself. The latter writing occupied some time in production, and the grating noise of the pencil in forming each word was distinctly audible. A chair opposite to me was raised some eighteen inches from the floor ; my slate was taken out of my hand, and produced at the opposite side of the table, where neither Dr. Slade nor I could reach it ; the accordion played all round and about me, while the doctor held it by the lower part, and finally, on a touch from his hand upon the back of my chair, I was levitated, chair and all, some inches.

Mr. Stainton Moses was himself a powerful medium, and this fact doubtless aided the conditions. He adds:

I have seen all these phenomena and many others

several times before, but I never saw them occur rapidly and consecutively in broad daylight. The whole séance did not extend over more than half an hour, and no cessation of the phenomena occurred from first to last. *

All went well for six weeks, and London was full of curiosity as to the powers of Slade, when there came an awkward interruption.

Early in September, 1876, Professor Ray Lankester with Dr. Donkin had two sittings with Slade, and on the second occasion, seizing the slate, he found writing on it when none was supposed to have taken place. He was entirely without experience in psychic research, or he would have known that it is impossible to say at what moment writing occurs in such séances. Occasionally a whole sheet of writing seems to be precipitated in an instant, while at other times the author has clearly heard the pencil scratching along from line to line. To Ray Lankester, however, it seemed a clear case of fraud, and he wrote a letter to *The Times*† denouncing Slade, and also prosecuted him for obtaining money under false pretences. Replies to Lankester's letter and supporting Slade were forthcoming from Dr. Alfred Russel Wallace, Professor Barrett, and others. Dr. Wallace pointed out that Professor Lankester's account of what happened was so completely unlike what occurred during his own visit to the medium, as well as the recorded experience of Serjeant Cox, Dr. Carter Blake, and many others, that he could only look upon it as a striking example of Dr. Carpenter's theory of preconceived ideas. He

* *The Spiritualist*, Vol. IX, p. 2.   † September, 16, 1876.

says: " Professor Lankester went with the firm conviction that all he was going to see would be imposture,
and he believes he saw imposture accordingly." Professor Lankester showed his bias when, referring to
the paper read before the British Association on
September 12 by Professor Barrett, in which he dealt
with Spiritualistic phenomena, he said, in his letter to
The Times : " The discussions of the British Association have been *degraded* by the introduction of
Spiritualism."

Professor Barrett wrote that Slade had a ready
reply, based on his ignorance of when the writing did
actually occur. He describes a very evidential sitting
he had in which the slate rested on the table with his
elbow resting on it. One of Slade's hands was held
by him, and the fingers of the medium's other hand
rested lightly on the surface of the slate. In this way
writing occurred on the under surface of the slate.
Professor Barrett further speaks of an eminent scientific friend who obtained writing on a clean slate when
it was held entirely by him, both of the medium's
hands being on the table. Such instances must surely
seem absolutely conclusive to the unbiased reader, and
it will be clear that if the positive is firmly established,
occasional allegations of negative have no bearing upon
the general conclusion.

Slade's trial came on at Bow Street Police Court on
October 1, 1876, before Mr. Flowers, the magistrate.
Mr. George Lewis prosecuted and Mr. Munton
appeared for the defence. Evidence in favour of the
genuineness of Slade's mediumship was given by

Dr. Alfred Russel Wallace, Serjeant Cox, Dr. George Wyld, and one other, only four witnesses being allowed. The magistrate described the testimony as "overwhelming" as to the evidence for the phenomena, but in giving judgment he excluded everything but the evidence of Lankester and his friend Dr. Donkin, saying that he must base his decision on "inferences to be drawn from the known course of nature." A statement made by Mr. Maskelyne, the well-known conjurer, that the table used by Slade was a trick-table was disproved by the evidence of the workman who made it. This table can now be seen at the offices of the London Spiritualist Alliance, and one marvels at the audacity of a witness who could imperil another man's liberty by so false a statement, which must have powerfully affected the course of the trial. Indeed, in the face of the evidence of Ray Lankester, Donkin, and Maskelyne, it is hard to see how Mr. Flowers could fail to convict, for he would say with truth and reason, "What is before the Court is not what has happened upon other occasions—however convincing these eminent witnesses may be—but what occurred upon this particular occasion, and here we have two witnesses on one side and only the prisoner on the other." The "trick-table" probably settled the matter.

Slade was sentenced, under the Vagrancy Act, to three months' imprisonment with hard labour. An appeal was lodged and he was released on bail. When the appeal came to be heard, the conviction was quashed on a technical point. It may be pointed out that though he escaped on a technical point, namely, that the words " by palmistry or otherwise " which appeared in the statute had been omitted, it must not be assumed that had the technical point failed he might not have escaped on the merits of his case. Slade, whose health had been seriously affected by the strain of the trial, left England for the Continent a day or two later. From the Hague, after a rest of a few months, Slade wrote to Professor Lankester offering to return to London and to give him exhaustive private tests on condition that he could come without molestation. He received no answer to his suggestion, which surely is not that of a guilty man.

An illuminated testimonial to Slade from London Spiritualists in 1877 sets out:—

In view of the deplorable termination of Henry Slade's visit to this country, we the undersigned desire to place on record our high opinion of his mediumship, and our reprobation of the treatment he has undergone.

We regard Henry Slade as one of the most valuable Test Mediums now living. The phenomena which occur in his presence are evolved with a rapidity and regularity rarely equalled. . . .

He leaves us not only untarnished in reputation by the late proceedings in our Law Courts, but with a mass of testimony in his favour which could probably have been elicited in no other way.

This is signed by Mr. Alexander Calder (President of the British National Association of Spiritualists) and a number of representative Spiritualists. Unhappily, however, it is the Noes, not the Ayes, which have the ear of the Press, and even now, fifty years later, it would be hard to find a paper enlightened enough to do the man justice.

Spiritualists, however, showed great energy in supporting Slade. Before the trial a Defence Fund was raised, and Spiritualists in America drew up a memorial to the American Minister in London. Between the Bow Street conviction and the hearing of the appeal, a memorial was sent to the Home Secretary protesting against the action of the Government in conducting the prosecution on appeal. Copies of this were sent to all the members of the Legislature, to all the Middlesex magistrates, to various members of the Royal Society, and of other public bodies. Miss Kislingbury, the secretary to the National Association of Spiritualists, forwarded a copy to the Queen.

After giving successful séances at the Hague, Slade went to Berlin in November, 1877, where he created the keenest interest. He was said to know no German, yet messages in German appeared on the slates, and were written in the characters of the fifteenth century. The *Berliner Fremdenblatt* of November 10, 1877, wrote: " Since the arrival of Mr. Slade at the Kronprinz Hotel the greater portion of the educated world of Berlin has been suffering from an epidemic which we may term a Spiritualistic fever." Describing his experiences in Berlin, Slade said that he began by fully converting the landlord of the hotel, using the latter's slates and tables in his own house. The landlord invited the Chief of Police and many prominent citizens of Berlin to witness the manifestations, and they expressed themselves as satisfied.

Slade writes: " Samuel Bellachini, Court Conjurer to the Emperor of Germany, had a week's experience with me free of charge. I gave him from two to three séances a day and one of them at his own house. After his full and complete investigation, he went to a public notary and made oath that the phenomena were genuine and not trickery."

Bellachini's declaration on oath, which has been published, bears out this statement. He says that after the minutest investigation he considers any explanation by conjuring to be " absolutely impossible." The conduct of conjurers seems to have been usually determined by a sort of trade union jealousy, as if the results of the medium were some sort of breach of a monopoly, but this enlightened German, together with Houdin, Kellar, and a few more, have shown a more open mind.

A visit to Denmark followed, and in December began the historic séances with Professor Zöllner, at Leipzig. A full account of these will be found in Zöllner's " Transcendental Physics," which has been translated by Mr. C. C. Massey. Zöllner was Professor of Physics and Astronomy in the University of Leipzig, and associated with him in the experiments with Slade were other scientific men, including William Edward Weber, Professor of Physics; Professor Scheibner, a distinguished mathematician; Gustave Theodore Fechner, Professor of Physics and an eminent natural philosopher, who were all, says Professor Zöllner, " perfectly convinced of the reality of the observed facts, altogether excluding imposture or prestidigitation." The phenomena in question included, among other things, " the production of true knots in an endless string, the rending of Professor Zöllner's bed-screen, the disappearance of a small table and its subsequent descent from the ceiling in *full light*, in a private house and under the observed conditions, of which the most noticeable is the apparent passivity of Dr. Slade during all these occurrences."

Certain critics have tried to indicate what they consider insufficient precautions observed in these experiments. Dr. J. Maxwell, the acute French critic, makes an excellent reply to such objections. He points out* that because skilled and conscientious psychic investigators have omitted to indicate explicitly in their reports that every hypothesis of fraud has been studied and dismissed, in the belief that " their implicit affirmation of the reality of the fact appeared sufficient to them," and in order to prevent their reports from being too unwieldy, yet captious critics do not hesitate to condemn them and to suggest possibilities of fraud which are quite inadmissible under the observed conditions.

Zöllner gave a dignified reply to the supposition that he was tricked in these cord-tying experiments: " If, nevertheless, the foundation of this fact, deduced by me on the ground of an enlarged conception of space, should be denied, only one other kind of explanation would remain, arising from a moral code of consideration that at present, it is true, is quite customary. This explanation would consist in the pre-

* " Metapsychical Phenomena " (Translation, 1905), p. 405.

sumption that I myself and the honourable men and citizens of Leipzig, in whose presence several of these cords were sealed, were either common impostors, or were not in possession of our sound senses sufficient to perceive if Mr. Slade himself, before the cords were sealed, had tied them in knots. The discussion, however, of such a hypothesis would no longer belong to the dominion of science, but would fall under the category of social decency." *

As a sample of the reckless statements of opponents of Spiritualism, it may be mentioned that Mr. Joseph McCabe, who is second only to the American Houdini for wild inaccuracies, speaks† of Zöllner as " an elderly and purblind professor," whereas he died in 1882, in his forty-eighth year, and his experiments with Slade were carried out in 1877–78, when this distinguished scientist was in the vigour of his intellectual life.

So far have opponents pushed their enmity that it has even been stated that Zöllner was deranged, and that his death which occurred some years later was accompanied with cerebral weakness. An inquiry from Dr. Funk set this matter at rest, though it is unfortunately easy to get libels of this sort into circulation and very difficult to get the contradictions. Here is the document :‡

Your letter addressed to the Rector of the University, October 20, 1903, received. The Rector of this University was installed here after the death of Zöllner, and had

* Massey's Zöllner, pp. 20–21.
† " Spiritualism. A Popular History from 1847," p. 161.
‡ " The Widow's Mite," p. 276.

no personal acquaintance with him ; but information received from Zöllner's colleagues states that during his entire studies at the University here, until his death, he was of sound mind ; moreover, in the best of health. The cause of his death was a hæmorrhage of the brain on the morning of April 25th, 1882, while he was at breakfast with his mother, and from which he died shortly after. It is true that Professor Zöllner was an ardent believer in Spiritualism, and as such was in close relations with Slade.

> (Dr.) KARL BUCHER, Professor of Statistics
> and National Economy at the University.

The tremendous power which occasionally manifests itself when the conditions are favourable was shown once in the presence of Zöllner, Weber, and Scheibner, all three professors of the University. There was a strong wooden screen on one side of the room:

A violent crack was suddenly heard as in the discharging of a large battery of Leyden jars. On turning with some alarm in the direction of the sound, the before-mentioned screen fell apart in two pieces. The strong wooden screws, half an inch thick, were torn from above and below, without any visible contact of Slade with the screen. The parts broken were at least five feet removed from Slade, who had his back to the screen ; but even if he had intended to tear it down by a cleverly devised sideward motion, it would have been necessary to fasten it on the opposite side. As it was, the screen stood quite unattached, and the grain of the wood being parallel to the axis of the cylindrical wooden fastenings, the wrenching asunder could only be accomplished by a force acting longitudinally to the part in question. We were all astonished at this unexpected and violent manifestation of mechanical force, and asked Slade what it all meant ; but he only shrugged his shoulders, saying that such phenomena occasionally, though somewhat rarely, occurred in his presence. As he spoke, he placed, while still standing, a piece of slate-pencil on the polished surface of the table, laid over it a slate, purchased and just cleaned by myself, and pressed the five spread fingers of his right hand on the upper surface of the slate, while his left hand rested on the centre of the table. Writing began on the inner surface of the slate, and when Slade turned it up, the following sentence was written in English : " It was not our intention to do harm. Forgive what has happened." We were the more surprised at the production of the writing under these circumstances, for we particularly observed that both Slade's hands remained quite motionless while the writing was going on.*

In his desperate attempt to explain this incident, Mr. McCabe says that no doubt the screen was broken before and fastened together afterwards with thread. There is truly no limit to the credulity of the incredulous.

After a very successful series of séances in St. Petersburg, Slade returned to London for a few days in 1878, and then proceeded to Australia. An interesting account of his work there is to be found in Mr. James Curtis's book, " Rustlings in the Golden City." Then he returned to America. In 1885 he appeared before the Seybert Commission in Philadelphia, and in 1887 again visited England under the name of " Dr. Wilson," though it was well known who he was. Presumably his *alias* was due to a fear that the old proceedings would be renewed.

* "Transcendental Physics," pp. 34, 35.

At most of his séances, Slade exhibited clairvoyant powers, and materialized hands were a familiar occurrence. In Australia, where psychic conditions are good, he had materializations. Mr. Curtis says that the medium objected to sitting for this form of manifestation, because it left him weak for a time, and because he preferred to give séances in the light. He consented, however, to try with Mr. Curtis, who thus describes what took place at Ballarat, in Victoria:

Our first test of spirit appearance in the form took place at Lester's Hotel. I placed the table about four or five feet from the west wall of the room. Mr. Slade sat at the end of the table furthest from the wall, whilst I took my position on the north side. The gaslight was toned down, not so much but that any object in the room could be clearly seen. Our hands were placed over one another in a single pile. We sat very still about ten minutes, when I observed something like a little misty cloud between myself and the wall. When my attention was first drawn towards this phenomenon, it was about the size and colour of a gentleman's high-crowned, whitish-grey felt hat. This cloud-like appearance rapidly grew and became transformed, when we saw before us a woman—a lady. The being thus fashioned, and all but perfected, rose from the floor on to the top of the table, where I could most distinctly observe the configuration. The arms and hands were elegantly shaped ; the forehead, mouth, nose, cheeks, and beautiful brown hair showed harmoniously, each part in concord with the whole. Only the eyes were veiled because they could not be completely materialized. The feet were encased in white satin shoes. The dress glowed in light, and was the most beautiful I ever beheld, the colour being bright, sheeny silvery grey, or greyish shining white. The whole figure was graceful, and the drapery perfect. The materialized spirit glided and walked about, causing the table to shake, vibrate, jerk and tilt considerably. I could hear, too, the rustling of the dress as the celestial visitant transiently wended from one position or place to another. The spirit form, within two feet of our unmoved hands, still piled up together in a heap, then dissolved, and gradually faded from our vision.

The conditions at this beautiful séance—with the medium's hands held throughout, and with enough light for visibility—seem satisfactory, provided we grant the honesty of the witness. As the preface contains the supporting testimony of a responsible Australian Government official, who also speaks of Mr. Curtis's initial extremely sceptical state of mind, we may well do so. At the same séance a quarter of an hour later the figure again appeared:

The apparition then floated in the air and alighted on the table, rapidly glided about, and thrice bent her beautiful figure with graceful bows, each bending deliberate and low, the head coming within six inches of my face. The dress rustled (as silk rustles) with every movement. The face was partially veiled as before. The visibility then became invisible, slowly disappearing like the former materialization.

Other similar séances are described.

In view of the many elaborate and stringent tests through which he passed successfully, the story of Slade's " exposure " in America in 1886 is not convincing, but we refer to it for historical reasons, and to show that such incidents are not excluded from our review of the subject. The *Boston Herald*, February 2, 1886, heads its account, " The celebrated Dr. Slade comes to grief in Weston, W. Na., writes upon slates which lie upon his knees under the table, and moves tables and chairs with his toes." Observers in an adjoining room, looking through the crevice under the door saw these feats of agility being performed by the medium, though those present in the room with him were unaware of them. There seems, however, to have been in this as in other cases, occurrences which bore the appearance of fraud, and Spiritualists were among those who denounced him. At a subsequent public performance for "Direct Spirit Writing" in the Justice Hall, Weston, Mr. E. S. Barrett, described as a "Spiritualist," came forward and explained how Slade's imposture had been detected. Slade, who was asked to speak, appeared dumbfounded, and could only say, according to the report, that if his accusers had been deceived he had been equally so, for if the deceit had been done by him, it had been without his consciousness.

Mr. J. Simmons, Slade's business manager, made a frank statement which seems to point to the operation of ectoplasmic limbs, as years later was proved to be the case with the famous Italian medium, Eusapia Palladino. He says: "I do not doubt that these gentlemen saw what they assert they did; but I am convinced at the same time that Slade is as innocent of what he is accused of as you (the editor) yourself would have been under similar circumstances. But I know that my explanation would have no weight in a court of justice. I myself saw a hand, which I could have sworn to be that of Slade, if it had been possible for his hand to be in that position. While one of his hands lay upon the table and the other held the slate under the corner of the table, a third hand appeared with a clothes-brush (which a moment previously had brushed against me from the knee upwards) in the middle of the opposite edge of the table, which was forty-two inches long." Slade and his manager were arrested and released on bail, but no further proceedings seem to have been taken against them. Truesdell, also, in his book, " Spiritualism, Bottom Facts," states that he saw Slade effecting the movement of objects with his foot, and he asks his readers to believe that the medium made to him a full confession of how all his manifestations were produced. If Slade ever really did this, it may probably be accounted for by a burst of ill-timed levity on his part in seeking to fool a certain type of investigator by giving him exactly what he was seeking for. To such instances we may apply the judgment of Professor Zöllner on the Lankester incident: " The physical facts observed by us in so astonishing a variety in his presence negatived on every reasonable ground the supposition that he in one solitary case had taken refuge in wilful imposture." He adds, what was certainly the case in that particular instance, that Slade was the victim of his accuser's and his judge's limited knowledge.

At the same time there is ample evidence that Slade degenerated in general character towards the latter part of his life. Promiscuous sittings with a mercenary object, the subsequent exhaustions, and the alcoholic stimulus which affords a temporary relief, all

acting upon a most sensitive organization, had a dele-
terious effect. This weakening of character, with a
corresponding loss of health, may have led to a
diminution of his psychic powers, and increased the
temptation to resort to trickery. Making every allow-
ance for the difficulty of distinguishing what is fraud
and what is of crude psychic origin, an unpleasant
impression is left upon the mind by the evidence
given in the Seybert Commission and by the fact that
Spiritualists upon the spot should have condemned his
action. Human frailty, however, is one thing and
psychic power is another. Those who seek evidence
for the latter will find ample in those years when the
man and his powers were both at their zenith.

Slade died in 1905 at a Michigan sanatorium to
which he had been sent by the American Spiritualists,
and the announcement was followed by the customary
sort of comment in the London Press. The *Star*,
which has an evil tradition in psychic matters, printed
a sensational article headed " Spook Swindles," giving
a garbled account of the Lankester prosecution at Bow
Street. Referring to this, *Light* says : *

Of course, this whole thing is a hash of ignorance,
unfairness and prejudice. We do not care to discuss it
or to controvert it. It would be useless to do so for the
sake of the unfair, the ignorant, and the prejudiced, and it
is not necessary for those who know. Suffice it to say
that the *Star* only supplies one more instance of the difficulty of getting all the facts before the public ; but the
prejudiced newspapers have themselves to blame for their
ignorance or inaccuracy.

* 1886, p. 433.

DR. MONCK

It is the story of the Davenport Brothers and Maskelyne over again.

If Slade's career is difficult to appraise, and if one is forced to admit that while there was an overpowering preponderance of psychic results, there was also a residuum which left the unpleasant impression that the medium might supplement truth with fraud, the same admission must be made in the case of the medium Monck, who played a considerable part for some years in the 'seventies. Of all mediums none is more difficult to appraise, for on the one hand many of his results are beyond all dispute, while in a few there seems to be an absolute certainty of dishonesty. In his case, as in Slade's, there were physical causes which would account for a degeneration of the moral and psychic powers.

Monck was a Nonconformist clergyman, a favourite pupil of the famous Spurgeon. According to his own account, he had been subject from childhood to psychic influences, which increased with his growth. In 1873 he announced his adhesion to Spiritualism and gave an address in the Cavendish Rooms. Shortly afterwards he began to give demonstrations, which appear to have been unpaid and were given in light. In 1875 he made a tour through England and Scotland, his performances exciting much attention and debate, and in 1876 he visited Ireland, where his powers were directed towards healing. Hence he was usually known as " Dr." Monck, a fact which naturally aroused some protest from the medical profession.

Dr. Alfred Russel Wallace, a most competent and honest observer, has given an account of a materialization séance with Monck which appears to be as critic-proof as such a thing could be. No subsequent suspicion or conviction can ever eliminate such an incontrovertible instance of psychic power. It is to be noted how far the effects were in agreement with the subsequent demonstrations of ectoplasmic outflow in the case of Eva and other modern mediums. Dr. Wallace's companions upon this occasion were Mr. Stainton Moses and Mr. Hensleigh Wedgwood. Dr. Wallace writes:

It was a bright summer afternoon, and everything happened in the full light of day. After a little conversation, Monck, who was dressed in the usual clerical black, appeared to go into a trance ; then stood up a few feet in front of us, and after a little while pointed to his side, saying, "Look."

We saw there a faint white patch on his coat on the left side. This grew brighter, then seemed to flicker and extend both upwards and downwards, till very gradually it formed a cloudy pillar extending from his shoulder to his feet and close to his body.

Dr. Wallace goes on to describe how the cloudy figure finally assumed the form of a thickly draped woman, who, after a brief space, appeared to be absorbed into the body of the medium.

He adds: "The whole process of the formation of a shrouded figure was seen in full daylight."

Mr. Wedgwood assured him that he had had even more remarkable manifestations of this kind with

Monck, when the medium was in a deep trance, and in full view.

It is quite impossible after such evidence to doubt the powers of the medium at that time. Archdeacon Colley, who had seen similar exhibitions, offered a prize of a thousand pounds to Mr. J. N. Maskelyne, the famous conjurer, if he could duplicate the performance. This challenge was accepted by Mr. Maskelyne, but the evidence showed that the imitation bore no relation to the original. He attempted to gain a decision in the courts, but the verdict was against him.

It is interesting to compare the account given by Russel Wallace and the experience later of a well-known American, Judge Dailey. This gentleman wrote : *

Glancing at Dr. Monck's side we observed what looked like an opalescent mass of compact steam emerging from just below his heart on the left side. It increased in volume, rising up and extending downward, the upper portions taking the form of a child's head, the face being distinguished as that of a little child I had lost some twenty years previously. It only remained in this form for a moment, and then suddenly disappeared, seeming to be instantly absorbed into the Doctor's side. This remarkable phenomenon was repeated four or five times, in each instance the materialization being more distinct than the preceding one. This was witnessed by all in the room, with gas burning sufficiently bright for every object in the room to be plainly visible.

It was a phenomenon seldom to be seen, and has enabled all who saw it to vouch for, not only the remarkable power possessed by Dr. Monck as a materializing medium, but

* *Banner of Light*, Dec. 15, 1881.

as to the wonderful manner in which a spirit draws out this position our hands were never moved till I untied the slates to ascertain the result.

Surely it is vain after such testimony to deny that Monck had, indeed, great psychic powers.

Apart from materializations Dr. Monck was a remarkable slate-writing medium. Dr. Russel Wallace in a letter to the *Spectator* * says that with Monck at a private house in Richmond he cleaned two slates, and after placing a fragment of pencil between them, tied them together tightly with a strong cord, lengthways and crosswise, in a manner that prevented any movement.

· I then laid them flat on the table without losing sight of them for an instant. Dr. Monck placed the fingers of both hands on them, while I and a lady sitting opposite placed our hands on the corners of the slates. From this position our hands were never moved till I untied the slates to ascertain the result.

Monck asked Wallace to name a word to be written on the slate. He chose the word " God " and in answer to a request decided that it should be lengthways on the slate. The sound of writing was heard, and when the medium's hands were withdrawn, Dr. Wallace opened the slates and found on the lower one the word he had asked for and written in the manner requested.

Dr. Wallace says :

The essential features of this experiment are that I myself cleaned and tied up the slates; that I kept my hands

* Oct. 7, 1877.

ALFRED RUSSEL WALLACE

on them all the time ; that they never went out of my sight
for a moment ; and that I named the word to be written,
and the manner of writing it after they were thus secured
and held by me.

Mr. Edward T. Bennett, assistant secretary to the
Society for Psychical Research, adds to this account:
" I was present on this occasion, and certify that
Mr. Wallace's account of what happened is correct."

Another good test is described by Mr. W. P.
Adshead, of Belper, a well-known investigator, who
says of a séance held in Derby on September 18,
1876:

There were eight persons present, three ladies and
five gentlemen. A lady whom Dr. Monck had never
before seen had a slate passed to her by a sitter, which she
examined and found clean. The slate pencil which was on
the table a few minutes before we sat down could not be
found. An investigator suggested that it would be a good
test if a lead pencil were used.

Accordingly a lead pencil was put on the slate, and the
lady held both under the table. The sound of writing
was instantly heard, and in a few seconds a communication had been written filling one side of the slate. The
writing was done in lead, and was very small and neat, and
alluded to a strictly private matter.

Here were three tests at once. (1) Writing was obtained without the medium (or any other person but the
lady), touching the slate from first to last. (2) It was
written with lead pencil at the spontaneous suggestion of
another stranger. (3) It gave an important test communication regarding a matter that was strictly private.
Dr. Monck did not so much as touch the slate from first
to last.

Mr. Adshead also speaks of physical phenomena occurring freely with this medium when his hands were closely confined in an apparatus called the " stocks," which did not permit movement of even an inch in any direction.

In the year 1876 the Slade trial was going on in London, as already described, and exposures were in the air. In considering the following rather puzzling and certainly suspicious case, one has to remember that when a man who is a public performer, a conjurer or a mesmerist, can pose as having exposed a medium, he wins a valuable public advertisement and attracts to himself all that very numerous section of the community who desire to see such an exposure. It is only fair to bear this in mind in endeavouring to hold the scales fair where there is a conflict of evidence.

In this case the conjurer and mesmerist was one Lodge, and the occasion was a séance held at Huddersfield on November 3, 1876. Mr. Lodge suddenly demanded that the medium be searched. Monck, whether dreading assault or to save himself exposure, ran upstairs and locked himself in his room. He then let himself down from his window and made for the police office, where he lodged a complaint as to his treatment. The door of his bedroom had been forced and his effects searched, with the result that a pair of stuffed gloves was found. Monck asserted that these gloves had been made for a lecture in which he had exposed the difference between conjuring and mediumship. Still, as a Spiritualist paper remarked at the time:

DR. MONCK

The phenomena of his mediumship do not rest on his probity at all. If he were the greatest rogue and the most accomplished conjurer rolled into one, it would not account for the manifestations which have been reported of him.

Monck was sentenced to three months' imprisonment, and is alleged to have made a confession to Mr. Lodge.

After his release from prison Monck held a number of test sittings with Stainton Moses, at which remarkable phenomena occurred.

Light comments:

Those whose names we have mentioned as testifying to the genuineness of Dr. Monck's mediumship are well known to the older Spiritualists as keen and scrupulously cautious experimenters, and Mr. Hensleigh Wedgwood's name carried much weight, as he was known as a man of science and was brother-in-law of Charles Darwin.

There is an element of doubt about the Huddersfield case, as the accuser was by no means an impartial person, but Sir William Barrett's testimony makes it clear that Monck did sometimes descend to deliberate and cold-blooded trickery. Sir William writes:

I caught the " Dr." in a gross bit of fraud, a piece of white muslin on a wire frame with a black thread attached, being used by the medium to simulate a partially materialized spirit.*

Such an exposure, coming from so sure a source, arouses a feeling of disgust which urges one to throw the whole evidence concerning the man into the wastepaper basket. One must, however, be patient

* S.P.R. *Proceedings*, Vol. IV, p. 38 (footnote).

and reasonable in such matters. Monck's earlier séances, as has been clearly shown, were in good light, and any such clumsy mechanism was out of the question. We must not argue that because a man once forges, therefore he has never signed an honest cheque in his life. But we must clearly admit that Monck was capable of fraud, that he would take the easier way when things were difficult, and that each of his manifestations should be carefully checked.

CHAPTER XIV

COLLECTIVE INVESTIGATIONS OF SPIRITUALISM

SEVERAL committees have at different times sat upon the subject of Spiritualism. Of these the two most important are that of the Dialectical Society in 1869–70, and the Seybert Commission in 1884, the first British and the second American. To these may be added that of the French society, Institut Général Psychologique in 1905–8. In spite of the intervals between these various investigations, it will be convenient to treat them in a single chapter as certain remarks in common apply to each of them.

There are obvious difficulties in the way of collective investigations—difficulties which are so grave that they are almost insurmountable. When a Crookes or a Lombroso explores the subject he either sits alone with the medium, or he has with him others whose knowledge of psychic conditions and laws may be helpful in the matter. This is not usually so with these committees. They fail to understand that they are themselves part of the experiment, and that it is possible for them to create such intolerable vibrations, and to surround themselves with so negative an atmosphere, that these outside forces, which are governed by very definite laws, are unable to penetrate it. It is not in vain that the three words " with one accord " are interpolated into the account of the apostolic sitting in the upper room. If a small piece of metal may upset a whole magnetic installation, so a strong adverse psychic current may ruin a psychic circle. It is for this reason, and not on account of any superior credulity, that practising Spiritualists continually get such results as are never attained by mere researchers. This also may be the reason why the one committee upon which Spiritualists were fairly well represented was the one which gained the most positive results. This was the committee which was chosen by the Dialectical Society of London, a committee which began its explorations early in 1869 and presented its report in 1871. If common sense and the ordinary laws of evidence had been followed in the reception of this report, the progress of psychic truth would have been accelerated by fifty years.

Thirty-four gentlemen of standing were appointed upon this committee, the terms of reference being " to investigate the phenomena alleged to be spiritual manifestations." The majority of the members were certainly in the mood to unmask an imposture, but they encountered a body of evidence which could not be disregarded, and they ended by asserting that " the subject is worthy of more serious attention and careful investigation than it has hitherto received." This conclusion so amazed the society which they represented that they could not get it to publish the findings, so the committee in a spirited way published them at their own cost, thus giving permanent record to a most interesting investigation.

The members of the committee were drawn from many varied professions and included a doctor of divinity, two physicians, two surgeons, two civil engineers, two fellows of scientific societies, two barristers, and others of repute. Charles Bradlaugh the Rationalist was a member. Professor Huxley and G. H. Lewes, the consort of George Eliot, were invited to co-operate, but both refused, Huxley stating in his reply that " supposing the phenomena to be genuine, they do not interest me "—a dictum which showed that this great and clear-headed man had his limitations.

The six sub-committees sat forty times under test conditions, often without the aid of a professional medium, and with a full sense of responsibility they agreed that the following points appeared to have been established :

" 1. That sounds of a very varied character, apparently proceeding from articles of furniture, the floor and walls of the room—the vibrations accompanying which sounds are often distinctly perceptible to the touch—occur, without being produced by muscular action or mechanical contrivance.

" 2. That movements of heavy bodies take place without mechanical contrivance of any kind or adequate exertion of muscular force by the persons present, and frequently without contact or connexion with any person.

" 3. That these sounds and movements often occur at the times and in the manner asked for by persons present, and, by means of a simple code of signals, answer questions and spell out coherent communications.

" 4. That the answers and communications thus obtained are, for the most part, of a commonplace character ; but facts are sometimes correctly given which are only known to one of the persons present.

" 5. That the circumstances under which the phenomena occur are variable, the most prominent fact being that the presence of certain persons seems necessary to their occurrence, and that of others generally adverse ; but this difference does not appear to depend upon any belief or disbelief concerning the phenomena.

" 6. That, nevertheless, the occurrence of the phenomena is not ensured by the presence or absence of such persons respectively."

The report briefly summarizes as follows the oral and written evidence received, which not only testifies to phenomena of the same nature as those witnessed by the sub-committees, but to others of a more varied and extraordinary character:

" 1. Thirteen witnesses state that they have seen heavy bodies—in some instances men—rise slowly in the air and remain there for some time without visible or tangible support.

" 2. Fourteen witnesses testify to having seen hands or figures, not appertaining to any human being, but lifelike in appearance and mobility, which they have sometimes touched or even grasped, and which they are therefore convinced were not the result of imposture or illusion.

" 3. Five witnesses state that they have been touched by some invisible agency on various parts of the body, and often where requested, when the hands of all present were visible.

" 4. Thirteen witnesses declare that they have heard musical pieces well played upon instruments not manipulated by any ascertainable agency.

" 5. Five witnesses state that they have seen red-hot coals applied to the hands or heads of several persons without producing pain or scorching, and three witnesses state that they have had the same experiment made upon themselves with the like immunity.

" 6. Eight witnesses state that they have received precise information through rappings, writings, and in other ways, the accuracy of which was unknown at the time to themselves or to any persons present, and which on subsequent inquiry was found to be correct.

" 7. One witness declares that he has received a precise and detailed statement which, nevertheless, proved to be entirely erroneous.

" 8. Three witnesses state that they have been present when drawings, both in pencil and colours, were produced in so short a time, and under such conditions as to render human agency impossible.

" 9. Six witnesses declare that they have received information of future events, and that in some cases the hour and minute of their occurrence have been accurately foretold, days and even weeks before."

In addition to the above, evidence was given of trance-speaking, of healing, of automatic writing, of the introduction of flowers and fruits into closed rooms, of voices in the air, of visions in crystals and glasses, and of the elongation of the human body.

The report closes with the following observations:

In presenting their report, your Committee, taking into consideration the high character and great intelligence of many of the witnesses to the more extraordinary facts, the extent to which their testimony is supported by the reports of the sub-committees, and the absence of any proof of imposture or delusion as regards a large portion of the phenomena ; and further, having regard to the exceptional character of the phenomena, the large number of persons in every grade of society and over the whole civilized world who are more or less influenced by a belief in their supernatural origin, and to the fact that no philosophical explanation of them has yet been arrived at, deem it incumbent upon them to state their conviction that the subject is worthy of more serious attention and careful investigation than it has hitherto received.

Among those who gave evidence. or read papers before the committee were: Dr. Alfred Russel Wallace, Mrs. Emma Hardinge, Mr. H. D. Jencken, Mr. Benjamin Coleman, Mr. Cromwell F. Varley, Mr. D. D. Home, and the Master of Lindsay. Correspondence was received from Lord Lytton, Mr. Robert Chambers, Dr. Garth Wilkinson, Mr. William Howitt, M. Camille Flammarion, and others.

The committee was successful in procuring the evidence of believers in the phenomena, but almost wholly failed, as stated in its report, to obtain evidence from those who attributed them to fraud or delusion.

In the records of the evidence of over fifty witnesses, there is voluminous testimony to the existence of the facts from men and women of good standing. One witness * considered that the most remarkable phenomenon brought to light by the labours of the committee was the extraordinary number of eminent men who were shown to be firm believers in the Spiritual hypothesis. And another † declared that whatever agencies might be employed in these manifestations, they were not to be explained by referring them to imposture on the one side or hallucination on the other.

An interesting sidelight on the growth of the movement is obtained from Mrs. Emma Hardinge's statement that at that time (1869) she knew only two professional mediums in London, though she was acquainted with several non-professional ones. As she

* Grattan Geary.   † E. L. Blanchard.

herself was a medium she was probably correct in what she said. Mr. Cromwell Varley averred that there were probably not more than a hundred known mediums in the whole kingdom, and he added that very few of those were well developed. We have here conclusive testimony to the great work accomplished in England by D. D. Home, for the bulk of the converts were due to his mediumship. Another medium who played an important part was Mrs. Marshall. Many witnesses spoke of evidential sittings they had attended at her house. Mr. William Howitt, the well-known author, was of opinion that Spiritualism had then received the assent of about twenty millions of people in all countries after personal examination.

What may be called the evidence for the opposition was not at all formidable. Lord Lytton said that in his experience the phenomena were traceable to material influences of whose nature we were ignorant, Dr. Carpenter brought out his pet hobby of " unconscious cerebration." Dr. Kidd thought that the majority were evidently subjective phenomena, and three witnesses, while convinced of the genuineness of the occurrences, ascribed them to Satanic agency. These objections were well answered by Mr. Thomas Shorter, author of " Confessions of a Truth Seeker," and secretary of the Working Men's College, in an admirable review of the report in *The Spiritual Magazine.**

It is worthy of note that on the publication of this important and well-considered report it was ridiculed

* 1872, pp. 3–15.

by a large part of the London Press. An honourable exception was the *Spectator*.

The Times reviewer considered it " nothing more than a farrago of impotent conclusions, garnished by a mass of the most monstrous rubbish it has ever been our misfortune to sit in judgment upon."

The *Morning Post* said: " The report which has been published is entirely worthless."

The *Saturday Review* hoped that report would involuntarily lead " to discrediting a little further one of the most unequivocally degrading superstitions that have ever found currency among reasonable beings."

The *Standard* made a sound criticism that deserves to be remembered. Objecting to the remark of those who do not believe in Spiritualism, yet say that there may be " something in it," the newspaper sagely observes: " If there is anything whatever in it beyond imposture and imbecility, there is the whole of another world in it."

The *Daily News* regarded the report as "an important contribution to the literature of a subject which, some day or other, by the very number of its followers, will demand more extended investigation."

The *Spectator*, after describing the book as an extremely curious one, added: " Few, however, could read the mass of evidence collected in this volume, showing the firm faith in the reality of the alleged spiritual phenomena possessed by a number of individuals of honourable and upright character, without also agreeing with Mr. Jeffrey's opinion, that the remarkable phenomena witnessed, some of which had not been traced to imposture or delusion, and the gathered testimony of respectable witnesses, 'justify the recommendation of the subject to further cautious investigation.'"

These are but brief extracts from longer notices in a few of the London newspapers—there were many others—and, bad as they are, they none the less indicate a change of attitude on the part of the Press, which had been in the habit of ignoring the subject altogether.

It must be remembered that the report concerned itself only with the phenomenal aspect of Spiritualism, and this, in the opinion of leading Spiritualists, is decidedly the less important side. Only in the report of one sub-committee is it recorded that the general gist of the messages was that physical death was a trivial matter in retrospect, but that for the spirit it was a rebirth into new experiences of existence, that spirit life was in every respect human ; that friendly intercourse was as common and pleasurable as in life ; that although spirits took great interest in worldly affairs, they had no wish to return to their former state of existence ; that communication with earth friends was pleasurable and desired by spirits, being intended as a proof to the former of the continuance of life in spite of bodily dissolution, and that spirits claimed no certain prophetic power. These were the main heads of the information received.

It will be generally recognized in the future that, in their day and generation, the Dialectical Society's Committee did excellent work. The great majority of the members were opposed to the psychic claims, but in the face of evidence, with a few exceptions, such as Dr. Edmunds, they yielded to the testimony of their own senses. There were a few examples of intolerance such as Huxley's unhappy dictum, and Charles Bradlaugh's declaration that he would not even examine certain things because they were in the region of the impossible, but on the whole the team work of the sub-committees was excellent.

There appears in the report of the Dialectical Society's Committee a long article by Dr. Edmunds, an opponent to Spiritualism, and to the findings of his colleagues. It is worth reading as typical of a certain class of mind. The worthy doctor, while imagining himself to be impartial, is really so absolutely prejudiced that the conceivable possibility of the phenomena being supernormal never is allowed to enter into his mind. When he sees one with his own eyes his only question is, " How was the trick done ? " If he cannot answer the question he does not consider this to be in favour of some other explanation, but simply records that he cannot discover the trick. Thus his evidence, which is perfectly honest as to fact, records that a number of fresh flowers and fruits, still wet, fell upon the table—a phenomenon of apports which was shown many times by Mrs. Guppy. The doctor's only comment is that they *must* have been taken from the sideboard, although one would have imagined that a large basket of fruit upon the sideboard would have attracted attention, and he does not venture to say that he saw such an object. Again he was shut up with the Davenports in their cabinet and admits that he could make nothing of it, but, of course, it *must* be a conjuring trick. Then when he finds that mediums who perceive that his mental attitude is hopeless refuse to sit with him again, he sets that down also as an evidence of their guilt. There is a certain type of scientific mind which is quite astute within its own subject and, outside it, is the most foolish and illogical thing upon earth.

It was the misfortune of the Seybert Commission, which we will now discuss, that it was entirely composed of such people, with the exception of one Spiritualist, a Mr. Hazard, who was co-opted by them and who had little chance of influencing their general atmosphere of obstruction. The circumstances in which the Commission was appointed were these. A certain Henry Seybert, a citizen of Philadelphia, had left the sum of sixty thousand dollars for the purpose of founding a Chair of Philosophy at the University of Pennsylvania with the condition that the said University should appoint a commission to " make a thorough and impartial investigation of all systems of morals, religion, or philosophy which assume to represent the truth, and particularly of modern Spiritualism." The personnel of the body chosen is immaterial save that all were connected with the University, with Dr. Pepper, the Provost of the University as nominal chairman, Dr. Furness as acting chairman, and Professor Fullerton as secretary. In spite of the fact that the duty of the Commission was to

" make a thorough and impartial investigation " of modern Spiritualism, the preliminary report coolly states :

The Commission is composed of men whose days are already filled with duties which cannot be laid aside, and who are able, therefore, to devote but a small portion of their time to these investigations.

The fact that the members were satisfied to start with this handicap shows how little they understood the nature of the work before them. Their failure, in the circumstances, was inevitable. The proceedings began in March, 1884, and a " preliminary " report, so called, was issued in 1887. This report was, as it proved, the final one, for though it was reissued in 1920 there was no addition save a colourless preface of three paragraphs by a descendant of the former chairman. The gist of this report is that fraud on the one side and credulity on the other make up the whole of Spiritualism, and that there was really nothing serious on which the committee could report. The whole long document is well worth reading by any student of psychic matters. The impression left upon the mind is that the various members of the Commission were in their own limited way honestly endeavouring to get at the facts, but that their minds, like that of Dr. Edmunds, were so formed that when, in spite of their repellent and impossible attitude, some psychic happening did manage to break through their barriers, they would not for an instant consider the possibility that it was genuine, but simply passed it by as if it did not exist. Thus with Mrs. Fox-Kane they did get well-marked raps, and are content with the thousand-times disproved supposition that they came from inside her own body, and they pass without comment the fact that they received from her long messages, written swiftly in script, which could only be read when held to the looking-glass, as it was from right to left. This swiftly-written script contained an abstruse Latin sentence which would appear to be much above the capacity of the medium. All of this was unexplained and ignored.

Again, in reporting upon Mrs. Lord the Commission got the Direct Voice, and also phosphorescent lights after the medium had been searched. We are informed that the medium kept up an " almost continuous clapping of hands," and yet people at a distance from her seem to have been touched. The spirit in which the inquiry is approached may be judged from the remark of the acting chairman to W. M. Keeler, who was said to be a spirit photographer, that he " would not be satisfied with less than a cherub on my head, one on each shoulder, and a full-blown angel on my breast." A Spiritualist would be surprised indeed if an inquirer in so frivolous a mood should be favoured with results. All through runs the fallacy that the medium is producing something as a conjurer does. Never for a moment do they seem to realize that the favour and assent of invisible operators may be essential—operators who may stoop to the humble-minded and shrink away from, or even make game of, the self-sufficient scoffer.

While there were some results which may have

been genuine, but which are brushed aside by the report, there were some episodes which must be painful to the Spiritualist, but which none the less must be faced. The Commission exposed obvious fraud in the case of the slate medium, Mrs. Patterson, and it is impossible to deny that the case against Slade is a substantial one. The latter days of this medium were admittedly under a cloud, and the powers which had once been so conspicuous may have been replaced by trickery. Dr. Furness goes the length of asserting that such trickery was actually admitted, but the anecdote as given in the report rather suggests chaff upon the part of the medium. That Dr. Slade should jovially beckon the doctor in from his open window, and should at once in reply to a facetious remark admit that his own whole life had been a swindle, is more than one can easily believe.

There are some aspects in which the Commission —or some members of it—seem to have been disingenuous. Thus, they state at the beginning that they will rest their report upon their own labours and disregard the mass of material already available. In spite of this, they introduce a long and adverse report from their secretary upon the Zöllner evidence in favour of Slade. This report is quite incorrect in itself, as is shown in the account of Zöllner given in the chapter treating of Slade's experiences in Leipzig. It carefully suppresses the fact that the chief conjurer in Germany, after a considerable investigation, gave a certificate that Slade's phenomena were *not* trickery. On the other hand, when the testimony of a conjurer is against a spiritual explanation, as in the comments of Kellar, it is given in full, with no knowledge, apparently, that in the case of another medium, Eglinton, this same Kellar had declared the results to be beyond his art.

At the opening of the report the Commission says: "We deemed ourselves fortunate at the outset in having as a counsellor the late Mr. Thomas R. Hazard, a personal friend of Mr. Seybert, and widely known throughout the land as an uncompromising Spiritualist." Mr. Hazard evidently knew the importance of ensuring the right conditions and the right type of sitters for such an experimental investigation. Describing an interview he had with Mr. Seybert a few days before the latter's death, when he agreed to act as his representative, Mr. Hazard says he did so only "with the full and distinct understanding that I should be permitted to prescribe the methods to be pursued in the investigation, designate the mediums to be consulted, and reject the attendance of any person or persons whose presence I deemed might conflict with the harmony and good order of the spirit circles." But this representative of Mr. Seybert seems to have been quietly ignored by the University. After the Commission had been sitting for some time, Mr. Hazard was dissatisfied with some of its members and their methods. We find him writing as follows in the Philadelphia *North American*,* presumably after vainly approaching the University authorities :

Without aiming to detract in the slightest degree from

* May 18, 1885.

the unblemished moral character that attaches to each and
every individual of the Faculty, including the Commission,
in public esteem, nor to the high social and literary standing
they occupy in society, I must say that through some strange
infatuation, obliquity of judgment, or perversity of intellect,
the Trustees of the University have placed on the Commission for the investigation of modern Spiritualism, a
majority of its members whose education, habit of thought,
and prejudices so singularly disqualify them from making
a thorough and impartial investigation of the subject which
the Trustees of the University are obligated both by contract and in honour to do, that had the object in view been
to belittle and bring into discredit, hatred and general
contempt the cause that I know the late Henry Seybert
held nearest his heart and loved more than all else in the
world beside, the Trustees could scarcely have selected
more suitable instruments for the object intended from all
the denizens of Philadelphia than are the gentlemen who
constitute a majority of the Seybert Commission. And
this I repeat, not from any causes that affect their moral,
social or literary standing in society, but simply because
of their prejudices against the cause of Spiritualism.

He further advised the Trustees to remove from
the Commission Messrs. Fullerton, Thompson, and
Koenig.

Mr. Hazard quoted Professor Fullerton as saying
in a lecture before the Harvard University Club on
March 3, 1885:

It is possible that the way mediums tell a person's
history is by the process of thought-transference, for every
person who is thus told of these things goes to a medium
thinking of the same points about which the medium talks.
. . . When a man has a cold he hears a buzzing noise in

his ears, and an insane person constantly hears sounds which never occur. Perhaps, then, disease of mind or ear, or some strong emotion, may be the cause of a large number of spiritual phenomena.

These words were spoken after the professor had served on the Commission for more than twelve months.

Mr. Hazard also quotes Dr. George A. Koenig's views, published in the *Philadelphia Press*, about a year after his appointment on the Commission:

I must frankly admit that I am prepared to deny the truth of Spiritualism as it is now popularly understood. It is my belief that all of the so-called mediums are humbugs · without exception. I have never seen Slade perform any of his tricks, but, from the published descriptions, I have set him down as an impostor, the cleverest one of the lot. I do not think the Commission view with much favour the examination of so-called spirit mediums. The wisest men are apt to be deceived. One man in an hour can invent more tricks than a wise man can solve in a year.

Mr. Hazard learned from what he considered to be a reliable source, that Professor Robert E. Thompson was responsible for this view which appeared in *Penn's Monthly* of February, 1880.

Even if Spiritualism be all that its champions claim for it, it has no importance for anyone who holds a Christian faith. . . . The consideration and discussion of the subject is tampering with notions and condescending to discussions with which no Christian believer has any business.

We have in these expressions of opinion a means of judging how unsuited these members of the Com-

mission were for making what Mr. Seybert asked for
—" a thorough and impartial " investigation of the
subject.

An American Spiritualist periodical, the *Banner
of Light*, commenting on Mr. Hazard's communication, wrote :

So far as we have information, no notice was taken
of Mr. Hazard's appeal—certainly no action was had,
for the members above quoted remain on the Commission
to this day, and their names are appended to this preliminary
report. Professor Fullerton, in fact, was and now is the
secretary ; one hundred and twenty of the one hundred and
fifty pages of the volume before us are written by him, and
exhibit that excessive lack of spiritual perception and knowledge of occult, and we might also say natural laws, which
led him to inform an audience of Harvard students that
" when a man has a cold he hears a buzzing noise in his
ears " ; that " an insane person constantly hears sounds
which never occur," and suggest to them that spiritual
phenomena may proceed from such causes.

The *Banner of Light* continues :

We consider that the Seybert Commission's failure to
follow the counsel of Mr. Hazard, as it was plainly their
duty to do, is the key to the entire failure of all their subsequent efforts. The paucity of phenomenal results, in
any degree approaching what might be looked for, even by
a sceptic, which this book records, is certainly remarkable.
It is a report of what was not done, rather than that of what
was. In the memoranda of proceedings at each session,
as given by Professor Fullerton, there is plainly seen a
studied effort to give prominence to everything that a
superficial mind might deem proof of trickery on the part
of the medium, and to conceal all that might be evidence
of the truth of his claims. . . . It is mentioned that when

certain members of the Commission were present all phenomena ceased. This substantiates the correctness of
Mr. Hazard's position ; and there is no one who has had
an experience with mediums, sufficient to render his opinion
of any value, who will not endorse it. The spirits knew
what elements they had to deal with ; they endeavoured
to eliminate those that rendered their experiments nuga-
tory ; they failed to do this through the ignorance, wilful-
ness or prejudice of the Commission, and the experiments
failed ; so the Commission, very " wise in its own conceit,"
decided that all was fraud.

*Light,** in its notice of the report, says what needs
saying as much now as in 1887 :

We notice with some pleasure, though without any
marked expectation of what may result from the pursuance
of bad methods of investigation, that the Commission pro-
poses to continue its quest " with minds as sincerely and
honestly open as heretofore to conviction." Since this is
so, we presume to offer a few words of advice founded
upon large experience. The investigation of these obscure
phenomena is beset with difficulty, and any instructions
that can be given are derived from a knowledge which is
to a great extent empirical. But we know that prolonged
and patient experiment with a properly constituted circle
is a *sine qua non*. We know that all does not depend on
the medium, but that a circle must be formed and varied
from time to time experimentally, until the proper con-
stituent elements are secured. What these elements may
be we cannot tell the Seybert Commission. They must
discover that for themselves. Let them make a study in
the literature of Spiritualism of the varied characteristics
of mediumship before they proceed to personal experiment.
And when they have done this, and perhaps when they have

* 1887, p. 391.

realized how easy it is so to conduct an examination of this nature as to arrive at negative results, they will be in a better position to devote intelligent and patient care to a study which can be profitably conducted in no other way.

There is no doubt that the report of the Seybert Commission set back for the time the cause of psychic truth. Yet the real harm fell upon the learned institution which these gentlemen represented. In these days when ectoplasm, the physical basis of psychic phenomena, has been established beyond a shadow of doubt to all who examine the evidence, it is too late to pretend that there is nothing to be examined. There is now hardly a capital which has not its Psychic Research Society—a final comment upon the inference of the Commission that there was no field for research. If the Seybert Commission had had the effect of Pennsylvania University heading this movement, and living up to the great tradition of Professor Hare, how proud would her final position have been ! As Newton associated Cambridge with the law of gravitation, so Pennsylvania might have been linked to a far more important advance of human knowledge. It was left to several European centres of learning to share the honour among them.

The remaining collective investigation is of less importance, since it deals only with a particular medium. This was conducted by the Institut Général Psychologique in Paris. It consisted of three series of sittings with the famous Eusapia Palladino in the years 1905, 1906, and 1907, the total number of séances being forty-three. No complete list of the sitters is available, nor was there any proper collective report, the only record being a very imperfect and inconclusive one from the secretary, M. Courtier. The investigators included some very distinguished persons, including Charles Richet, Monsieur and Madame Curie, Messrs. Bergson, Perrin, Professor d'Arsonal of the College de France, who was president of the society, Count de Gramont, Professor Charpentier, and Principal Debierne of the Sorbonne. The actual result could not have been disastrous to the medium, since Professor Richet has recorded his endorsement of the reality of her psychic powers, but the strange superficial tricks of Eusapia are recorded in the subsequent account of her career, and we can well imagine the disconcerting effect which they would have upon those to whom such things were new.

There is included in the report a sort of conversation among the sitters in which they talk the matter over, most of them being in a very nebulous and non-committal frame of mind. It cannot be claimed that any new light was shed upon the medium, or any new argument provided either for the sceptic or for the believer. Dr. Geley, however, who has probably gone as deeply as anyone else into psychic science, claims that "les expériences"—he does not say the report—constitute a valuable contribution to the subject.* He bases this upon the fact that the results chronicled do often strikingly confirm those obtained in his own Institut Métapsychique

---

* " L'Ectoplasmie et la Clairvoyance," 1924, p. 402.

working with Kluski, Guzik, and other mediums. The differences, he says, are in details and never in essentials. The control of the hands was the same in either case, both the hands being always held. This was easier in the case of the later mediums, especially with Kluski in trance, while Eusapia was usually a very restless individual. There seems to be a half-way condition which was characteristic of Eusapia, and which has been observed by the author in the case of Frau Silbert, Evan Powell, and other mediums, where the person seems normal, and yet is peculiarly susceptible to suggestion or other mental impressions. A suspicion of fraud may very easily be aroused in this condition, for the general desire on the part of the audience that something should occur reacts with great force upon the unreasoning mind of the medium. An amateur who had some psychic power has assured the author that it needs considerable inhibition to keep such impulses in check and to await the real power from outside. In this report we read: " The two hands, feet, and knees of Eusapia being controlled, the table is raised suddenly, all four feet leaving the ground. Eusapia closes her fists and holds them towards the table, which is then completely raised from the floor five times in succession, five raps being also given. It is again completely raised whilst each of Eusapia's hands is on the head of a sitter. It is raised to a height of one foot from the floor and suspended in the air for seven seconds, while Eusapia kept her hand on the table, and a lighted candle was placed under the table," and so on, with even more conclusive tests with table and other phenomena.

The timidity of the report was satirized by the great French Spiritualist, Gabriel Delanne. He says:

> The reporter keeps saying " it seems " and " it appears," like a man who is not sure of what he is relating. Those who held forty-three séances, with good eyes and apparatus for verification, ought to have a settled opinion—or, at least, to be able to say, if they regard a certain phenomenon as fraudulent, that at a given séance they had seen the medium in the act of tricking. But there is nothing of the sort. The reader is left in uncertainty—a vague suspicion hovers over everything, though not supported on any serious grounds.

Commenting on this, *Light* says : *

> Delanne shows by extracts from the Report itself that some of the experiments succeeded even when the fullest test precautions were taken, such as using lamp-black to discover whether Eusapia really touched the objects moved. Yet the Report deliberately discounts these direct and positive observations by instancing cases occurring *at other times and places* in which Eusapia was *said* or *believed* to have unduly influenced the phenomena.
>
> The Courtier Report will prove more and more plainly to be what we have already called it, a " monument of ineptitude," and the reality of Eusapia's phenomena cannot be seriously called in question by the meaningless phrases with which it is liberally garnished.

What may be called a collective investigation of a medium, Mrs. Crandon, the wife of a doctor in

* 1909, p. 356.

Boston, was undertaken in the years 1923 to 1925 by a committee chosen by the *Scientific American* and afterwards by a small committee of Harvard men with Dr. Shapley, the astronomer, at their head. The controversy over these inquiries is still raging, and the matter has been referred to in the chapter which deals with great modern mediums. It may briefly be stated that of the *Scientific American* inquirers the secretary, Mr. Malcolm Bird, and Dr. Hereward Carrington announced their complete conversion. The others gave no clear decision which involved the humiliating admission that after numerous sittings under their own conditions and in the presence of constant phenomena, they could not tell whether they were being cheated or not. The defect of the committee was that no experienced Spiritualist who was familiar with psychic conditions was upon it. Dr. Prince was very deaf, while Dr. McDougall was in a position where his whole academic career would obviously be endangered by the acceptance of an unpopular explanation. The same remark applies to Dr. Shapley's committee, which was all composed of budding scientists. Without imputing conscious mental dishonesty, there is a subconscious drag towards the course of safety. Reading the report of these gentlemen with their signed acquiescence at each sitting with the result, and their final verdict of fraud, one cannot discover any normal way in which they have reached their conclusions. On the other hand, the endorsements of the mediumship by folk who had no personal reasons for extreme caution were frequent and enthusiastic. Dr. Mark Richardson of Boston reported that he had sat more than 300 times, and had no doubt at all about the results.

The author has seen numerous photographs of the ectoplasmic flow from " Margery," and has no hesitation, on comparing it with similar photographs taken in Europe, in saying that it is unquestionably genuine, and that the future will justify the medium as against her unreasonable critics.

PRINTED BY CASSELL & COMPANY, LIMITED, LA BELLE SAUVAGE, LONDON, E.C.4
F30.3.26